THE BEAUTY OF TIME TRAVEL

THE WORK OF RAMDANE TOUHAMI
AND THE AGENCY ART RECHERCHE INDUSTRIE
FOR OFFICINE UNIVERSELLE BULY

OFFICINE UNIVERSELLE
BULY

AU
6 RUE BONAPARTE PARIS VI

gestalten

TABLE OF CONTENTS

TABLE OF CONTENTS

FORE[V]

by Ramdane Touhami

Slowly but surely, we will come to see opening a store as an act of resistance

WORD

In today's world it may well appear that stores are opened mainly for mercantile reasons, to satisfy a commercial desire. What's more, people generally tend to view the neighborhood store as futile, if not obsolete, in this age of e-commerce, rather than consider the services and social interactions that they provide. And yet, opening a store in the 21st century remains essential. Slowly but surely, we will come to see opening a store as an act of resistance: to the internet, to the disappearance of our social ties, and to the desertification of our city centers. During this unprecedented healthcare crisis, and in the wake of lockdowns and restrictions on moving about in public, we all saw the highly social role that our neighborhood shops played. How many of us used the excuse of buying a baguette as a way to escape from the house for a few minutes, our permissions to leave the house in hand? How many of us rediscovered the pleasure of chatting with our fruit and vegetable seller? But even aside from this crisis, we must remember that many people live alone and that on any given day, their local baker or pharmacist may be the only people they talk to. Our neighborhood shops are, thus, vital. It is frightening to imagine a world where people's only social interaction is receiving a package or take-out delivery, or perhaps taking an Uber ride.

LET'S SAVE RETAIL!

Opening a store fulfills our need to preserve, to the greatest extent possible, those places where we can socialize. For those of us who belong to the pre-millennial generation, we could never have imagined that love would become such a business, in the form of dating apps where people seldom appear to meet anymore. People used to go to bars and restaurants, or even just try to pick someone up in public. This kind of direct, human interaction is disappearing in Western countries, and this is why I believe that opening a physical store is key to a country's mental health and wellbeing. Hence, the following thoughts on the need to revamp retail commerce, to reinvent how we think about it, and to consider the impact that this might have on our lives.

One of the most crucial aspects of setting up a store today is hiring the most qualified people possible, or at least people that can be trained over the long term, so that we revive the actual profession of selling. It's a shame to reduce this to being a cashier. Being a salesperson has become a temporary job, but it used to be a veritable career that allowed people to develop highly specific skills. Salespeople have become the last step, like an anus in a digestive system; they are often the worst paid in the company where they work, and the least respected. The people who run the company have to take responsibility so that they can once again be proud of the complexity and diversity of knowledge and expertise that their profession demands. For example, at Buly, we pay our salespeople 30–40% above market rate, because we know that these are ultimately our most important employees. We have taken the time to train them in various languages, calligraphy, and in *origata*, the Japanese art of paper folding and packaging. We are simply trying to reconsider the multitude of practices that this professional actually involves.

A true salesperson knows all the products intimately, takes the time to listen, to advise, to explain, and to suggest. This person has acquired skills and expertise in this domain, and can also transmit them. Just as during the phases of designing and fabricating a store, we should not treat the moment of sale as something to be completed as quickly as possible; it should instead be something that is done as best as possible, by taking one's time. As I said before, buying something can be summed up as an exchange of time. And as a salesperson, I am giving you my time to sell you a durable product, which took time to design and make.

This relationship is now highly imbalanced; we buy something quickly and very expensively that was made in just a few seconds. We have to do everything we can to rediscover the exceptional nature of this exchange between the salesperson and the customer around the product. And this applies to any domain! Just as when the vegetable seller explains a recipe, tells us a story, or gives us advice on storage, we realize that we are dealing with someone who knows the entire history of various kinds of tomatoes; these kinds of interactions can be fascinating each and every time. Or imagine your local fishmonger who has your phone number and knows what you like, and who calls you to tell you "I just got some phenomenal sea bass from Brittany for you!" This elevates a simple commercial gesture to the level of social interaction, the sharing of experiences, which is precisely what is missing from supermarkets and large retail stores.

If we want to ward off the Retail Apocalypse, we have to reintroduce a notion of surprise and selection, to be better than the internet. The internet represents an utter lack of human interaction, where everything is automated, and which offers a selection one could make oneself and find elsewhere. Of course it's nigh impossible to be cheaper, but we can provide better service. We can explain where the product comes from, who made it, and why it costs what it does. We can look for things that people don't necessarily know about and which they can discover in the store. We have to rely on our customers' intelligence and natural curiosity; they want to learn and understand, not just buy. We also have to change our windows every week, consider our displays and interior layout, create new pathways, train our sales staff, and pay them well. Ultimately, we have to create a community of trust around our store.

This concerns all kinds of businesses, and not just high-end ones. You can be extremely creative with a kebab shop and give customers looking for this kind of product an exceptional experience, one that doesn't just copy the kebab joint down the street! Unlike most everywhere else, by injecting our creativity into places where it matters, we can raise intellectual and aesthetic standards. Let's take the French-style kebab at the restaurant Grillé, which is made with high-quality veal, incredible fries, a spectacular sauce, and a special bread. Yes, it's slightly more expensive than a regular kebab, but they have raised the bar considerably. Instead of a kebab, they call it a grillé, which is actually the translation into French of the Turkish word kebab. Outsmarting the internet also means no longer competing on the basis of price alone, and not necessarily viewing everything as immediately accessible. Making these efforts is the price we have to pay to save our neighborhood stores.

RAMDANE TOUHAMI'S ENTREPRENEURIAL ADVENTURES

A social journey

There is a design mythology of how to take over a historical brand, how to respect the brand truth and make it attractive now. Through his creative and professional path, Ramdane Touhami will share his career adventures, the rules to respect, and his sources of inspiration.

Ramdane Touhami, portrait by the photographer Marsy Hild Thorsdottir, 2019.

Everything began in 1993 with an iconoclastic T-shirt which stated "Teuchy," his first success in the skating and hip-hop scene. In the enthusiastic hubbub, Ramdane launched "King Size:" the first French skating clothing line with the motto of "French savoir-faire finally comes to skateboarding."

In 2003, Ramdane Touhami successfully reinvented the men's department of the London institution Liberty. In 2007, he revamped the oldest candle-maker in the world, the French company Cire Trudon. Meticulous research gave him a thorough knowledge of the brand's 200-year history. The first step he took was to restore the brand's original name, which is linked to its founder, Cire Trudon, and to write an official industrial history of the brand. The second step, the most important one, was to create new products that would form part of the brand legacy. The third step was to redesign the Parisian store in a "historical" vein to host the new product lines and to welcome new customers. Until 2007, Cire Trudon was sold only in France, but by 2009, with the development of its wholesale business, it had become available in 59 countries.

Ramdane Touhami brought his knowledge and skills to bear once more with the launch of Officine Universelle Buly in 2014. Buly has been steadily reinventing French beauty products. Ramdane Touhami and his team work daily on developing the heritage of Buly, a 19th-century beauty brand, drawing inspiration from the excellence of its past to offer the best possible experience in the present day. The brand's history is celebrated through the authentic decor of its stores: with its traditional apothecary counters of yore and the refined aura of master perfumers, all the boutiques are known for their uniqueness. As Ramdane Touhami once said: "I don't think one can call me an art director. Let's just say that I feel more responsible than an art director perhaps because I had industrial experience from a young age. I am not the sort of person to make artistic 'gestures.' I think like an investor, like an entrepreneur... When I approach a brand or a new territory, I go at it with the logic of an entrepreneur, with the idea that what is beautiful and what is good isn't a luxury or a whim, but the quickest and surest way to sell well, to sell better." Here's the story of the beginnings of his creative journey...

"When I approach a brand or a new territory, I go at it with the logic of an entrepreneur, with the idea that what is beautiful and what is good isn't a luxury or a whim, but the quickest and surest way to sell well, to sell better."

Ramdane Touhami

RAMDANE TOUHAMI
IN HIS OWN WORDS

"For me, beauty is not limited to things that adorn the skin. Beauty lies in lettering, furniture, space, and the enchantment of people's manners. I was brought up in Montauban, in the southwest of France, by Moroccan-French parents. Growing up, I felt deprived of a sense of excitement, of anything that could win over my heart. My mother worked as a maid at a late-19th-century manor that belonged to a judge. My father was a farmer who took care of the manor's farm, especially its apple orchard.

The owner lived in Paris and came down to his country estate only occasionally, during his vacations. But for farmers, working with nature means that there is no day off. Nature is always changing and demanding to be tended to. The farmer's life is all about labor, from Monday to Sunday. Even as a four-year-old child, each day involved a form of labor as I walked six kilometers each day to go to school. Color TV only came into our lives when I was 12 years old. Even in the late 1980s, with no internet, no social media, life in the countryside was contained within a very small radius; there was hardly any access to information about things happening outside our town. But there was one thing I always looked forward to: our annual visit to the French capital. Each year, after the end of the harvest, my father was temporarily freed from looking after the farm day in and day out. For one month, my father and our family would head to the Parisian suburb where my mother's family lived. Holding my grandfather's hand, I visited the mosque in Paris, walked around the covered passageways, and stared up at the grand architecture, thrilled by the city's majesty. Everything I saw in Paris was something happening in another world for me. In the 1980s, no one from my neighborhood in Montauban went to Paris. For people in this village in the southwest of France, the things outside their daily lives were from another planet. Paris didn't exist in the minds of the people in my community. I don't remember all the details of the buildings in Paris or of the manor where we lived, but I was in ecstasy whenever I saw grand interiors, decorations, and a general ambience that was far removed from my upbringing. These formative experiences made a lasting impression on me, later allowing me to conjure up an aesthetic mood based on the 19th century and to create my own imaginary world. But it would take time for someone to help me retrieve these memories."

Teuchy sweatshirt, 1993
(teuchy is a slang word for weed).

A SOCIAL
JOURNEY

"I went to school in Montauban, somehow without ever experiencing a sense of joy. Living in an era when class distinctions in society and discrimination against certain ethnic groups were very marked, I couldn't hold my head high. I was sort of an outcast. I felt inferior to Others, and always kept my voice hidden. But when in 1992, at the age of 17, I created a T-shirt that said 'Teuchiland,' which means the land of cannabis, appropriating the word from my favorite outdoor label Timberland, people loved the idea. They treated me as if I were a rock star. For the first time in my life, I felt that my creativity could give joy to others. I was elated. That's how I cut my teeth. Producing 100 T-shirts a month generated a fortune for me in just a few years. But then I was kidnapped by gangs and robbed of all the cash I had earned. Left feeling nowhere, I crawled my way up to Paris, homeless. You learn many things when you become homeless. My daily life was about being careful, protecting myself, and scrutinizing everything around me. This experience developed my awareness of danger, whether I was getting into trouble or not, and it gave me insight into the essence of things. I have spent my life crawling up from rock bottom. I am like a war-horse. I think I went through the toughest times, and there is no predicament that scares me.

In the 1990s in Paris, people were looking for a new kind of store experience. I was one of the first to use the term 'concept' store. I love the format of retail, which is about creating a space for a customer's shopping experience. You go to a store with a certain intention, but you encounter unexpected things along the way. I am fascinated by a sense of wonderland. In 1997, I created a retail emporium called L'Épicerie, one of the first concept stores in France, with items ranging from clothing to furniture, objects, music, and magazines, and curations with fashion designers Marc Jacobs and Jeremy Scott. It was the same year that the 'concept' store Colette was set to open its doors on Rue Saint-Honoré. You can imagine how I wanted to pick a fight with a similar concept store. However, I met its head of media relations, Victoire de Taillac, who would later become my wife (officially in May 2010) and help me retrieve the formative memories of my childhood. I went radical on L'Épicerie, throwing extravagant parties that eventually bankrupted the brand by 1999. At the same time, in 1998–99, I was consulted on the restyling of one section of the oldest department store in the world, Le Bon Marché, which had lost the contemporary vibe that it had at the time of its founding in 1852. A businessman from Japan, Rikuzo Suzuki, who owned a Japanese retail holding company called Sazaby, noticed what I was doing. His wife Sophie de Taillac, Victoire's elder sister, introduced me to this businessman who became interested in my approach to retail and offered me the job of shaking up one of his retail brands called And A."

L'Epicerie, Paris, picture by Artus de Lavilléon, 1997.

UNDER THE SPELL OF JAPAN

"My first visit to Japan in 1996 had a lasting effect on my creative work. It was a revelation for me to encounter the creations of designer Rei Kawakubo of Comme Des Garçons and of Jun Takahashi of Undercover. It would be too banal to categorize them as merely designers, because their creations are not limited to just fashion design. From the clothes to the stores where these clothes are displayed, the music that fills these stores, every detail with which the customers come into contact has been meticulously thought out by the creators themselves, who are uncompromising in their vision, and thus, very consistent. Nowadays, many fashion designers have incorporated this approach, but in 1995, no one thought of communicating brand identity in this way. I think people follow and support these brands for this very reason. They identify with the brand's philosophy, even more than with the person who creates it."

PARFUMERIE GENERALE
AND
CIRE TRUDON

"Back in Paris, in 2001, together with Victoire, I started Parfumerie Générale, a multi-brand store where people could learn about, try on, and buy beauty items. Then, in 2003, I was asked to become artistic director of the menswear department at the century-old department store Liberty of London, which had lost its former sense of rarity and novelty. There are a lot of things you have to work on when you are sprucing up a brand. Not only did I select merchandise, but I also changed staff, oversaw the window displays, and designed men's clothes myself to complete the holistic universe I wanted to create. In this situation, with the brand in decline, the owner was willing to move on and thus give the artistic director this freedom.

In 2005, my lawyer approached me about shaking up France's oldest candle-maker, Cire Trudon, which had been founded in 1643. Originally named Trudon, the name was used from 1643 to 1884, and then changed when the candle-maker was sold to another owner. Trudon was a candle manufacturer to France's royal family. Candles, which were the only source of artificial light in those days, were immensely important. It is no wonder that Jean Le Rond d'Alembert, co-editor with Diderot of the first encyclopedia, devoted some 20 pages to the art of candle-making. If you step into a French church, you will find Trudon candles. That's how important Trudon was to French society. It had always been, at least while the candle was our primary source of artificial light. But Trudon became debt-heavy, nearly filing for bankruptcy in an age when our lives began to be dominated by LEDs. But I was interested in the fact that Trudon has been a part of our society for nearly 380 years. I knew there were reasons why it had stood the test of time. Given Cire Trudon's heritage, without wanting to distort its history, I thought I would create a candle that didn't exist before, a candle that would transport you to another world. I went with a perfumer to Versailles to take in the smell of the palace and the gardens. I stepped into an old library and wandered around souks in Morocco. Each city and place has its own distinctive smell that tickles people's noses and reveals the story of that particular place. I translated these scents of various places into candles so that people could be at home and, at the same time, feel as if they were being taken on a journey. To embody the scent of a place in a candle was an idea that no other candle-maker had at the time that we launched the new Cire Trudon in 2007. I also introduced a glass case for the candle to make the olfactory experience safer. Encasing beeswax in a glass container meant that we had to find a new way to make the candles. We developed new ways of inserting cotton wicks and pouring the molten wax into the glass. The first Cire Trudon scented candle was launched in November 2007, and became enormously successful. I didn't change the product per se, which fundamentally remained a candle, but I changed the way people experienced the candle. To make this experience as engaging as possible, the catalog, the store, and the product display all needed to reinforce this mythology."

Inside view of the Parfumerie Générale store (2001–2004).

LIVING WITH HISTORY

"Being so intensely involved with these heritage brands gives me the illusion that I am living with history. This is not entirely inaccurate. My wife, Victoire de Taillac, comes from one of the oldest families in France. The Taillacs, whose family tree dates back to the 15th century, includes the famous Porthos, one of the musketeers that Alexandre Dumas described in his 1844 novel 'The Three Musketeers.' Knowing her and the world in which she grew up helped bring back the formative childhood memory of the manor where I grew up. Victoire and her behaviour became a mirror of my perception of beauty. Each day, seeing her, talking to her, living with her, I feel as if I am in a dialogue with a history that has continued since the 15th century. Visiting her family estate in Gascogne, in the southwest of France, which was built in the 19th century, immerses me in parallel worlds of a past and a present. At this estate, we live surrounded by family portraits from the 17th century that gaze down and smile at us. This transports me to another era. It resuscitated my formative childhood memory of peeking into the owner's manor house, enchanted and breathless, feeling whisked away to another world, something that has had a major effect on my sense of aesthetics. Still today, I have one foot in the present, and the other in the past, where, it turns out, it has stayed all along."

HOW TO REVAMP A BRAND?

Officine Universelle Buly through three centuries

Costume of a perfumer. Anonymous engraving. Paris, musée Carnavalet.

Perfume houses—those fragrant testaments to the passage of time. They embody the spirit of an era and the ephemerality of trends, leaving in their wake the impression of fragrance as a source of beauty. Perfume is, essentially, an essence, and perfume-makers all have one thing in common: they advance the customs of an era, determining the makeup of those customs; they strive to create new paradigms. Some perfume houses of the past have had a direct influence on the way scent is understood today, both on a cultural level—who should wear perfume? How? Why?—as well as on a personal level, in that they taught us how to enchant, how to embellish our person or amplify our presence. Some houses have triumphed, again and again, at establishing these olfactory norms, while others have been subject to the vagaries of entrepreneurial life. Other houses have seen their glorious mirrors stained with the tarnish of old age, only to learn (to everyone's surprise) that it lends them a certain cachet. The only way to fully bring back to life a period in which competition was matched only by innovation is to revive one of the great witnesses to that time: the perfume house of yesteryear. A trivial conversation, a chance encounter, sometimes has the power to change everything and to guide destiny—to fuse, as if by trickery, the magnificence of times past with our present day. In 2012, Ramdane met Arnaud Montebourg, the French Minister of the Economy and Industrial Renewal at the time. At the end of their meeting, the two would decide the fate of one of the oldest Parisian perfume houses, that of the Jean-Vincent Bully, vinaigrier-parfumier. It took a single phrase to bring two centuries together, linked by nothing but the enduring allure of Parisian elegance, charm, and chic. "You're a real César Birotteau, Ramdane," Montebourg declared to the man he'd just met.

THE 19ᵀᴴ CENTURY CAN BE SEEN AS A HISTORICAL STAGE ON WHICH PERFUME PLAYED A LEADING ROLE: WHERE PERFUME DONNED A FLAMBOYANT COSTUME MADE OF THE FRENCH "ART DE VIVRE" AND PERFORMED AGAINST A DAZZLING CULTURAL BACKDROP, APPLAUDED BY A FRESHLY CAPTIVATED PUBLIC.

But what's behind this literary reference? The character in question, Mr Birotteau, is a curious figure who appears in one of the sociological portraits painted by Balzac in 1837. César Birotteau is a small-time, provincial perfumer who, as it turns out, doesn't possess "an iota of knowledge about natural history or chemistry."[1] Balzac recounts the perfumer's rise, his heyday, and then a series of unforeseen events: after some ill-fated investments, Birotteau has to be bailed out by the king. But he dies tragically before he can reap the benefits of his freshly restored glory. Admittedly, the portrait is not very flattering. But all comparisons aside, the work traces an unrelenting pursuit of success and is an ode to resilience. From the ashes of the perfumer's past honors, "this character... acquires the status of a hero; a moment of misfortune transforms his life into something sacred," writes the scholar Danièle Dupuis. Amidst a backdrop of dawning capitalism and in an era marked by relentless competition and a wave of innovation, Auguste Popinot—Birotteau's clerk—makes an ingenious discovery that saves the fallen perfumer, allowing him to be given a new lease on life by the king. This story is not so much a literary invitation to entrepreneurship than it is a reminder of the ambition and confidence necessary for success.

1. Balzac, *Grandeur et décadence de César Birotteau*, p. 222.

Bully advertising poster, dated
1920s (from private collection).

And so with that chance encounter as a starting point, the plot was set in motion: Ramdane Touhami headed for the archives along the Seine, the National Archives, that famed library containing catalogs of perfumers and other records of major patent rulings. The details he found in these documents would radically influence and guide his creative process: as documents piled up, the historical investigation took on the feverish pitch of a thriller, with all the elements making a stronger and stronger case for reviving this bygone era. The 19th century can be seen as a historical stage on which perfume played a leading role: where perfume donned a flamboyant costume made of the French *art de vivre* and performed against a dazzling cultural backdrop, applauded by a freshly captivated public. With this rich history, the stage managers of Time parted the curtains on an opening scene, revealing Paris and her scents as they dictated, in magnificent fashion, the commandments of beauty.

IN THE WAKE
OF
CESAR BIROTTEAU

The origins of Balzac's hero are often disputed. The archivist Rosine Lheureux prefers the interpretation that Louis Toussaint Piver, a perfumer and influential figure of the time, was the inspiration for the character. "Balzac frequented Piver's store because the perfumer had created a custom fragrance for the writer. Piver wasn't sure how to name his company, alternating between perfumer-distiller, perfumer-chemist and soap distiller, and finally opted for the title of perfumier-vinaigrier (maker of perfumes and scented vinegars)."[2] Madeleine Ambrière-Fargeaud[3] points out that Piver's catalog—which Balzac edited in 1827—was a source of material and inspiration for the author. Meanwhile, the historian Claude Pasteur sees the ambitious Antoine Caron reflected in Balzac's character. Caron was a royalist at the head of an illustrious perfume house of the same name. In contrast, the academic Romain Vaissermann sees Caron as the model for Ragon, the young hero's master and apprentice perfumer in César Birotteau. But then, from this thicket of clues scattered throughout France's archives, a singular figure emerges: Monsieur Bully. At the beginning of the 19th century, a merchant perfumer by the name of Claude Bully invented a *vinaigre de toilette*, a vinegar-based fragrance that he described as an "aromatic, hygienic, anti-mephitic vinegar." The *vinaigre de toilette* revolutionized beauty care. It was designed to fight body odors, cure disease (eg. mephitism), and nourish the skin. We see similar claims made about a number of César Birotteau's inventions. Initially reserved for members of the aristocracy, Bully's *vinaigre de toilette* achieved widespread popularity. Jean-Vincent Bully, his son, brought public recognition and scientific validity to the brand: "With the backing of doctors and scientists, Bully's vinegar was granted two patents in 1809, another for improvements in 1814, and his products were showcased at the 1823, 1827, and 1849 World Fairs, as well as at the Great Exhibition in London (in 1851), where it was the only invention to be granted a special prize," according to the *Illustrated History of the World's Fair* in 1855.[4] This image of success, however, was met with a brutal fate: Jean-Vincent lived to see his business ruined and plundered.

2. Rosine Lheureux, *Une histoire des parfumeurs 1850–1910* (*A History of Perfumers 1850–1910*), p. 54.

3. Madeleine Ambrière-Fargeaud, *Balzac, le commerce et la publicité* (*Balzac: Trade and Advertising*), Revue L'année balzacienne.

4. Charles Robin, *Histoire illustrée de l'exposition universelle*. Review, 1974.

AT THE BEGINNING OF THE 19TH CENTURY, A MERCHANT PERFUMER BY THE NAME OF CLAUDE BULLY INVENTED A 'VINAIGRE DE TOILETTE,' A VINEGAR-BASED FRAGRANCE THAT REVOLUTIONIZED BEAUTY CARE.

ANSELME POPINOT.

Anselme retourna chez lui, fit pour cinquante mille francs
de billets.......

CÉSAR BIROTTEAU.

Portrait of Anselme Popinot, a staff member
of César Birotteau, engraving by Bertal &
F Leblanc, *César Birotteau, volume X of La
Comédie humaine*, Furne, 1844.

Illustration for *César Birotteau*
by Honoré de Balzac.

César Birotteau by Honoré de Balzac, first edition, 1837 (private collection).

It is the end of July 1830: Paris is in the throes of revolution. The crowd is armed and erects barricades throughout the city. The Palais des Tuileries, where King Charles X lived, is taken by storm. The Swiss Guard, charged with protecting the king, scatters and flees. The crowd is angry. "Bully, in his carelessness, left his store open. The fugitives rushed in, hiding in the back room and under the counters. The mob invaded the store," reports the newspaper *Le Temps*.[5] In the wake of this tragic episode, only debris and broken bottles remained, and "the precious vinegar, the object of the perfumer's dreams of fortune, flowed into the gutters."[6] Jean-Vincent Bully became an enemy of the people: his request for reparations was seen as an act of partiality and he was refused any compensation for the losses he endured. Everything, from his honor to his finances, had to be rebuilt from the ground up. This same resilience inspired Balzac's writing, with the difference being that Bully was "a victim of politics and probity"[7] while Birotteau's fall was due to his reckless choices and legendary rashness.

Jean-Vincent Bully ended up selling his invention "for a trifling sum,"[8] became an administrative clerk, and swore to redeem himself through sacrifice and hard work. He earned his living at the offices of *La Quotidienne*, a monarchist-legitimist newspaper founded by one of his former clients, the Count of Lostange. Bully led a life of sacrifice and deprivation: he ate very little and spent his nights in his chair at the office. During this time, the Lords A and M Landon became the sole proprietors of the disgraced perfumer's formulas. They obtained the exclusive right to produce and label the fabled lotion called "Au Temple de Flore," marketed by the perfume house bearing the same name. The gentlemen even opened a boutique at 67 rue Montorgueil. And, in a final blow to the disgraced Bully, the *Encyclopedic Dictionary of the Industrial Arts* published that "this good man met the sad fate of many inventors: he died a pauper while his invention brought fortune several times over to those who were able to put it to use." This was precisely what happened: the Lords Landon leveraged their noble title to obtain the prestigious Medals of the Universal Exhibitions along with the glorious fruits of such a prize. In 1867, the house received an award for its toothpaste powder, then in 1878 it was awarded a grand prize. Ironically, for decades the Landon family had to face imposters who counterfeited the famous *vinaigre de toilette*. After a long legal battle, Landon had to concede defeat against his former employee, Leroux. The Court of Appeals in 1881 granted Leroux the right to market the precious vinegar as long as the label contained the words "composed according to Claude Bully's recipe, made by Leroux."[9] A real slap in the face.

"The fall of César Birotteau strongly resembles that of Jean-Vincent Bully", insists Eugénie Briot, historian of the French perfume industry in the 19th century. "It's a mash-up: Balzac drew on different sources to inform his hero. Deeply ingrained in the popular imagination of the time was the idea that a perfumer could easily amass a fortune, more quickly and spectacularly than any other profession. Perfume is a scented breeze, a fleeting sensation that convinces the shopper to squander their money. *Grandeur et décadence de César Birotteau* is a title that very aptly describes the turbulent trajectory of perfume-making in the 19th century."

5. *Le Temps*, August 18 1937.

6. *Ibid.*

7. *Ibid.*

8. Eugène-Oscar Lami, *Dictionnaire encyclopédique et biographique de l'industrie et des arts industriels. (The Encyclopedic and Biographical Dictionary of Industry and the Industrial Arts).*

9. Law Journal: La Loi (The Law); May 11, 1882.

Vinaigre de Toilette bottle by Jean-Vincent Bully, post 1889 (private collection).

THE SCENT
OF
AN EMPIRE

In the year 1800, perfumery was by no means a uniform industry. The profession had been fragmented by a series of historical precedents, which determined that several kinds of businesses had the right to craft perfume. Thus, apothecaries; perfumers; pharmacists; druggists; surgeon-barbers; master glove-makers; vinegar makers; and distillers all had their hands on this sweet-smelling treasure. Year in year out, the law would try to dictate who could be part of this motley crew. But the question remained: who should be allowed to make perfume?

HENCEFORTH, PERFUME WOULD ASSUME A PURELY COSMETIC FUNCTION. THAT SAID, MANY PERFUME-RELATED ITEMS WERE STILL MANUFACTURED BY APOTHECARIES. IT WAS A VERITABLE HODGEPODGE!

"Under the Ancien Régime, the guilds played an important role in the crafting and manufacture of perfume. Several of them fought over the right to sell perfume, namely the glove-makers (who doubled as perfumers) and the merchants," explains Eugénie Briot. The glove-makers in particular were required to adhere to extremely precise standards and conventions—a result of their place of importance at the Court of Versailles. Perfumed gloves were the height of refinement under Louis XV, after a short fall from grace under the reign of Louis XIV. Merchants only had permission to sell perfume, so they were involved purely in the marketing side of things. "Apothecaries and barbers joined the sweet-smelling fray: until the 19th century fragrance was considered a medicine, a hygienic and therapeutic product. In the catalogs of Bully, Dissey or Piver, their product range was extremely wide-ranging and varied: inks; bleach; drugstore items; combs and brushes; haberdashery goods; barber's supplies; gloves for household needs; and perfumed goods. The perfumers' task, then, was to build a luxury image that would allow them to narrow their focus to perfume products alone."[10]

10. Eugénie Briot,
La fabrique des parfums
(*The Making of
Perfume*), p. 260.

It was believed that bad smells made you sick and only the prophylactic virtues of perfume could protect you. Then, Pasteur's discoveries revealed that disease was not caused by bad smells, but by pathogens. From this point on, perfume would no longer be seen as having the ability to protect or cure. People lost faith in the idea that disease produced an unpleasant odor and pleasant scents could cure disease. Henceforth, perfume would assume a purely cosmetic function. That said, many perfume-related items were still manufactured by apothecaries. It was a veritable hodgepodge! After the French Revolution, a new law (Loi Le Chapelier) opened up trade: the contemporaries of Claude and Jean-Vincent Bully (Dissey, Piver, Houbigant, Gellé,

Automaton doll created for the promotion
of Jean-Vincent Bully's *Vinaigre de Toilette*,
19th century (private collection).

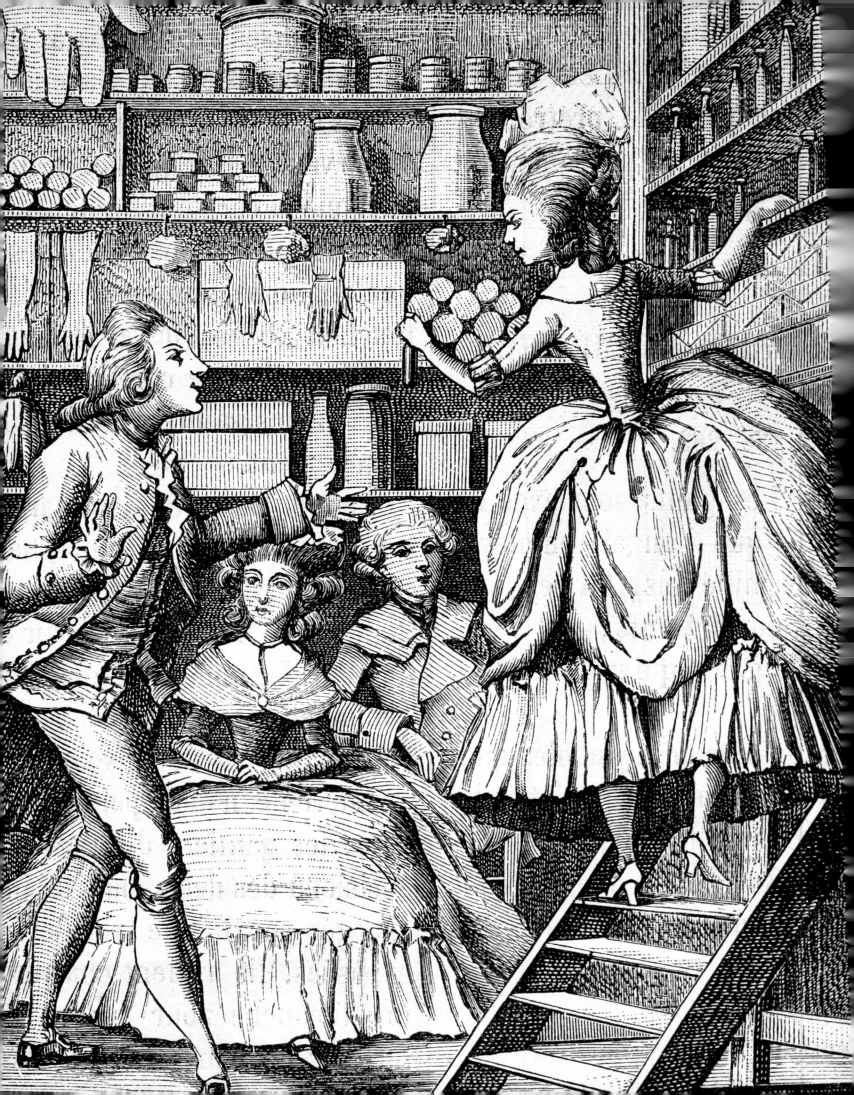

Lubin, Legrand and others) all had the right to manufacture perfumes despite the fact that they were members of opposing guilds. As such, distillers and vinegar-makers sold perfumed products that were more closely related to hygiene than to perfumery in the strict sense of the term.[11] While heady perfumes were adored by Josephine de Beauharnais, they were abhorred by Napoleon I, who would only settle for eau de cologne. The precious cologne never left his side: the long cylindrical bottles slipped easily into his boots when he went to battle.[12] History does not tell us whether the bottles he took with him were the source of legislative inspiration. What we do know, though, is that during his reign, the emperor introduced radical changes to the basic laws governing pharmaceuticals: the law, introduced on the April 21, 1803 introduced a strict legislative framework: there would be a national testing board, years of study regulating the profession, professional codes of conduct, etc.

11. Interview with Eugénie Briot.

12. Annick Le Guérer, *op. cit.* p. 178.

WHILE HEADY PERFUMES WERE ADORED BY JOSEPHINE DE BEAUHARNAIS, THEY WERE ABHORRED BY NAPOLEON I, WHO WOULD ONLY SETTLE FOR EAU DE COLOGNE.

The pharmacist assumed a primary role in preparing and dispensing medicines. As such, a real philosophical and semantic shift occurred: perfumery temporarily took its place among scented hygiene products, endowed with less therapeutic value. On August 18, 1810, Napoleon signed a law that put an end to the marriage between perfumery and pharmaceuticals. His aim was to protect consumers from the widespread sale of harmful drugs being pedaled by quacks and charlatans. With this law, therapeutic formulas would now have to be presented to a commission for approval; so-called "secret" remedies were prohibited. The commission made sure that products made no claims to medicinal properties, and it required manufacturers to disclose the product's ingredients. As a consequence, the perfumers were forced to label their inventions as "scented products," since marketing them as such enabled them to avoid full disclosure of their formula.[13] When Claude Bully filed his first patent in 1809, and later his improvement patent in 1814, he took care to specify the formulation in detail in order to benefit from exclusive rights for a period of five years and to establish the date of its discovery in the event of counterfeiting. Although commissions and applications were set up through official channels, the patents referred to by the Ministry of the Interior were marked WGG (Without Government Guarantee), the wording of which warned the public that the State, despite the patent approval, could not vouch for the invention. There was some ambiguity regarding this new legal landscape, in which the law of 1810 and those relating to registered patents coexisted. It should be remembered here that patenting was, above all, a matter of dating the ownership of one's invention and bringing it to the attention of the authorities. These patents for inventions appear to be the first legal weapon used by perfumers in order to protect themselves from the evils of competition. Such documents served as a basis for the Lords Landon, Bully's successors, during their various legal crusades.

13. Annick Le Guérer, *op. cit.* p. 178.

Perfumers' store in the 18th century, engraving.

HYGIENE AND SCENT FROM POLITICAL VIRTUE TO THE PERFUMER'S CABINET

At the turn of the century, the offerings were abundant and the selection was vast. A new cult devoted to hygiene and its civilizing properties emerged. Perfumery shifted into an era of health and wellbeing, and it started to compete with the claims made by pharmacies. A rivalry developed between pharmacists and perfumers concerning the manufacture and sale of hygiene products, which had become household amenities. This rivalry faded, though, as a new flourishing market emerged, in which everyone took their rightful place.[14] Hygiene began to center around essential products: *vinaigre de toilette*, soap products, and eau de cologne. It is not surprising that perfumers wanted a piece of the commercial boom. Bully Vinegar was no exception: ubiquitous advertising promoted his product's benefits on the skin, claiming the vinegar "restores radiance and suppleness." The product could be used for "ladies' hygiene, bathing, bruises, rheumatism, and as protection against epidemics and certain 'mephitisms,'" such as cholera. It claimed to be "far superior to eau de cologne and other alcohol-based eaux, whose irritating properties it simply did not possess." The product was also ideal "for children's hygiene" according to the same advertisements. As for the famous eau de cologne, perfume specialist Annick Le Guérer has traced its beginnings back to 1620, the year it was released by Florentine perfume-maker Santa Maria Novella. The fragrance was then imported into France after the secret formula was passed on to Jean-Marie Farina in 1806.

The dubious origins of cologne were a source of mistrust among the French: did it come from Cologne (a city belonging to the hated enemy, the Prussians)? Or was it a French product because the secret formula had been acquired by Farina, a Frenchman? This feud benefited the scented vinegar industry and even led to appearances in the newspapers of the time: "We had to fluff,

14. Rosine Lheureux,
op. cit. p. 196.

Bully Vinegar was no
vertising promoted his pro
claiming the vinegar "resto

15. Jules Curry, *Lettres et petites histoires en prose rimée.* (*Letters and little stories in lyrical prose*).

16. Taken from a note written by a Picard reporter at the 1889 World's Fair.

then perfume, the featherbed using Jean-Vincent Bully's eau de parfum. This was easy enough, but we had to use a pair of pincers—on account of the Prussian linen—so as not to sully our hands."[15] It even turned into a "fashion craze"[16] of sorts and some people passed the vinegar off as a substitute for eau de cologne. But was this really the case?

The newspapers during the Belle Epoque and the inter-war period continued to praise Bully's scented vinegars. *Pêle-Mêle* in 1904 claimed that "the best *vinaigre de toilette*… bears the name of Bully vinegar." In the summer of 1937, *Le Figaro* mentioned in its beauty section: "Don't forget to buy a bottle of… Bully vinegar, the object of world renown for nearly a century."

Scented vinegars were less astringent and contained less alcohol than an eau de cologne. The latter was used to perfume the water used for your beauty regime and it caused an invigorating sensation, while vinegar was meant to be applied directly to the skin, thanks to its softening properties. Both were used to perfume and cleanse the air. The advent of shampoo in the 20th century marked the end of an era for scented vinegar. An increase in purchasing power led people to lose interest in multi-purpose products. Instead, they opted for products that would fulfill a single cosmetic need; they wanted to emulate the wealthy bourgeoisie who filled their vanities with a whole assortment of beauty care products.[17]

17. Interview with Eugénie Briot.

As for soap, hygiene became an intensely political issue, and consequently, soap became highly prized for its popular appeal and its hygienic properties. The goal, at the time, was to civilize the people, conferring virtue upon them in the process. The idea was this: if the masses are clean, their morals will improve. The 19th century was battered by major epidemics—in 1832 a cholera outbreak in Paris killed indiscriminately, blind to the distinctions of class. The rich needed protection from contagion, and so Paris and France had to be cleaned up—and urgently. Basic hygiene was taught at school and in the army, and public showers and baths were erected. Soap was a civilizing agent through which redemption could be found. It was not just it a product—it was a form of salvation.[18]

18. Interview with Eugénie Briot.

Soap and perfume—both placed in wash basins to perfume water for freshening up—were the domain of master perfumers. They drove away bad smells and the diseases associated with them, leaving the body clean. The historian Alain Corbin in his book *Le miasme et la jonquille* (*Miasma and the Daffodil*) even describes the act of smelling good as a marker of social status: a bar of soap allowed people to distance and distinguish themselves from others through smell. More than

exception: ubiquitous ad— duct's benefits on the skin, zes radiance and suppleness.

anything, one didn't want to be mistaken for a member of the working class, the underprivileged, the poor. To avoid this, a group identity with cleanliness at its core had to be established. Soap, however, brought with its cleansing bubbles a formidable economic competitor, and suddenly France was in trouble! English soap, with its beautifully crafted curves and excellent composition, was preferred in France—a painful bruise on France's national pride. Production standards in France were no longer satisfactory and Marseilles produced nothing but poor-quality soap. As for that German "garbage," people wouldn't even go near it.[19] Soap caused a veritable trench warfare! But alas, perfumers used their ingenuity to conquer the hearts and the skin of the French: new manufacturers cropped up in Paris, and, with their new fragrances, the battle was won.

19. Interview with Eugénie Briot.

CONQUERING A CENTURY 1800–1900

The 19th century was a period of considerable growth for the perfume industry. In the 1800s, as we've already seen, perfume was associated with beauty regimens and good hygiene. Perfume held a mirror up to its time, and in turn the greatest authors of this era—Huysmans, Zola, Baudelaire, Maupassant, to name a few—gave perfume a leading role: the fundamentals of what we know today began taking shape and were tested out. New chemical techniques emerged, and the world saw the dawn of marketing and a craze for prestigious world fairs. New fragrances and social conventions took hold.

1800: At this time, the French perfume industry is defined by its thriving artisanal guilds, and perfumery is a flourishing sector. There is no professional continuity between the achievements of the 18th century and the 1820s. A new era is beginning to dawn.[20]

20. Rosine Lheureux, *Une histoire des parfumeurs en France 1850-1910 (A History of Perfumers in France 1850-1910)*.

1820: A generation of pioneers become the founders of modern perfumery. Their legacies will later be enshrined by post-modern and contemporary perfumers alike. Among them Piver, Legrand, Taveau, Gellé, Pinaud, Guerlain. France distinguishes itself from its main competition, England. The aristocratic clientele begin to buy French fragrances and soaps again, and this sparks a revival in perfumery during the Restoration (1815-1830). Perfumers are trying to make a product that is as beloved and as widely used as powder had been in the previous century.[21] Sales are structured around merchant-manufacturers, where the division between the crafting of fragrances and selling them is totally porous. At the time, Paris is a capital city with only 12 arrondissements and 46 quartiers, or neighborhoods. In the streets, romantic poems are read in wide stretches of greenery: Hugo, Lamartine, Musset, Nerval are the standard bearers of the romantic period. When Parisians go to the opera in the rue Le Peletier (Garnier did not exist back then), women wear buns in an "Apollo knot," and men don capes and top hats. The people hurry to hear Méhul, Spontini, Boieldieu, Rossini, Chopin, Listz, Halévy.

21. *Ibid.*

Above and below, various advertisements printed in *Le Novelliste* and *Charivari*, BNF collection.
In the middle, a warning about Bully's Vinaigre de Toilette counterfeits, published in a Parisian gazette. It says that a back-label must be required on the product.

TAPIS DE LYON — TEXTILES VÉGÉTAUX
LAFOND, ANDRÉ & GOURDONNIER
LYON-VAISE. RUE DE LA SPARTERIE.

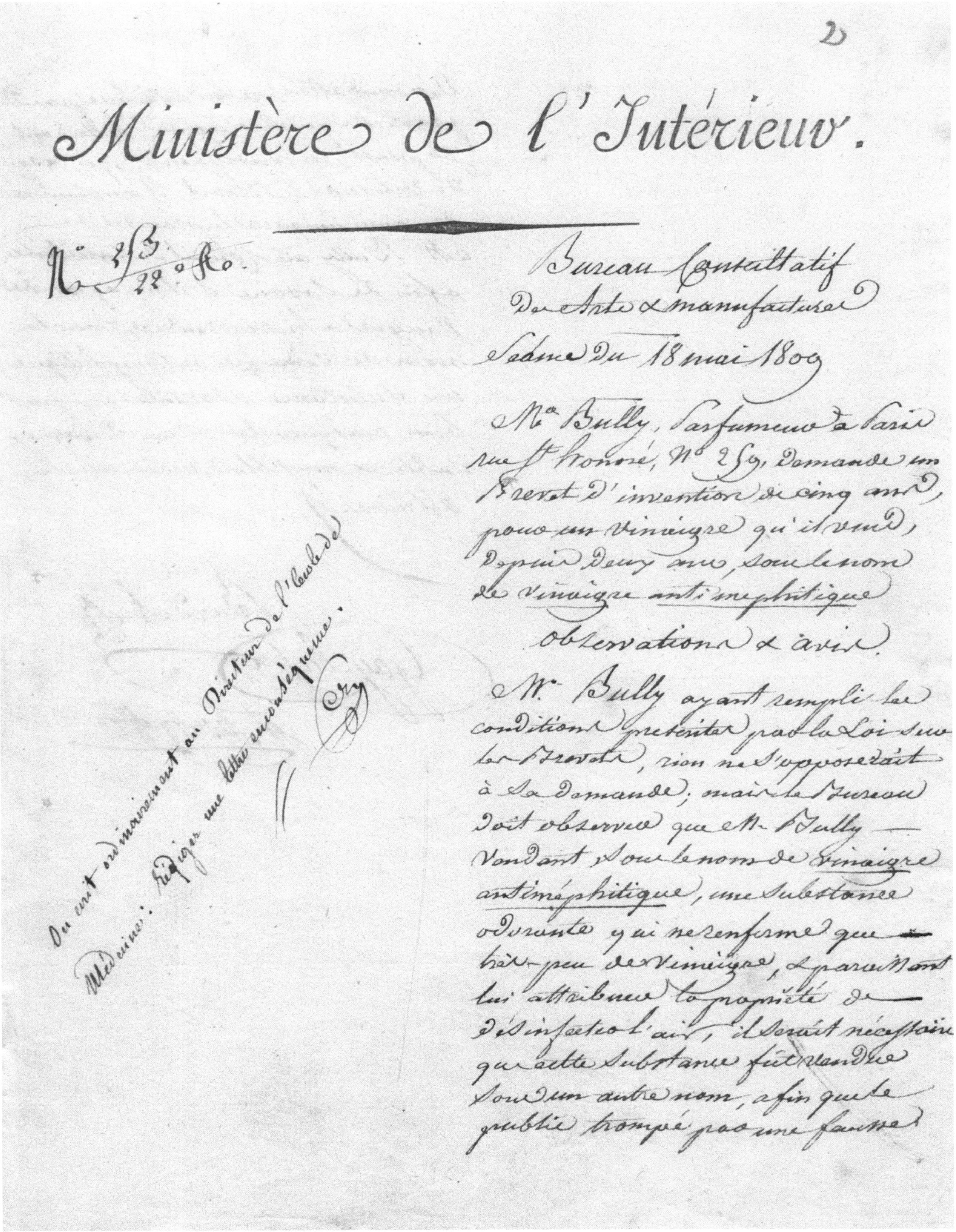

2)

Ministère de l'Intérieur.

N° ...

Bureau Consultatif
Des Arts & manufactures
Séance du 18 mai 1809

M.r Bully, Parfumeur à Paris
rue S.t Honoré, N° ..., Demande un
Brevet d'invention de cinq ans,
pour un vinaigre qu'il vend,
depuis Deux ans, sous le nom
de vinaigre anti mephitique

Observations & avis

M.r Bully ayant rempli les
conditions prescrites par la Loi sur
les Brevets, rien ne s'opposerait
à Sa Demande; mais le Bureau
Doit observer que M.r Bully
Vendant, Sous le nom de vinaigre
antimephitique, une substance
odorante qui ne renferme que
très-peu de vinaigre, & paraissant
lui attribuer la propriété de
désinfecter l'air, il Serait nécessaire
que Cette Substance fut vendue
Sous un autre nom, afin que le
public trompé par une fausse

1878 World Fair in Paris. French section. Perfumery, furniture, and accessories: the carpets. Paris (7th arrondissement), 1878.

Claude Bully's application for a patent to improve his *Vinaigre de Toilette*, 1814. Issued September 20, 1814, archives of INPI, the French National Institute of Industrial Property.

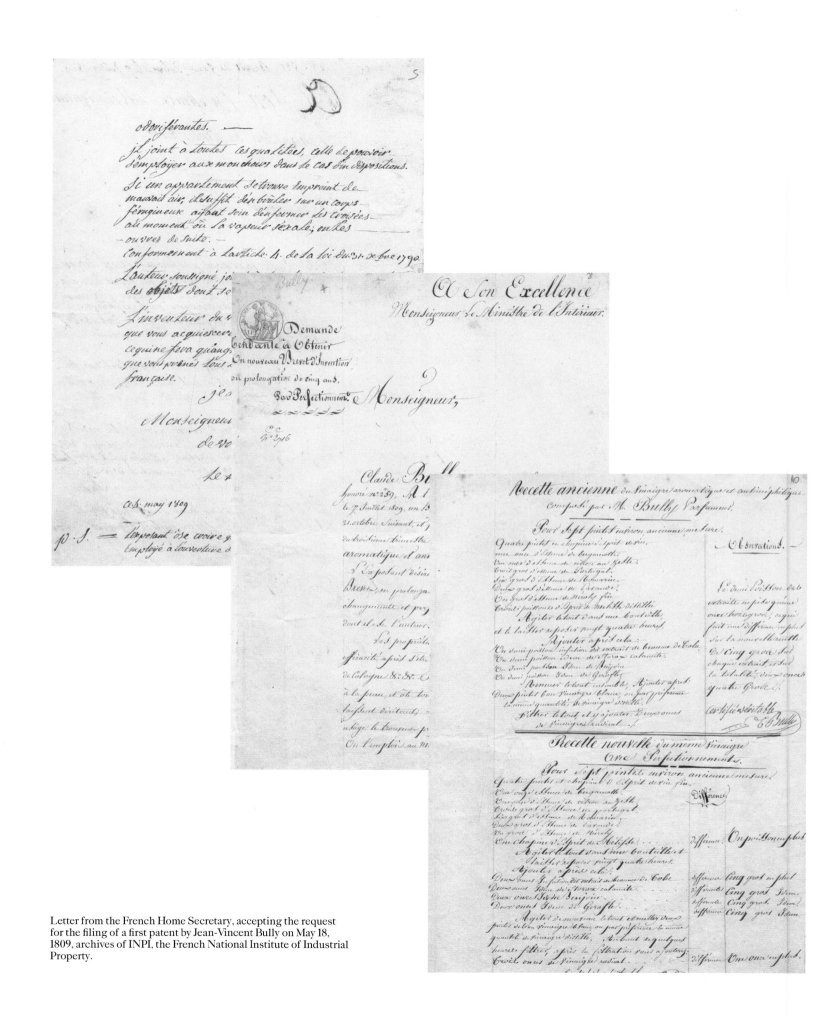

Letter from the French Home Secretary, accepting the request for the filing of a first patent by Jean-Vincent Bully on May 18, 1809, archives of INPI, the French National Institute of Industrial Property.

Balzac's first writings are published, and new museums open their doors: the Musée du Luxembourg, dedicated to contemporary art, opens, and another, named Versailles, opens its doors in 1830, when Louis Philippe undertook the ambitious project of converting the royal residence into a heraldic archive dedicated to the glories of France.

PERFUME HELD A MIRROR UP TO ITS TIME, AND IN TURN THE GREATEST AUTHORS OF THIS ERA— HUYSMANS, ZOLA, BAUDELAIRE, MAUPASSANT, TO NAME A FEW—GAVE PERFUME A LEADING ROLE.

22. Eugénie Briot, *op. cit.*

Circa 1860, perfumery grows increasingly industrialized: steam engines revolutionize the production process. Perfumers draw inspiration from the tools used in soap-making, pharmaceuticals, and distillation[22] and begin to use them to their advantage. New names appear: Cottance, Raynaud, Lavandier, Millot, Klotz, Bourjeois, Roger & Gallet. Perfumery becomes an international phenomenon with the advent of the World Expositions. Considered major events at the time, these expositions, or fairs, offer a unique opportunity to showcase France's *savoir-faire*. Perfumers exhibit their goods, awash in an aura of splendor, unfettered by the limitations of national borders. It is these very same fairs that will crown the achievements of Jean-Vincent Bully in 1867 and 1878. The times, however, are marked by ambivalence: perfume has seduced Europe's Royal Courts but it has also drawn the ire of the people. Perfumery is, first and foremost an aesthetic art, and aesthetic arts were thought to corrupt one's morals. The size of the market also drastically changes: the market is no longer restricted to local buyers—foreign competition now has to be accounted for. Perfumers develop special iconography and conventions, and a new generation of merchants enter the scene. A perfumer's path is increasingly shaped by the specter of profit and less by passion or legacy. Perfumery, fashion, and clothing grow more intertwined by the day.[23] Retail and production cease to inhabit the same space. Stores now boast luxurious window displays and have carefully crafted interiors. Paris is expanding and gradually separating itself from that "Old Paris" allure. The medieval buildings are destroyed, and cut-stone buildings, with their chiseled edges, line every street.

23. *Ibid.*

Late 19th century: This is the Golden Age. Fragrance is widely beloved and the rules of luxury are being rewritten. A disconnect between a perfume's intrinsic value and its retail price emerges. The industry establishes a visual vocabulary that is still in use today. The market is increasingly dominated by all things Parisian and the provincial brands are pushed out. Toothpastes and hair products leave the perfume shop and join the shelves of the drugstore. Paris steps into the spotlight: now a city of global renown, it adopts the nickname the "City of Light" following the World Exposition of 1900, which, coincidently, also marks the birth of that indelible iron beacon, the Tour Eiffel.

A REVOLUTION: THE ALCHEMISTS OF FRENCH ELEGANCE

Perfume-makers depended on the city of Grasse for its supply of flowers and other raw and semi-finished goods. The town's supply increased significantly following the irrigation of the Siagne Canal in the 1850s.[24] However, by then, the industry had seen the light of chemical science:[25] synthetic molecules opened up new horizons for perfumers; fragrance no longer depended on natural materials like flowers and could be derived instead from artificial compounds. The fragrance industry increasingly adopted a philosophy based on the chemical mechanics of scent. This development, which originated in Germany, quickly spread to England and France. Everybody benefited from it: perfumers expanded their aromatic vocabulary and manufacturers were able to produce more without having any seasonal constraints and without having to rely on natural compounds, which were both expensive and finite in quantity. Soap-makers, meanwhile, could lower their production costs and retail prices—the middle and working classes had, at long last, access to soap.[26]

24. G Pillivuyt, *Histoire du parfum [...], collection de la parfumerie Fragonard (A History of Perfume, the Fragonard perfumery collection)*, Paris, cited by Rosine Lheureux, p. 60.

25. Eugénie Briot, *op. cit.*

26. Annick Le Guérer, *Histoire du parfum (The History of Scent)*.

Bully brochure celebrating the 100th anniversary of the brand in 1909 and describing products of the brand, from the Historical Library of the City of Paris (BHVP). Note, during the rebirth of the brand in 2014, a graphic error was inserted on a batch of labels: it anchored Buly in 1803, the year when the statue of the Place Vendôme was built and where the Pont des Arts, the first metal bridge in France, was created in the immediate vicinity of rue Bonaparte.

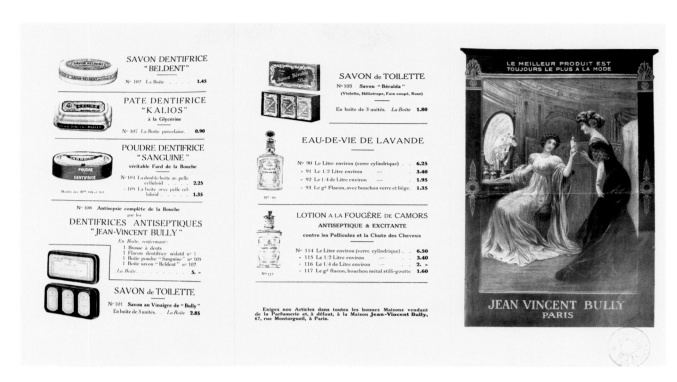

"WE HAD TO FLUFF, THEN PERFUME, THE FEATHERBED USING JEAN-VINCENT BULLY'S EAU DE PARFUM."

Jules Curry

Next page: World Fair in 1900, Paris. The perfumery at the Champs de Mars. *Le Panorama*, new production, n°15.

FASHION, VIRTUE,
AND
THE DEVIL

The world of fragrance captured and distilled society's trends, but it reflected the divisive, fire-and-brimstone mores of the time. In spite of the boom in sales and perfume's newly acquired prestige, the 19th century was very much of two minds about all things scented. The body and its various smells became a site on which society imposed the social conventions of the time. A culture of performative morality developed around scent, driven by the upper classes. "At the end of the 19th century, you certainly didn't want to be mistaken for a loose woman!" quips Eugénie Briot. It was unthinkable to go against these diktats and certain age-based rules. A woman, if she were to break one these unwritten rules, would face damning judgment about her morals or her rank (musk and tuberose, for example, were forbidden scents and signified a supreme lack of taste). For ladies of good rank, the use of heliotrope, rose or narcissus[27] was much preferred. Men should under no circumstances use an atomizer, lest they appear effeminate. No one was spared! Men could wear fragrance but only if it was subtle and discernable at close range. This was accomplished by using scented cosmetic products and not perfume. To disregard this cardinal rule would assign him the label of an "invert" (an old-fashioned term used for homosexuals). Let's not forget that this distrust centered mainly around a fleeting and ostentatious product. The perfume bottle was "something that could be exhibited, an object one would go out of their way to show off." [28] A strict hierarchy of good and poor taste settled in, where vulgar and classy smells alike underwent the ruthless scrutiny of tastemakers. The Baroness of Staff, a notable arbiter of taste at the time, warned: moderation and good judgment are of utmost importance. "Do not apply too much perfume. It can be a serious nuisance to your neighbors." And, so, the tone was set. At the ball, in the theater, in subdued drawing rooms filled with hushed conversation, "the principle of modesty had to be respected." [29] Anyone who violated this rule was the subject to public indignation, chastisement, and possibly even a flight to the opposite corner of the drawing room. Queen Victoria, on an official visit to Paris in 1855, was tactless enough in the eyes and sensitive noses of elegant Parisians to wear a fragrance "with a disqualifying hint of musk" [30] —how could she! Worse, perfume became scandalous as soon as it no longer evoked hygiene, but rather femininity. It was viewed as a tool of seduction, so young women were told to be clean, and only mothers should wear perfume. Any departure from the prescribed use of fragrance welcomed suspicions of certain cardinal sins:[31] pride and lust were strongly condemned during the Second Empire, at a time when people associated fragrance with incense at church and religious salvation.[32] Despite the profusion of perfumes, doctors regularly warned against attending balls, whose air was clogged with the scent of perfume![33] Pasteur's discoveries put an end to fragrance's image as something that could protect its wearer, denying scent any prophylactic properties: "The smell of perfume is dangerous... for the brain and flesh. It leads the mind astray." [34]

Morality prevailed. These manmade scents were no longer the cause of evil, and instead fragrance became inherently evil itself: any and all scents were seen as harmful to people and their organs. The concert halls with their incredible "cacophony of smells" were a veritable scourge. This evil had to be fought in a hygienic way, namely with appropriate ventilation during

27. Madame Celnart, *Manuel des dames ou l'Art de l'élegance (A Lady's Handbook, or the Art of Elegance)*, cited by Eugénie Briot, p. 218.

28. Eugénie Briot, *op. cit.* p. 213.

29. *Ibid.* p. 216.

30. Alain Corbain, *Le miasme et la jonquille (Miasma and the Daffodil)*, p. 323.

31. Eugénie Briot, p. 238.

32. Erika Wicky and Andrea Oberhuber, *Du mauvais usage des parfums (The Misuse of Fragrance)*.

33. Interview with Eugénie Briot.

34. The Countess of Gencé, *Le cabinet de toilette d'une honnête femme (An Honest Woman's Washroom)*, cited by E. Briot p. 238.

35. Érika Wicky &
Andrea Oberhuber,
op. cit.

36. Interview with
Eugénie Briot, *op. cit.*

fashionable events. Upon its opening, the Théâtre des Champs-Elysées was considered state-of-the-art for its ability to remedy the problem.[35] These multiple setbacks would ultimately have no effect on the glorious history of perfumery. It would quickly move past these injustices, trading them in for a dazzling destiny. Little by little, perfume became widely accepted, thanks to brands who used their symbolic power and moral authority[36] to win over consumers. Perfume houses soothed customers' consciences just as they guaranteed their good taste. Ultimately, this gave them incredible power to dictate the rules of the game.

Collection of medals received as a reward for the innovations of Jean-Vincent Bully: Médailles des Expositions,
National Exhibition of French Industrial Products, for the years 1849, 1878 (private collection).

THE BEGINNINGS OF MARKETING

To sell perfume is to leverage publicity. Balzac even spoke of "commercial poems." Advertising and exposure are integral parts of the process. According to the historian Danielle Dupuis, César Birotteau, like many of his contemporaries, learned to harness the power of advertising. The hero of Balzac's novel launched "his 'Double Paste of Sultan' and his 'Carminative Balm' to great fanfare." How could anyone deny themselves this extra boost, so crucial to improving sales and visibility? In order to improve sales, companies' poster campaigns and magazine inserts regularly invoked scientific approval. The hope was to reassure the public and give any fragrance a stamp of credibility.

THE CUSTOMER WANTED SOMETHING EXTRA FOR THEIR PURCHASE: PROOF OF QUALITY AND DISTINCTION. SINCE IT'S IMPOSSIBLE TO EXPERIENCE PERFUME FROM AFAR, MARKETERS HAD TO TRANSLATE ITS ESSENCE INTO IMAGES, TRANSFORMING IT INTO A NETWORK OF SIGNIFIERS THAT EXPRESSED ELEGANCE.

The end of the 19th century marked the real advent of "The Brand." The competition between Parisian perfume houses was fierce: the strategy of setting a brand apart from its competitors became a battle waged with words, images, and smells—the importance of which simply could not be ignored. Price lay at the heart of this new marketing strategy: the more expensive the product, the more refined it was perceived to be. That extra touch was the key to any sale. "Do you want a purple perfume? Many were affordable, but Violette by Guerlain, with all the imagery and symbolism that went with it, was not," writes Eugénie Briot. In the press, the Faits-Paris (forerunners of the advertorial, essential advertisements thinly disguised as gossip columns), would place the label "very expensive" next to fragrances. The customer wanted something extra for their purchase: proof of quality and distinction. Since it's impossible to experience perfume from afar, marketers had to translate its essence into images, transforming it into a network of signifiers that expressed elegance. By developing their brand through a visual approach, perfumers have built empires whose names will never fade.

Advertising for Bully displayed on a Parisian building, early 20th century.

Advertising for Jean-Vincent Bully, *Le Journal Le Petit Troyen*, September 3 1925.

43. Rosine Lheureux,
op. cit. p. 33.

44. *Ibid.* p. 78.

45. *Ibid.* p. 35.

46. Eugénie Briot,
op. cit. p. 253.

47. Interview with
Eugénie Briot.

The perfume store and the manufacturing process became entirely separate in the second half of the 19th century. The boutique served one purpose only: to sell perfume. Perfume boutiques were filled with precious decorations and opulent interiors where audacity and creativity reigned supreme. The reception area was comfortable, the staff very attentive. Engravings show us that sometimes there were more staff than customers! Cabinets made of precious wood (lemon, cherry, pear, mulberry) are filled with glass bottles and jars. The clientele came for their little bottle of ecstasy, and left filled with a feeling of abundance. Bottles and jars sometimes reached all the way to the ceiling, sometimes they sat in glass cabinets near the saleswomen, never too far from the highly fashionable sales counters.[43] Some boutiques used a flashy, maximalist aesthetic: engravings graced the walls, and everywhere were curios, Chinese vases, and Louis XIII or XVI furniture. The decorations were largely based on bourgeois conventions:[44] traditional cabinetry, parquet flooring in the Hungarian or Versailles style. Moldings and ornamental paintings introduced pediments, cornices, and architectural columns into the commercial space. Around 1890, boutiques started to fashion themselves as "perfume parlors" and Guerlain was a pioneer in this field. Boudoirs and small parlors were all the rage and embodied a new luxury: it was no longer in the perfumer's interest to demonstrate his greatness by displaying his workshop or showing off an impressive range of products. The boutique, instead, became a cabinet of curiosities that exuded an air of calm and repose.[45]

At the same time, fragrance was also sold in *les grand magasins* (the precursors to modern-day department stores). With perfume and cologne on the shelves of Samaritaine, Printemps, and Bon Marché the rules of commerce were completely shaken up. Small retailers had to adapt to the new rules as well, particularly the introduction of fixed retail prices and discounted sales.[46] *Caravanserais* with their large bazaars (Galeries Saint-Martin; Les grandes Parfumerie des rues de Rennes, ND de Lorette, Clichy; Moncey) spurred a revival, and inexpensive, high-quality fragrances entered the market. An explosion of perfumes filled store shelves and even spilled into the streets, where it attracted the attention of the middle-class clientele. The perfume industry had come to understand that, as the market grew more and more fragmented, it was possible to sell the same product to different target groups. The only condition was that you present it using different rhetoric and aesthetics. This was the advent of luxury and the magic of perfume, whose resonance was all the more powerful because it was rooted in our history, our personalities, and our passions. Perfume: that senseless and irrational alchemy, a thing beyond price.[47]

PERFUME: TO BRING HUMANS AND GODS INTO SCENT OF PERFUME (AMBROSIA AND NECTAR). THIS BLIME TO PERFUME AND THOSE WHO MAKE IT.

Perfume shop La Perle, in Paris. 1919.

AEROSOLS AND ATOMIZERS: FRAGRANCE IN THE 20TH CENTURY

The traditions and customs of the fragrance industry underwent a major shake-up: fashion designers entered the scene and broke up the industry's monopoly on making and selling perfumes. However, in the 1900s, it was an entirely different playing field: perfumery started to align itself with chemistry and industrial processes, with fashion labels and artists. Something that was of secondary importance in fashion houses became an incredible asset: couture labels and their charming staff possessed a certain image. This was the century of visual mass media, where notoriety went hand in hand with acclaim from the press, publicity, and appearances on television and in film. Paul Poiret in 1911 is a leading figure of this new movement with his fragrance La Maison de Rosine. The great names of couture would follow the trend in the 1920s: Worth, Jean Patou, Jeanne Lanvin, Chanel, Molyneux, Lucien Lelong... the difference here being that the perfumes were marketed under their brand[48] to reach a wider audience. Gabrielle Chanel didn't need to be a wordsmith to name her new fragrance Chanel N°5 — the sheer power of the brand was enough to lend the perfume a halo of excellence.[49]

"Following this fragmentation of the industry, the perfumers of the past would not survive: almost all of them went extinct following the Second World War. In the disaster's wake, only a few survivors were recorded: Guerlain, Roger & Gallet. In the 1970s and 1980s, traditional perfumers would patiently bide their time until the emergence of niche perfumery in 1990: new brands such as Annick Goutal, l'Artisan Parfumeur, and Serge Lutens emerged. Their marketing adopted, down to the very last detail, the conventions of 19th-century perfumers. The customer now had an alternative to image-based perfumery and fashion brands, who create an image for a perfume rather than marketing the inherent qualities of the scent itself. These new brands' names, their labels, and their bottles adopted an old-fashioned style, and advertisement was minimal and restrained: these perfumers relied almost exclusively on coverage in the press. The creation of boutiques with alluring interior design took pride of place: the gardens of the Palais Royal de Lutens became an iconic retail space, and what mattered now was how journalists talked about it. What's more, the perfume conglomerate, the result of perfume houses being bought up by large corporations, brought a new awareness to the act of purchasing... Who exactly profits from this sale? The conventions of this new niche perfumery called for the use of authentic products, quality materials, and carefully honed techniques with the highest of standards. What made a product marketable now centered on what was in the product and not the hype surrounding it. This was in stark contrast to the fashion labels who sold their perfume with "smiles and movie stars and not perfume,"[50] as the fragrance specialist Eugénie Briot points out.

48. Anne-Sophie Trébuchet-Breitwiller, *Parfum et mode, l'histoire d'un paradoxe (Perfume and Fashion, the Story of a Paradox)*.

49. *Ibid*

50. *Ibid.*

In 2014, the adventure of the Officine Universelle Buly (with an "L" dropped from "Bully" to avoid offending any English-speaking customers) was about to begin. The stores of Claude and Jean-Vincent Bully remained but a memory, ringing with the echo of Balzac. Meanwhile a Vinagre Aromatico Tipo de Bully with the very same formula continued to exist in Latin America due to the vagaries of licensing; the work of the Bully family had endured, except outside the borders of France. It was due time to give Bully's creations a proper home once again, this time at Number 6, rue Bonaparte. "One day, a man will pick up a book and... everything will begin again," Marguerite Duras liked to say. Had it not been for César Birotteau, the boutique, its decor, the enduring spirit of Jean-Vincent Bully, might still be waiting in the wings, waiting to be returned to their former glory. But, thankfully this was not the case. Alas, the stage has been set: places everyone! Curtains!

This was the advent of luxury and the magic of perfume, whose resonance was all the more powerful because it was rooted in our history, our personalities, and our passions.

Officine Universelle Buly, rue Bonaparte, Paris.

THE REAL AND WORLDS THAT IN A BRAND

Umberto Eco, an Italian novelist, cultural critic, and philosopher, described in his essay, "Travels in Hyperreality," a contemporary culture filled with fantasy environments, created to be better than reality. The founders of Officine Universelle Buly, Ramdane Touhami and his wife Victoire de Taillac have together created an exquisite, better-than-real universe, a place in which reality can no longer be distinguished from fantasy. Walk into an Officine and you are magically transported to a fantastical 19th-century Paris.

IMAGINARY COLLIDE

Hyperreality according to Officine

The tale of Buly started sometime in the 1970s in Southern France, where a young boy of Moroccan descent was living in a 19th-century château. The boy's father was a farmer. His mother was the keeper of the château, which belongs to a wealthy French judge. "When you grow up in the countryside as an outsider you spend a lot of time by yourself," recalls Ramdane Touhami. "Creating my own world came naturally to me, almost like it was a necessity to survive. I remember the first powerful story I made up, it was the myth of a haunted cage. My mother was taking care of a 19th-century estate. There was an attic. One day, when I was eight, maybe nine, I went up to the attic by myself. I had a beautiful old oil lamp, the kind you see in historical movies. I held up the lamp to the walls and, as I was walking along, I discovered traces, lines carved into the wall that looked as if someone had marked the passing days into the plaster with a knife. Immediately a film started playing in my head. I imagined that during the Second World War, the Germans had taken over this castle. I knew that the Germans had occupied parts of this area during the war. I imagined that they had locked up their prisoners here, who counted their days of captivity by etching into the walls. I started exaggerating this fantasy, inviting other kids from the neighborhood, and my cousins, to come by so I could show them the attic and tell them its story. It thrilled me to see how excited they were by my story, how they followed, expectantly, every turn of my voice. In Arab society we have a great oral culture. We pass knowledge on verbally. We spend nights telling each other stories. From an early age, I learned that everyone has a story to tell, but only the one who tells the best story rules the banquet."

The story of Officine Universelle Buly is rooted in the 19th-century, in a world whose aesthetics reflect the formative memories of Touhami's childhood and also in the origins of his wife and business partner Victoire de Taillac whose family tree dates back to the famous Porthos, one of the musketeers that Alexandre Dumas portrayed in his 1844 novel *The Three Musketeers*, and whose family estate was built in the 19th century.

It is not just the aesthetic codes of the 19th century that attract Ramdane Touhami. It is the notion of a world in which elegance prevailed, a formal elegance but also the elegance of etiquette. It was the beginning of retail. A time best captured by French writer Emile Zola in his novel *Au Bonheur des dames (The Ladies' Paradise)* published in 1883, a story set in the world of Paris's first department store when, in the reign of Napoleon, production of crafted commodities became a Parisian speciality.

Since then, no other city in the world has carried the banner of beauty, luxury, and style like Paris. Officine Universelle Buly was named after Jean-Vincent Bully, who inspired César Birotteau's character in a novel written by Honoré de Balzac in 1837 as seen previously. Based on this tale, in 2014 the first Officine opened in Paris, on the Left Bank, in rue Bonaparte, giving us the magical sensation that the original Jean-Vincent Bully apothecary had never closed its doors.

Each store is the gateway to a world where scents and sceneries take you on a journey. Every direction your nose and eyes turn, you learn something exciting about the world of beauty, you want to surrender. The mission is to ensure that ancient beauty rituals and recipes won't disappear. The Touhamis' positioned themselves as guardians, blending their own stories with the Jean-Vincent Bully narrative: "It all started with my mother and my own experience," says Ramdane Touhami. "When I was a boy, my mother didn't allow us to use anything synthetic or industrial. I remember thinking that my friends all smelled so good, coated in clouds of whatever was in fashion in the 1980s. Instead, she put Rasul on my hair, or argan oil. I never smelled good. I always smelled like food. When I left home, one of the first things

I bought for myself was perfume. I remember bathing in it. I was obsessed, I bought soaps, shower gels, deodorants, and wrapped myself up in it. I think you could smell me for miles around. This obsession came from my childhood trauma, being bullied because I smelled like the kitchen, and not like Calvin Klein, Givenchy or Armani or whatever the fashion was.

Through Officine, I rediscovered my mother's recipes and other ancient rituals. The truth is, my mother was right, no synthetic product is as good for you as a natural one. We modify them according to the expectations of our present time. This time they're good for you, and they smell good too." Each of these ancient recipes that Officine meticulously preserves takes you on a journey to an exciting destination. Take for example camellia seed oil. Traditionally it was used by the Japanese to protect their hair. The legend goes that the Japanese owe their famously beautiful, shining hair to the use of *tsubaki* oil (camellia oil), which is extracted from camellia seeds. To include it in their range of products, Ramdane Touhami travelled to find the best camellia plantation in the world, which is on Goto Island in the south of Japan, a place so famous for its flowers that they annually celebrate its petals with a camellia festival.

He is particularly keen on this idea of travel to the source: "Every product we manufacture teaches you something, if nothing else, about where the ingredients come from. You travel in your mind to the place of their origin, you learn how they were traditionally used, and what they are good for. The sales staff know all our products intimately. They take the time to explain, to advise, and suggest, but also to listen. Customer care is a role that we highly praise. We can explain where the product comes from, who made it, and why it costs what it does. We push for the transmission of artistic know-how, advocating the pleasure of seeing local artisans create things that are beautiful, and which are so because they exist within a historical and geographical context. Fabricating everyday objects, under respectful conditions, allows a worker to feel that he or she is creating something beautiful, useful, and personal. Take, as an example, our range of 168 combs. When I first went to the comb factory in Switzerland, the last manufacturers of handcrafted acetate combs in Europe, I remember the owner telling me, 'Today we make five different models of combs, but we used to make 168.' She was 86 years old, and together with her late husband, they had started the factory in the 1950s. When I asked why she reduced her range, she said it was because the market had changed. I looked at her knowing that, economically speaking, this might not be a smart choice. I asked her, 'How many different combs can you do?' '168,' she said. 'Okay,' I answered. 'Let's do them all.'"

Alongside its manufactured products, Buly also sells raw materials, like powder and clay, sharing recipes with its customers and teaching them how to prepare their own face mask or body scrub at home. It's a protest against the amnesia brought on by our era of cultural uniformity. "We travel the world to source our natural clays and oils. We believe that the habits and beauty rituals that humans have practiced for centuries must be kept alive and passed on."

"Like every great storyteller, you never want your audience to be disappointed or bored. If they are, you lose them. The more satisfying a story is, the more you learn, the more you want to know," says Ramdane Touhami. For a story to be successful, it must indulge in details. The more precisely it is said, the more colorful the circumstances are, the clearer the picture in the mind becomes. The product descriptions awaken in you a desire to become part of the story. For example, learning about the Japanese minebari wood comb. Each comb is delicately hand-carved in Japan by a talented craftsman.

The legend is that there was once a young girl named Oroku, who suffered from continuous severe headaches. One day she prayed to the gods for a cure. The gods visited her and told her to make a comb out of a minebari tree, then to use it in her hair. Oroku did as the gods told her. She was cured, and the minebari tree comb became famous for its healing powers.

Ramdane Touhami keeps on developing new products. And has even reimagined the brand's core product: back in the 19th century, when Jean-Vincent Bully opened his apothecary-style perfumery, all you could buy was perfumes. In homage, Ramdane Touhami wanted to create more than just another perfume. Officine imagined a scent that smelled like the purest extract of its fragrance. With this end in view, they invented the first water-based perfume in the world. "With an alcohol-based perfume you can smell the alcohol, but when you mix a scent with water you only find its natural scent. The olfactory memory is the strongest sensation we have," says Victoire de Taillac, whose favourite scent is rosewater. "When we built the palette for the water-based perfumes it was essential to create a rose scent that would truly smell like a pure rose." Inhaling Damask rose gives you the impression that you have stepped into a rose garden. You can smell the aromas from the leaves, the stems, the flowers, and the soil. In your mind you see thousands of glowing petals. A beautiful, subtle colliding of the real and imaginary, which takes place in your head as soon as you step into the Buly universe.

"Like every great storyteller, to be disappointed or bored. The more satisfying a story is, you want to know," says R

you never want your audience
If they are, you lose them.
the more you learn, the more
amdane Touhami.

DOES LOGO MATTER?

The ongoing metamorphosis of a visual identity

Close up on the Huile Antique label, showing printing details and embossment on the golden medals won at World Expositions by Jean-Vincent Bully, 2019.

À TOUTES LES
EXPOSITIONS

As the self-proclaimed "industrial aesthetician" and designer Raymond Loewy humorously said in the title of his 1952 book, "Ugliness is a Hard Sell." Ramdane Touhami is clearly thinking the same thing when he says: "I view beauty as a game that lets your imagination run free. This storytelling element rooted in the 19th century is important for Officine." Historicism is at the heart of Officine Universelle Buly's visual identity, which is highly evocative and very much rooted in a past inspired by the traditions of the French art of living, but which is also open to the future and to the whole world, through a sense of journeying and the inclusion of beauty care products from every continent. This complex, intentionally paradoxical message for the brand is transmitted through all its visuals: images and photographs, product names, labels, a wide range of original, exclusive typefaces, the colors and shapes of boxes, bottles, tubes, candles, and other products, not to mention the boutiques as a whole, each one of which is different and yet, driven by the same philosophy.

Close up on the Lait Virginal label, showing printing details and embossment on the golden medal, 2019.

WHEN A SIGN
BECOMES A TRAP

The logo is just a small part of this identity, one to which Ramdane Touhami does not assign more than a little importance: "The term 'brand' originates from the age-old custom of burning a hot iron stamp on cattle to prove their ownership. As our society has gradually become dominated by a capitalist economy, the term is now used to identify objects manufactured by a certain company and to testify to the notion of authenticity attributed to that company. Most of us have succumbed to the myths surrounding brands. This was in the age of ownership, which allowed the owner to associate him/herself with the myth of brand. Now, and in the future, as people show less of an obsession with possessing and increasingly put value on sharing, how do you create a brand that can still generate a sense of myth around itself?"

The challenge lies in not becoming trapped within a fixed form of logotype: "A logo is the first thing that graphic design students learn how to make. A logo is ultimately a rule, and rules are made to be broken. It embodies marketing in the 20th century, a bit stiff and retrograde. Officine already has a dozen or so logos, all of them different. This is because I'm not selling a logo. I'm selling a view of the world, a way of doing things, a good product. I don't want customers to buy an oil or a perfume simply because they like the logo. It's also a question of constantly questioning everything, of living with a sense of constant change. For example, the typeface etched onto our combs has undergone several metamorphoses. Each boutique now has its own graphic signature on the letterhead it uses. The guiding principle is of an "incoherent coherence." We are betting on people's intelligence, that this isn't the main thing for them. A brand universe should never be boring. Today at the Officine, we are obsessed with creating new graphics. We refuse to adhere to codes or precise graphics charts. We want to avoid falling into the trap of limiting our horizons. Once a creative work is finalized and validated, everyone can copy it. With Buly, I want to complicate and change things constantly: typefaces, our products, even our paper bags."

"I'M NOT SELLING A LOGO. I'M SELLING A VIEW OF THE WORLD. A WAY OF DOING THINGS. A GOOD PRODUCT."

Ramdane Touhami

Close up on the Eau Superfine label, showing printing details and embossment on the golden medals and the central gilded title, 2019.

LES
PLUS HAUTES RECOMPENSES
ONT ÉTÉ OBTENUES

SU

LOTIO

Officine Universelle Buly
coat of arms sticker used
since 2018.

BOREDOM
IS
THE ENEMY

Codes, signs, and symbols abound in the imagery that the brand creates. And even though the visual identity remains very harmonious with the world of beauty, it never confines itself to a single image; it instead offers a multitude of images. For Ramdane Touhami, surprise is another key element in addition to reinvention and perpetual motion: "You have to surprise and especially not bore yourself, visually speaking. Success does not prevent change. Some of our classics, like Eau Superfine or Huile Antique, have changed in appearance several times over. Everything can, by its very nature, be perfected and changed. And our clients are far from upset by these changes; they are instead always delighted by the new versions, which they often find to be even more beautiful than the previous ones." Improvisation and intuition also play an important part in the process of changing the visual identity—as does the adrenaline stimulated by an urgent need, one of the main drivers of creativity for Ramdane Touhami. But the truth is that this identity, which is the result of a highly personal process, feels extremely coherent and natural. It bears its creator's signature at every step. A further particularity concerns its size: Officine is one of the only "global" beauty brands that doesn't hire teams of designers or outside consulting firms to come up with its visual identity. This is quite an exception in the world of luxury. The brand's director is its artistic director, who also sees himself as a "typologist," a devotee of letters and a creator of typefaces. Ramdane Touhami collects them and has surrounded himself with a permanent team of graphic designers for the particularly precise requests and orders he makes throughout the year. His inspiration often comes from the most unexpected places: "One of our logos was inspired by the one that Jean-Vincent Bully created for his cashiers at the 1867 World's Fair. Our last one came from an old wine bottle. For example, 80% of our typefaces come from old gravestones in cemeteries. The Guitry typeface came from a kind of painted box for German films from the 1920s and 1930s that I happen to collect. Another very typical pre-war typeface was created on the basis of the engraved lettering at the Italian poet Gabriele D'Annunzio's mausoleum on Lake Garda. Other ideas have sprung from an old box of rice powder, a door for a public bathhouse, or even commemorative plaques seen on the street. Sometimes we imagine an entire alphabet on the basis of just four letters. We have invented or reinvented all these typefaces; Buly does not use any typeface that doesn't belong to us."

SURPRISE IS ANOTHER KEY ELEMENT IN ADDITION TO REINVENTION AND PERPETUAL MOTION.

SYMBOLS
AND
COATS OF ARMS

In their diversity, all codes, signs, and labels nevertheless follow the same law: the history, re-invention, and continuation of Jean-Vincent Bully's legacy. Ramdane Touhami nuances this with the unexpected choices that this fertile territory of historical archives yields: "Living with history doesn't mean replicating things from the 19th century. Officine is not a replica of a historical era. Rather, in creating products, stores, and an identity, I researched motifs and ornaments from various bygone eras that inspired me to create my own history for the new Buly. Some elements were taken from the past as-is, while others are merely the fruit of my imagination. I realized later on that this echoes "hyperreality," the post-modern state described by Jean Baudrillard and Umberto Eco: the creation of another reality, the illusion that the product or the building has been there for centuries, when in actuality, it was made in our time. When we embarked on creating a new history for Officine Universelle Buly, I used an invented setting from the first third of the 19th century as a general backdrop. From day one, Victoire and I knew which products to include in the collection. In line with early 19th-century skincare customs, we included face cream, toner, and face cleanser as basic items. But we didn't want to look like a beauty brand. Describing beauty with words like "face toner" or a "facial cream" seems banal and lacking in imagination. Beauty should allow you to imagine, to indulge in your own sense of fantasy. Out of my fascination with history, I have been collecting 18th and 19th-century commercial labels, which tell you a lot about the society and its customs in those days. In 19th-century Paris, the beauty industry was quite advanced in terms of advertising's attempts to bring women under its spell. In the age of Romanticism in Europe, society still rigorously followed codes of etiquette. Before the French revolution, beauty was a domain thought to be reserved for the nobility, who spent exorbitant amounts of time fetishizing their external appearance. Aristocrats did everything to take care of their appearance by having scientists and chemists research the latest beauty secrets, and making sure that these secrets were never leaked to others. Beauty secrets became accessible to a much wider swathe of the population after the revolution, when Napoleon I promoted what we now call open innovation. The beauty industry began to grow at an unprecedented rate. To attract a clientele aspiring to a sense of elegance, the description of beauty items regularly became quite imaginative, much more than what they are now."

"BEAUTY SHOULD ALLOW YOU TO IMAGINE, TO INDULGE IN YOUR OWN SENSE OF FANTASY."

Ramdane Touhami

Seal sticker with a yellow sun, used for the
closure of boxes of glass bottles.

Officine Universelle Buly's coat of arms
sticker with a red curtain with gold
details, used from 2014–2018.

A COUNTER CURRENT

In the last several years, the identities of the world's best-known brands—Balenciaga, Celine, Yves Saint Laurent, Burberry, Balmain, and Berluti, just to name a few—appear to have been refashioned according to the same model to appear "more modern" (using simple, minimalist upper case letters in a "distilled" sans serif bold font). They end up being totally standardized, the unfortunate result of which is that they become symbolically interchangeable. Officine strives to be different and works in the exact opposite direction. For Ramdane Touhami, creating one's own register, one's own world is essential; Buly has no desire to participate in this competition for a false modernity. It wants to be in a class of its own. Singularity is the guiding principle at Officine, and what clients find so attractive is the sense of history and of journeying, a notion of an "elsewhere" in the fullest sense of the term. Instead of always dwelling on the same thing, Buly wants to surprise, to go off the beaten path. But this also means making a promise. For Ramdane Touhami, Officine's thinly veiled promise is a sense of mystery submerged in an imaginary past: "Historical brands have huge potential because they have a certain mystique that remains unrevealed. People are mesmerized by the *Venus di Milo* because part of her torso isn't there. The missing piece in the puzzle lets people imagine what this fragment would have looked like. People can continue its history, each with their own 'hyper-story' in their mind."

SINGULARITY IS THE GUIDING PRINCIPLE AT OFFICINE. AND WHAT CLIENTS FIND SO ATTRACTIVE IS THE SENSE OF HISTORY AND OF JOURNEYING. A NOTION OF AN "ELSEWHERE" IN THE FULLEST SENSE OF THE TERM. INSTEAD OF ALWAYS DWELLING ON THE SAME THING.

Seal stickers for gift wrapping.

French sociologist Dr Agnès Rocamora is a reader in social and cultural studies at the London College of Fashion. A leading investigator of consumer culture, Rocamora talks to Jina Khayyer.

Why are brands with a history forever exciting?

AR Although novelty matters, lasting appeal is rooted in heritage. Having a past gives a brand authenticity and credibility. It promises long-established truths. I strongly believe that it is not the appeal of the past, per se, that seduces the customer but the storytelling that is used to teleport the past into the present. Brands that have a history sell stories. Their narratives create imaginary worlds in which idealised versions of their products are created, transformed from mere commodities into something precious. The French sociologist Pierre Bourdieu argued that stories allow us to transcend the materiality of a product allowing an increase of its value. Bourdieu was also well known as a philosopher and anthropologist. His work was primarily concerned with the dynamics of power in society and the nature of social life. He established a connection between the value of a product and its symbolic production. Like Bourdieu I believe it's crucial to tell the story of how things are manufactured. Information gives the biggest increase of value. The success of every brand and product is built on strong symbolic production. Buly has been very skillful in putting in place the best possible narration and building a future on a fabulously told past with a strong how-and-where-it's-made tale.

JK Any kind of beauty ritual is a behaviour we have learned from family and friends, so applying cosmetic products is already loaded with stories. Repeating these rituals connects us to those emotional memories. Symbols also evoke memories: if the look of a beauty brand reminds me of what I've seen in my mothers' or grandmothers' bathroom, does it make me feel more familiar with the brand?

AR Yes. Semiotics, such as the logo and any other symbol used by a brand, play an important role. They help to create and articulate meaning. They are a bridge between your personal emotional connections and the values the brand is promising you. The idea of an ancestral truth, that these beauty products are made from recipes which have been passed down for generations, surviving time, is convincing. In a way it seems like a paradox for an industry, like the beauty industry, interested only in youth and beauty to rely on old recipes and old stories. Yet it is precisely that which gives integrity to the product, making it believable and therefore desirable. An extreme example would be: if it worked on Cleopatra, it's sure to work on me. Ancestral products have timeless appeal. There is a mystery surrounding them. An alluring combination of myth and magic secrets unveiled to give us beauty. Finding beauty is a never-ending quest. It doesn't get old or dated. To be beautiful is an immortal desire, so the narrative of unlocking a forgotten source of beauty and reviving it, with the best of the past and all the possibilities of now, is irresistible.

JK We are all made up from memories, yet every memory is personal and intimate. Scents are a powerful evoker of memories, as soon as we smell something we have a visual. How does a brand access this private space in our heads?

AR As a sociologist I always think, what is the social dimension that goes beyond the private? Memories are a coming together of a series of social experiences which relate to space, place, and time, where the body and senses of the individual crystallize into one memory. On one hand, smell is deeply private. Yet, as it was created in a social environment, at a certain place, in a certain time, with certain people, it is a social memory too. In fact, smell is one of the most important social memories. To access any kind of private memory you have to be able to spin a tight web with these social threads.

JK   The culture codes are what make us who we are. They invisibly shape how we behave in our personal lives, even when we are completely unaware of our motives. Is there a way to crack the codes that guide our actions and understand why we live and buy as we do?

AR   There is a way, yes. Sociology is all about understanding why people do what they do and buy what they buy. Depending on your class, your gender, your ethnicity, your sexuality, you make certain choices and those choices impact buying patterns. At the moment I'm reading a lot about the data-fiction of fashion. The future is turning towards algorithms. But, to be honest, if you really want to decode patterns, what you need is a good sociologist. That is what we do, find out why people want what they want. We analyze social parameters, such as class, sex, ethnicity, and try to understand what they have in common. Although our social and economic backgrounds determine what we consume, the communality between groups determines why we want it. We consume things to articulate our individual and social identity. What we consume shows our affiliation. We desire what is desired by the people we desire. We want it because it is wanted.

JK   Symbols instantly create images in our heads that we evaluate: I like, I don't like. Each image is associated with a set of stereotypes formed by the cultural codes we grew up with. Which codes did Buly incorporate?

AR   I think the historical time and context in which Buly was created was crucial. It was the beginning of an extremely digitized reality, where images on screens started to become a high currency. It was the beginning of Instagram and the beginning of our understanding that just looking good on a photo can bring so much more success. Instagram changed perceptions. I have heard designers say that they only created a certain collection or item because it looked good on-screen, on Instagram. Social media changed consumerism because things can be consumed visually before they are consumed physically. This had a massive impact on visual aesthetics. Buly launched at this historic turning point. Its founders understood early on how important it is to have Instagrammable products. Another thing that Buly mastered, which is as important, is the packaging: it becomes an object in its own right. It is as alluring as its content. In some cases you can even reuse it like, for example, the marble candle holder and bell jar which encase their scented candles. Buly has raised this approach to the highest art form, selling goods which are consumed as much for their visual appeal as for the high quality of the product. It's clear to me that Buly strives for a constant dialogue between visual image and quality.

JK   Which other semiotic-tools does Buly use successfully?

AR   Buly bridges luxury with tribalism by proposing a DIY-chemist fantasy, with their natural beauty powders and clays. The brand invites you to make your own, the result is you feel that you have a completely own, and as a result you feel personalized product. In this global climate, where everything is mass-produced, details like this add an intimate dimension to your purchase. Buly allows their customer backstage access, inviting them to interact. It's a beautiful *mélange* of the private and the public. Also, their wording is really good. I actually have a Buly hand cream on my desk as we speak. A friend of mine gave it to me for Christmas. It's called Pommade Concrète. I like the word *pommade* (in English it translates as ointment)—not many people use that word anymore. It connects me to an ancestral memory, therefore it feels precious as memories are precious.

JK   I'm saying Buly, leaving out an important part of the name and brand identity: Officine Universelle Buly à Paris. Aristotle believed that symbols are as powerful as the spoken word when it comes to evoking ideas and images in the mind. What is it about the symbolism of Paris that makes the French capital so enticing to everybody?

AR   How many other cities have been put into so many literary books, songs, films, paintings? There is a vast enterprise of mythologizing Paris. We talked about culture codes earlier; Paris codes have high symbolism. Paris is an asset in itself. Paris is a brand, the most appealing brand in the world. When you buy something in Paris, or anything made in Paris, it feels as if you buy Paris itself, as if you wear Paris, as if you smell like Paris—eventually it will make you feel like a real *parisienne*. I'm amazed how Paris never loses its charm. Myths sell. The Paris myth is one of the most lucrative myths ever. The very mention of Paris in combination with a product makes it art, luxury, beauty, and puts a veil on its commercial reality. You are not buying a thing, you are taking home a bit of Paris.

JK   Baudrillard believed that the simulacrum, the idealized version of a thing, gives the customer more happiness than the thing itself. Do you agree?

AR   In the case of Buly I would say the reality is that Buly lives up to its myth. A simulacrum is never just a simulacrum. When we buy a product, we have an actual product, it's real. If the product falls apart, the simulacrum falls apart. The fashion and beauty industry are a matter of reality. We are happy to dream, play, anticipate, and live by the simulacrum, but the quality of an object matters to the consumer. Products have to be more than just a fantasy. They have to live up to the story they tell.

"*Paris is a brand, the most appealing brand in the world.*"

Dr Agnès Rocamora

HOW TO CREATE A HISTORICAL COLLECTION WITH LITTLE TO GO ON

Continuing the work of Jean-Vincent Bully

Still-life of products from Officine Universelle Buly including
the Baume des Muses, La Douzaine Parfumée of the Louvre,
the Scented Decorative Pencils and the book *An Atlas of Natural Beauty*.

Without wanting to wear out or misuse the

said: when your temple of beauty has been b...

about the temple's rituals, its components,

is to think of the product range and its beauty

this respect, Officine Universelle Buly is

century and more contemporary aspirations. S...

the present sets the tone for a new conception of

is very clear on this point: "Officine wants

advantages of a skincare treatment and the ben...

essential elements of beauty, and Buly's proa...

us as a brand is as bewildering as it is simp...

it doesn't add value to the existing products.

monly accepted and give our customers that ex...

Ramdane Touhami offer a roadmap for creat...

…logy of religion, it must nevertheless be
…to perfection, all that remains is to think
…nd its figures. The crucial next step, then,
…roducts through a given historical lens. In
…e result of a careful balance between the 19th
…e perpetual pendulum between the past and
…modern cosmetology. Ramdane Touhami
…o offer people a feeling of enchantment. The
…ficial properties it has on your skin are the
…cts are charged with this task. What defines
…e: we don't add a new product to our range if
…"We have to push the limits of what is com-
…ra something." Victoire de Taillac and
…ng a beauty empire: the Buly Emporium.

THE BULY RANGE
AND ITS
SOURCE OF SEDUCTION

As Victoire de Taillac sees it, Buly is reviving the age-old conventions and professional traditions of the perfume industry during the reign of Napoleon: "The aim of a perfumery in Napoleon's time was to enrich the perfumer's business in the strictest sense, which caused them to sell a whole host of different specialty items under one roof. The advent of modernity would whittle down this rich mixture of offerings, but in the beginning of the 1810s, it's important to remember that perfume shops had the right to sell products dedicated to beauty and hygiene, and so they were closely intertwined with other professions. At the time, their shelves and display cabinets contained haberdashery products—brushes, sponges, and a whole range of scissors—alongside products from herbology, where the bounty of nature was harnessed to make medicines for the body. The approach, then, that we wanted to take was obvious: the future Officine would be a trifecta of fragrance, raw materials, and beauty accessories. From this point of view, the "Officine" in our name, French for "pharmacy" or "dispensary," was the embodiment of an old-fashioned business, with its seductive and archaic aesthetics, working at the forefront of pharmaceutical practices. The "Universelle" in our name refers to the fact that we bring together beauty traditions from all over the world: Officine appeals to all of mankind, drawing excellence from them."

THE PERPETUAL PENDULUM BETWEEN THE PAST AND THE PRESENT SETS THE TONE FOR A NEW CONCEPT OF MODERN COSMETOLOGY.

Eau Triple Sumi Hinoki, a fragrance with smoked cypress accords,
in its glass bottle, by Officine Universelle Buly.

"A GOOD FRAGRANCE SHOULD FI[T THE]
PERSON. PERFUME SHOULD NEI[THER ANNOUNCE ITS]
ARRIVAL, NOR LINGER BEHIND [AND SHOULD]
NEVER OVERPOWER. IF THESE R[ULES ARE FOLLOWED, NO]
FRAGRANCE WILL APPEAL TO EV[ERYONE, NOR WILL IT BE]
UNPLEASANT. WHETHER THE SCEN[T CHANGES]
WITH THE MOVEMENT OF YOUR [BODY]
AS YOU MAKE YOUR WAY THROUGH [A ROOM OR]
DEST AND GENUINE, NEVER INTR[USIVE, PER-]
SISTENT YET NEVER OBSTINATE-

ONE'S PERSONALITY AND THEIR
ER ANNOUNCE THE WEARER'S
EM TOO INTENSELY. IT SHOULD
LES ARE FOLLOWED, THEN YOUR
RYONE, AND NO ONE WILL FIND IT
EMANATES FROM YOUR WRIST, OR
HAIR, OR SUBTLY, IN YOUR WAKE,
A ROOM, IT SHOULD BE BOTH MO-
SIVE. A GOOD FRAGRANCE IS PER-
POLITELY PERCEPTIBLE." *Extract from the Buly catalog*

"THIS WAS TRULY ARCHEOLOGICAL WORK WE WERE DOING. WE WENT THROUGH THE HISTORY OF PERFUME WITH A FINE TOOTH COMB IN ORDER TO FIND ESSENCES THAT WERE STEEPED IN HISTORY."

Ramdane Touhami

Lait Virginal, a perfumed body lotion in its glass bottle, by Officine Universelle Buly.

FLUID MECHANICS: PERFUME, SOAPS, AND SELF-CARE

As Ramdane Touhami explains, the creative process for Buly's products followed a very clear progression: "During the first months of development, Officine was all about perfume and scent. Our research focused on which fragrance compounds were in vogue under the reign of Napoleon Bonaparte. Heady, airy, floral perfumes were subjected to an intense olfactory vetting. This was truly archeological work we were doing: we went through the history of perfume with a fine-tooth comb in order to find essences that were steeped in history.

I hate the word "synthesis" and its derivatives—they are equally synthetic. Nothing should be synthetic. We have made it a point of honor to select natural formulas and aromatic compounds. We studied historical perfumes and their hygienic properties with the help of reference books, perfume collections, fragrance historians, and relics preserved in specialized libraries. From the fragrances selected by the perfumers of the time, rose, violet, and heliotrope emerged pinnacles of French refinement. Our idea was to continue the selection of essences and aromatic plants through the lens of the four continents. We opened Officine in 2014 with a collection of water-based fragrances to be applied to the skin, unique because they are non-irritating and long-lasting. Based on the principle of emulsions (cosmetics that resemble an opaline solution), the fragrances had only eight variations compared to the current 14. These unique scents have been transformed into beauty bars, combining the benefits of both soap and perfume to provide a longer-lasting fragrance. With this we have truly reached the heart of the master perfumer's profession! The success was overwhelming, and other products were even more surprising: a widespread craze caused sales of Laits Virginaux et Huiles Antiques (Perfumed Milks and Oils) to skyrocket. It was crucial for us to develop these incredibly refined scents, seeing that they were once widely available in perfumers' catalogs, back when milks and creams were traditionally used to lotion the body. This approach to perfumes and scented beauty products allows the customer to apply a fragrance in a series of successive applications, in an almost impressionistic manner. As soon as a scent delights the senses of our customers, many of them ask for a scented version of another product. This lateral use of scent allows them to apply creams, oils, and intensely creamy milks with the same feeling of satisfaction. Our philosophy of perfume is to masterfully balance innovation with restraint. It demands that fragrance be hinted at rather than imposed. It is the fullness of an elegantly crafted fragrance. Anything related to scent is of utmost importance to us. Interior fragrance is an entire area of the business that we developed during our previous ventures at Cire Trudon.

We did not want to let go of this expertise. Candles, the Alabaster collection, and scented matches—whose woody surface is impregnated with scent, an idea that no manufacturer wanted to develop with us!—fuel our quest for innovation while drawing on the creations of the past. Perfumes for automobiles or scents that preserve the smell of a brand-new sneaker, these are the starting points for our scented inventions. Officine must embrace this conservative avant-gardism, an oxymoron that compels us to push the envelope of what is possible, both in terms of application and in terms of scented compounds."

THE NUTS
AND BOLTS
OF ACCESSORIES

For Ramdane Touhami, the most important thing to remember at Buly is the unbreakable link between beauty rituals and fragrance: "It is crucial that we offer durable accessories to make everyday life beautiful: vetiver root brushes, acetate combs, minebari, horsehair brushes for exfoliation, copper accessories for stimulating lymphatic drainage, etc. Accessories are no longer meant to be utilitarian, disposable objects. Instead they have become beautiful, timeless objects for self-care. They are part of an exhaustive inventory, with 400 products in our display cabinets and windows. Fifteen or so semi-precious stones are transformed into astonishing accessories that increase the benefits of our creams and skincare products. Our combs were carefully crafted in the last remaining comb factory in Europe and are undoubtedly the largest selection in the world produced by a single bran—they offer 190 products in total. As a beauty emporium, we are committed to bringing together a collection of rare objects gleaned from the four corners of the world: combs made from Alnus firma wood from Kiso, a densely wooded region in the heart of the Japanese islands; nail clippers from the Niigata forge, renowned for its sumptuous metalwork; hand-painted porcelain perfume diffusers from Arita. These ingenious treasures have the distinction of coming from the best craftsmen and not from some short-lived start-up. Traditionally used for the incredible way they feel on the skin, our sponges were brought to us from the Greek island of Kalymnos, infamously named the "Island of Widows" because of the perilous nature of retrieving these spongy treasures. Higher up, in the mountains, the incense of the monks of Athos contains the secrets of a censer that only men are allowed to light. In great secrecy, I went there to discover their traditions. In a world where there are so many trades with so much amazing knowledge, it is far more worthwhile to discover and celebrate traditional skills of the past, than to start a new company to make a product.

"THESE INGENIOUS TREASURES HAVE THE DISTINC-TION OF COMING FROM THE BEST CRAFTSMEN AND NOT FROM SOME SHORT-LIVED START-UP."

Ramdane Touhami

Bath Brush by Officine Universelle Buly.

"ALREADY PERFUMERS WERE EXPRESSING THE UNIVERSAL DIMENSION OF HYGIENE-RELATED PERFUMERY. THE UNIVERSALITY OF BEAUTY ON THE ONE HAND, THE UNIQUENESS OF EACH PERSON'S SKIN ON THE OTHER."

Victoire de Taillac

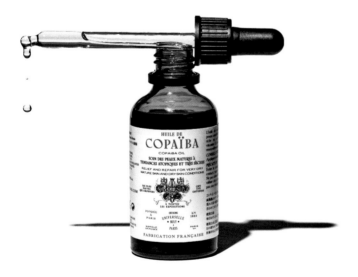

Argan Kernel Oil and Peony Powder by Officine Universelle Buly.

THE SKIN AND ITS MYRIAD QUESTIONS

Victoire de Taillac also supports Buly's global vision concerning the world of beauty: "Old perfumery catalogs contained broad categories that were broken down into various cosmetic needs. There were numerous product lines for the mouth, face, for men, and women, all richly illustrated. Already perfumers were expressing the universal dimension of hygiene-related perfumery. The universality of beauty on the one hand, the uniqueness of each person's skin on the other. It was essential that we continue this tradition, and to do this we had to clearly define each problem that needed to be treated. Our facial care products include treatments to purify, beautify, and soothe the skin, in the form of creams, waters, and floral lotions. The latter have the technical appeal of containing the natural compositions of times gone by and have the added benefit of not using any of today's most controversial and questionable chemical compounds. These skincare products follow modern techniques (they use vegetable glycerine, oils, butters, and natural preservatives) and our dental care products have some very original flavors, which are sometimes very unconventional compared to the current market practices. Incorporating apple, ginger, cucumber or mint tea into your dental routine can be very surprising. But surprise is good! Today, innovation is at the heart of an increasingly intense and commercial process. The dictates of business call for a relentless search for novelty, for new technologies. Officine Universelle Buly, however, remains committed to things that have stood the test of time: true to our heritage, we seek to learn from past generations. We have sought out oils that have been an integral part of certain communities for a very long time, for example in Benin [West Africa] where two sisters grow shea trees to extract their butter following traditional methods; or women in Morocco who cultivate argan oil in the same way as they did 1,000 years ago. In Egypt, we met the producers of black cumin oil, which is sacred in the Qu'ran for its ability to "protect from everything except death itself." In India, we looked for aloe vera, whose countless virtues have been appreciated for over 6,000 years, while in the West, in Brazil, copaiba is grown from the trunks of trees in the Amazon forest, where the inhabitants treasure its ability to soothe irritated skin. Our travels have led us to passionate, experienced nature lovers, including those on Fukue Island (Goto Islands, off the west coast of Japan) who grow camellia seed oil, waking up at 4am to watch the daily extraction process. There is now ample evidence to justify preserving certain customs, without resorting to chemistry to effectively serve the needs of self-care. We are not averse to technology, but if methods have stood the test of time, why would we want to replace them with new ones? These ancient beauty practices are the consequence of needing to remedy one's own ailments, using locally available ingredients, without the presence of any pharmacies or factories. At the time, there was no L'Oréal or P&G; people made their own soap and used oil extracted from locally harvested nuts to apply to the skin, body, and the hair. This, rather brilliantly, has been described as the slow-cosmetics movement. Officine offers the essence of these traditions from all over the world in the form of butters, clays, powders, and plant oils."

A SHORT PRIMER ON LOOKING YOUR BEST

Just as important as the ingredients that go into our products is the way our products look. Buly: where the emphasis is on style, on seduction through a rhythmic phrase, on the right and pleasant word for every occasion. This is a fundamental idea for Ramdane Touhami: "Basically, beauty is everyone's business. When we wake up in the morning, we wash our faces and brush our teeth. We comb our hair. These are basic routines that keep us healthy and, above all, help us to take care of ourselves. Beauty should not be a luxury that can be purchased like a high-end fashion brand. The very notion of luxury is changing. For Officine, beauty is about making customers happy through care and that's why I never use the word 'anti-ageing' in beauty products. Buly protects you from the hysterical obsession with ageing by not reminding you of it. Who came up with the erroneous claim that getting older is not beautiful? Beauty is more than the appearance of our skin. We are emotional and irrational beings and Officine Universelle Buly approaches beauty through this very lens, the one that speaks to our emotions and our souls. When you reach 80, do you expect your skin to be as flawless and taut as it was when you were 20? Do you think this is beauty? Beauty should be determined by how great you feel. If you feel delighted and objectively more radiant using certain beauty products, what else do you need? I want to offer our customers an immersive experience so that everyone can feel fabulous by using products that work."

"FOR OFFICINE, BEAUTY IS ABOUT MAKING CUSTOMERS HAPPY THROUGH CARE AND THAT'S WHY I NEVER USE THE WORD 'ANTI-AGEING' IN BEAUTY PRODUCTS. BULY PROTECTS YOU FROM THE HYSTERICAL OBSESSION WITH AGEING BY NOT REMINDING YOU OF IT." *Ramdane Touhami*

Opiat Dentaire, a fluorine-free mint, coriander, and cucumber-flavored toothpaste.

THE ART OF NAMING
OUR PRODUCTS

How can we make our everyday moments more magical? Can beauty be a journey? How can we strike a balance between harmony and innovation?" These are questions that the creators of Officine are constantly asking themselves, as Victoire de Taillac explains: "Can the beauty accessory, which has nothing superfluous about it, lead us to a euphoric state? The beauty industry uses and sometimes misuses harsh or demoralizing terms such as Skin Toner or Emulsifying Cream to emphasize the effects of the product. Officine focuses more on the world that the wording evokes. Lait Virginal brings to mind immaculate skin, like that of the Virgin Mary. Our Savon Superfin, with its latin prefix 'super' evokes quality that is unmatched. We believe in names that have nothing in common with the typical beauty product: they never have to be down-to-earth; instead, they attempt to soar above the clouds, evoking a celestial infinity. Much like *Alice in Wonderland* and its aura of nonsensical fantasy, Officine plays with a world that goes beyond one's sense of logic. Our customers are taken on a literary journey through our olfactory world and, rather than selling a mere product, we offer them a whole universe of evocations. The catalog becomes a compendium of allegories: everyday products are enhanced by a captivating lexicon, steeped in the exquisite. A lipstick becomes a Baume des Muses full of cheeky sophistication; a moisturizing hand cream is called Pommade Concrète... A whole litany of oils and powders detail which effects they have on the skin. Toothpaste becomes Opiat Dentaire, a treatment much appreciated by Napoleon, who himself was a key figure in political hygiene with his 'tooth kit.' Ramdane Touhami was adamant about naming products this way, and he initially opted for names exclusively linked to Napoleonic mythology for Buly's interior perfumes (Généraux d'Empire, Campagne d'Italie, etc.) This historical anchoring brought in an impressive number of clients who were admirers of the emperor. They even demanded soaps and labels printed with his likeness! For the water-based body fragrances, we worked on a floral, sunny symbolism, and in this respect Fleur d'Oranger de Berkane invites us to travel to an ancient Moroccan city: 'A snowstorm of dazzling petals on the dry hills covered with orange trees, the honeyed puffs of wind going through the branches of neroli, made green again by the waters of March, carried by the galloping horses from the sea to the shivering basins of the mosques in Cordoba. The Andalusian spring, white with flowers, comes rushing into the shade of the palaces, setting the sequined and gold-threaded drapes around the betrothed's baths a-gleaming.'

As for Makassar, an Indonesian fragrance in vogue since the 17th century, we have placed it in a literary context: 'Blowing from the horizon, warm winds and their powdery trail barely brush the surface and shake the forest of sails of the lambos, the twilight air blue with tobacco and burnt incense.'

At Buly, we believe scent is mediated through words. Inviting the mind into the experience makes you dream, and it reflects your own conception of beauty. Let's not forget the localized nature of fragrance: Damask Rose, Scottish Lichen, and so on. It is an invitation to discover new lands, to spark your imagination, and to immerse yourself in these places. If you feel transported, you will feel a rush of euphoria and the perfume will have achieved what it set out to do. Anyone can, without buying anything, take away this feeling of delight thanks to the catalog, which is distributed free of charge in our shops."

HOW CAN WE MAKE OUR EVERYDAY MOMENTS MORE MAGICAL? CAN BEAUTY BE A JOURNEY?

Pommade Concrète, one of the best-sellers of Officine Universelle Buly, a nourishing hand and foot cream, enriched with shea butter and beeswax.

Eau Superfine, a soothing floral face toner with rose water in a glass bottle by Officine Universelle Buly.

The scented candle Retour d'Egypte, in its black marble jar with a Buly-stamped glass bell jar to preserve the integrity of its scent.

"WHEN YOU WAKE UP IN THE MORNING AND YOU HAVE A BEAUTIFULLY DESIGNED TUBE OF TOOTHPASTE IN YOUR BATHROOM CABINET, SUDDENLY THIS MUNDANE ACT CAN BRING YOU A MOMENT OF EXHILARATION."

Ramdane Touhami

The products catalog by Officine Universelle Buly.

DESIGN: THE CATALOG AS LITERARY ANTHOLOGY

The catalog is the cornerstone of the brand's universe, according to Victoire de Taillac: "The magically illustrated Buly catalog is a gospel that tells the story of the brand's universe, both material and immaterial. It is entirely conceived and designed in French, and its translation into English, Korean, Japanese, Chinese, etc. is a difficult task, as the word play is so complex that it often has no meaning in another language! A rigorous adaptation is implemented every week using a squadron of translators.

We regularly update this document in search of the perfect tone, so that our customers feel at home in our world. It is a beacon of our expertise and carries our message into people's homes. Ramdane Touhami even talks about a Buly portable bible—which is saying something!" And for him, it's as much about words as it is about images: 'Thinking about the catalog means thinking about the iconography. I wanted the bottles to have an almost unreal dimension, with richly ornamental labels that contribute to the narrative. These visual objects are of utmost importance, as they are the first point of reference for anyone who doesn't know the brand. Their appearance must stir people's emotions and make them feel immersed in 19th-century Paris... long before they apply the product to their skin. During the research phase, I used mythological figures or religious iconography to decorate the bottles. This kind of classical beauty is widely present in my personal collection of old shop labels from every time period. As a synthesis of various eras, I began to draw fonts by hand before placing my favorite ornamental motifs here and there. Studying archives (old photographs, Buly products, invoices, correspondence) provided me with the inspiration to make the packaging more realistic. The glass bottles are decorated with arched shapes, the perfume bottles with sharp geometrical forms typical of the Art Nouveau period. All are alabaster-colored to prolong a feeling of purity, while emphasizing the labels by playing on the contrast. I thought as much about the product, its bottle, and its undeniable power to enhance any space it inhabits. A journey through beauty. When you wake up in the morning and you have a beautifully designed tube of toothpaste in your bathroom cabinet, suddenly this mundane act can bring you a moment of exhilaration. This is what we aim to do with our oral care products (the famous Opiats Dentaires or Eau de la Belle Haleine). When the first activity of the day delights you, your whole day looks different. For this to happen, the design must follow a certain logic. The snake and the caduceus have been associated with medicine since the time of the ancient Greeks as a symbol of healing. For the bottle of our cleansing water (known as Eau Rectifiée) I designed an illustration reminiscent of an ancient pump mechanism for extracting water. The products are either packaged in a metal tube or a glass bottle. Buly is inspired by the practices of apothecaries in the 19th century, at a time when plastic did not exist. It is not our policy to loudly proclaim that we are ethical or that we are trying to achieve sustainable development goals. We simply make things from materials that were available in the past. From product design to packaging and naming, every detail of Buly is purposeful and nothing is left to chance. When I see my customers keeping their empty Buly bottles because they like the design, I know we've done something right. We don't need to lecture them for them to be aware of the life cycle of the products they buy. Instead of ending up at the bottom of the sea, Buly products get a second life."

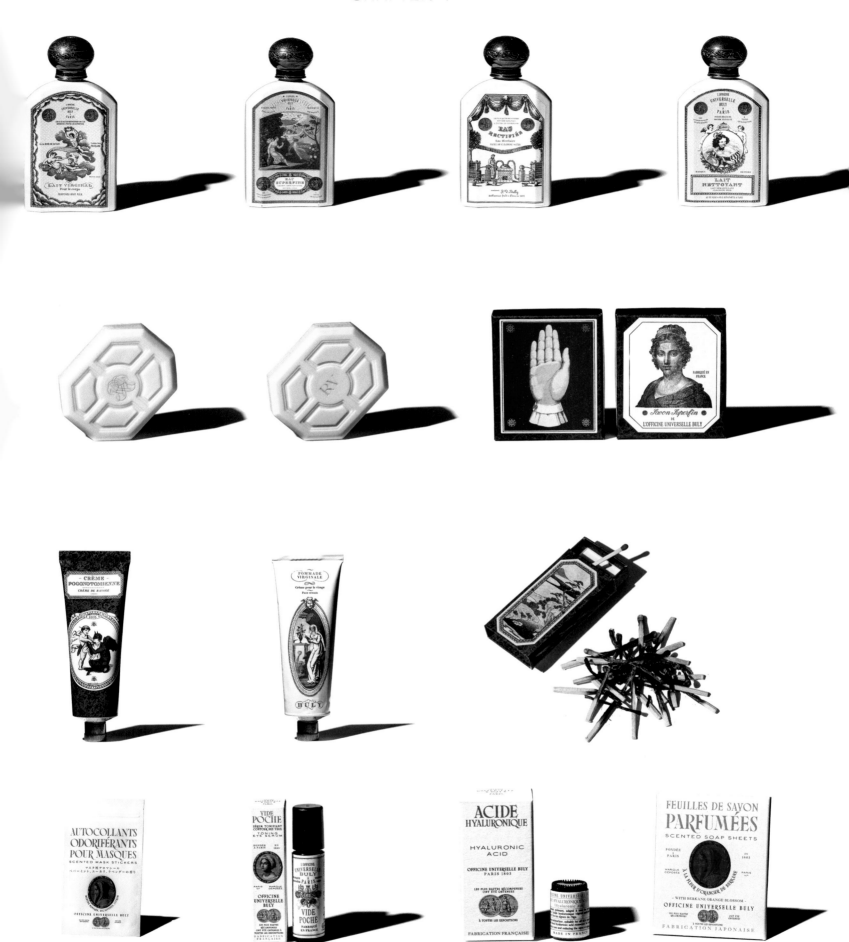

Still-life of products from Officine Universelle Buly including perfumes, scented candles, tubes, soaps, and facial care.

The Crillon Hotel coffret, designed for its prestigious bathrooms.

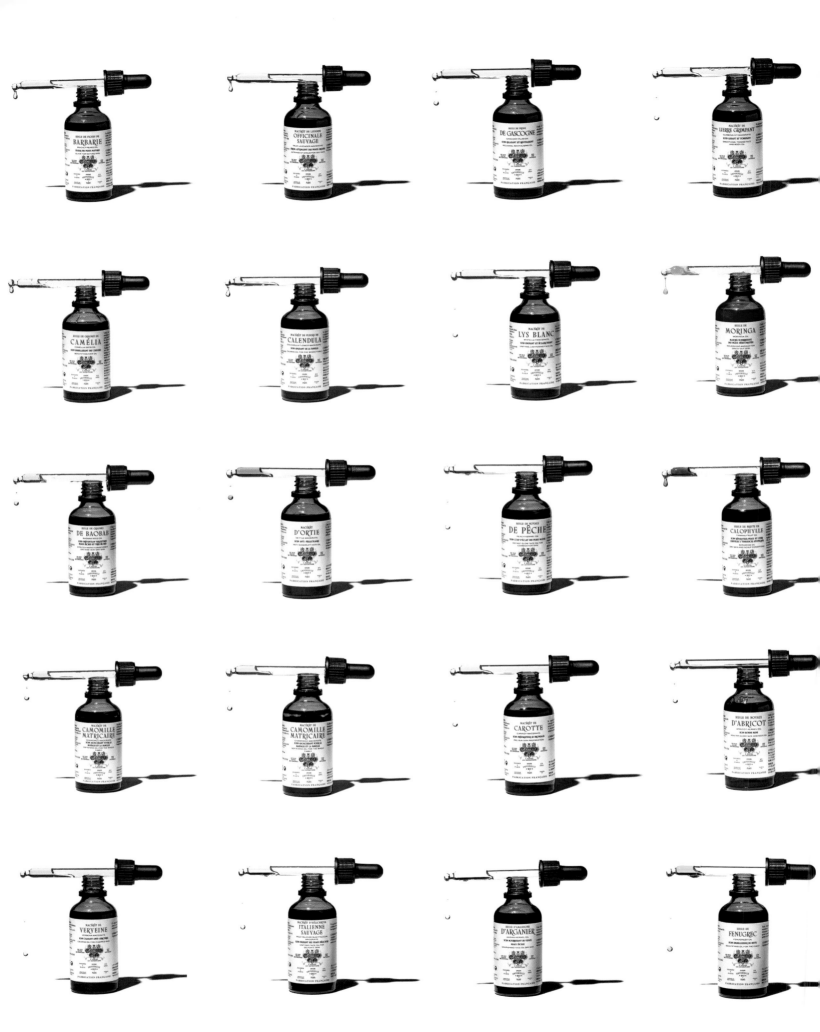

100

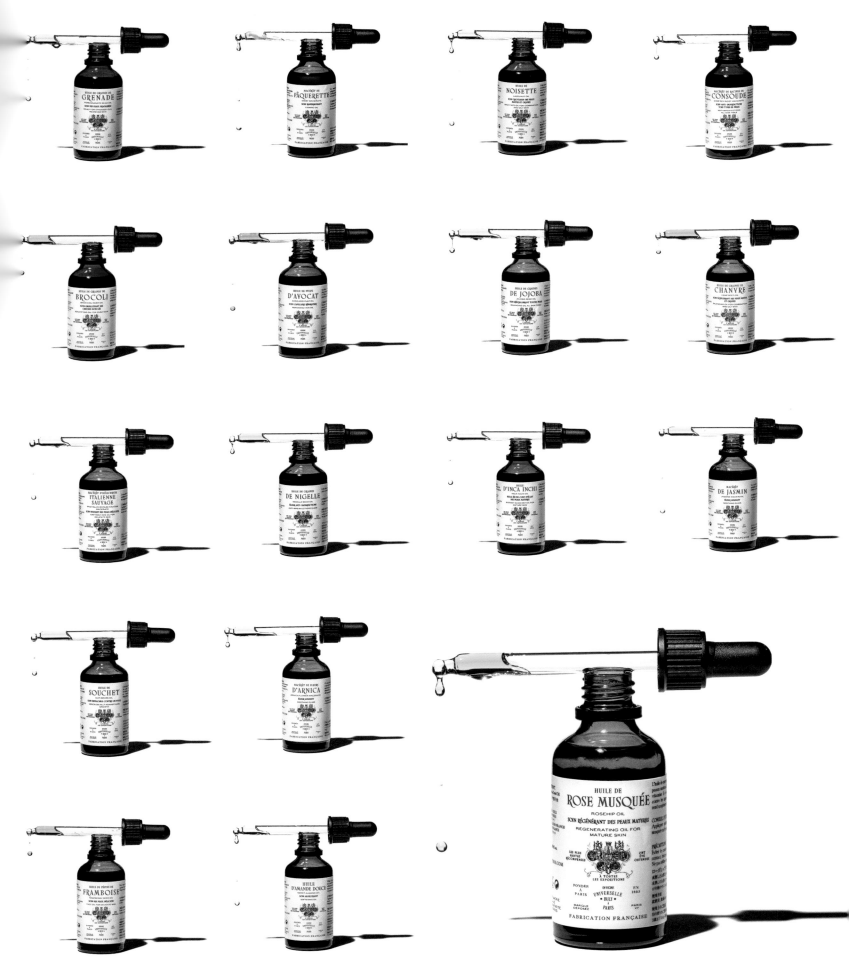

Packshots of organic plant oils from Officine Universelle Buly.

Still-life of raw natural powders and clays from Officine Universelle Buly.

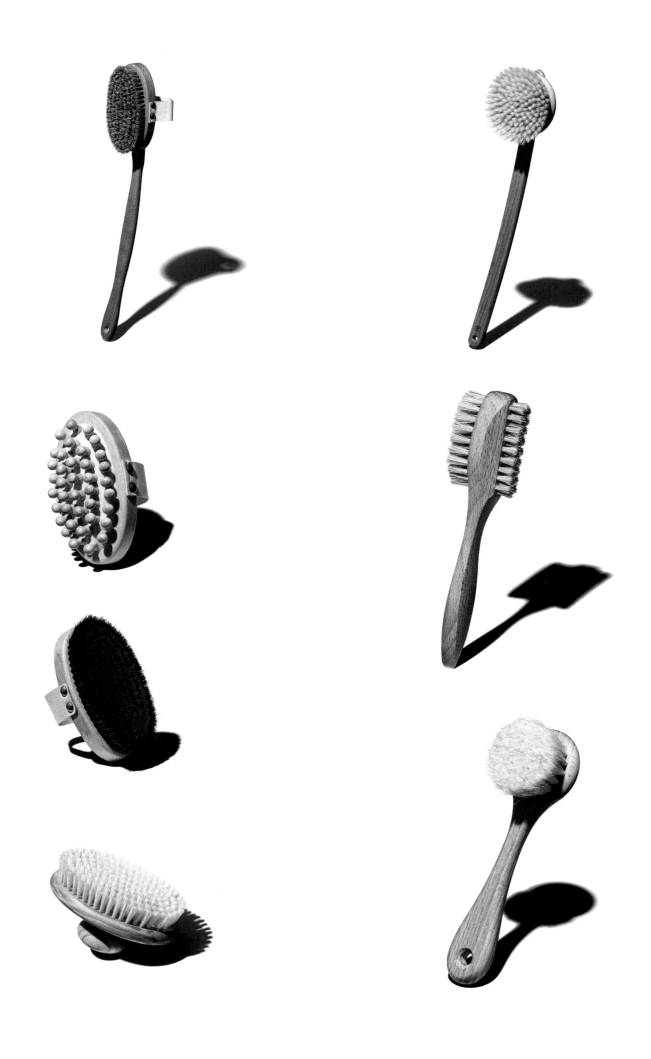

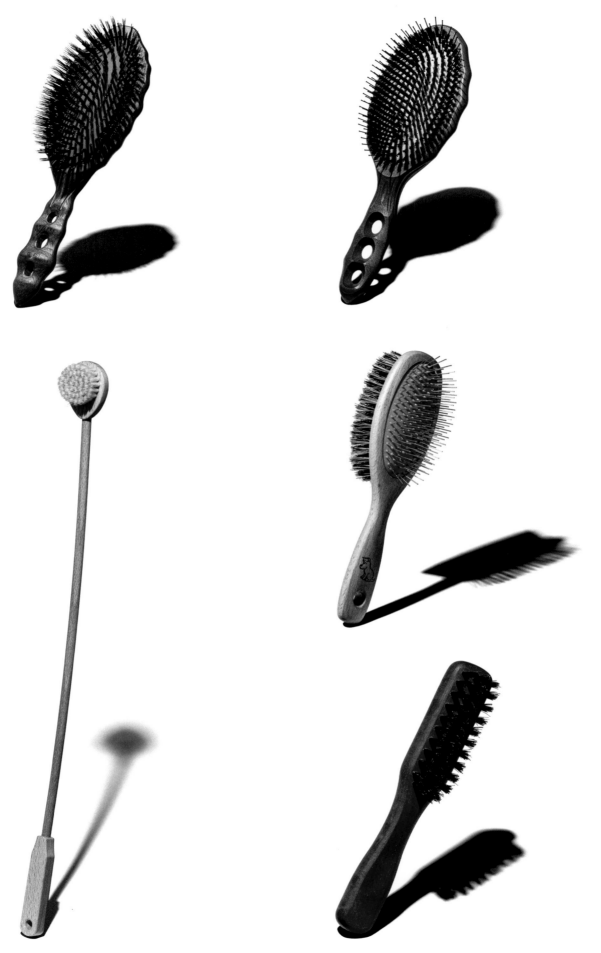

A collection of brushes from Officine Universelle Buly.

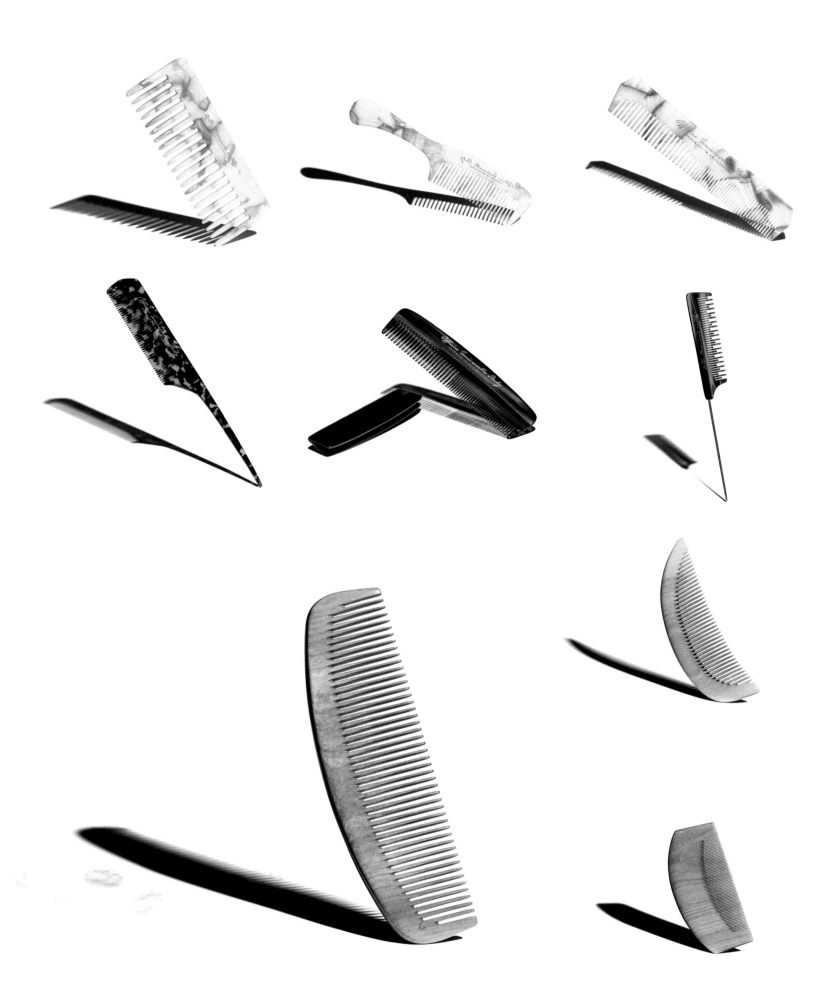

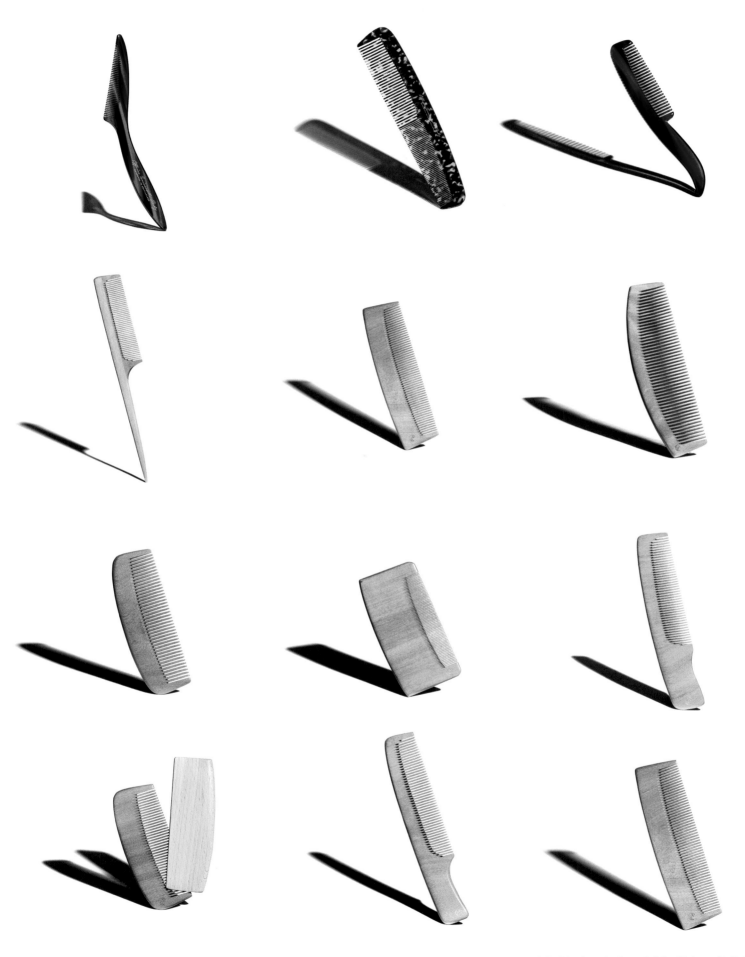

Still-life of combs from Officine Universelle Buly.

Still-life of face brushes and bath accessories from Officine Universelle Buly.

IS THE PAST A SOLUTION TO THE FUTURE?

The Pre-pl

White opaline bottle with bevelled edges, 200 ml capacity, with a zinc, aluminum, magnesium, and copper alloy cap, used since 2014 by Officine Universelle Buly.

stic Society

Not every progress is an improvement. There was a world before plastic, before industrialization, before mass-production, before the false promise of capitalism led us to believe that we can consume without limit or consequence. Plastic has become ubiquitous in our daily lives, but in its short history, a transformation from miracle material, one that could take the shape of anything, to environmental disaster, has been rapid. The solution sounds simple: a world without plastic. But plastic is a material with many benefits. It plays a critical role in maintaining food quality and reducing food waste, and the trade-offs between plastics and potential substitutes, or complete bans, can create negative impacts.

The answers are not straightforward. What we can do is cut down our use of plastic. When Victoire de Taillac and Ramdane Touhami started their research for Buly they discovered that, while synthetic materials may be necessary for the food industry, the cosmetics industry can do without it. It became one of their founding principles for the brand to be plastic-free.

From 2014, Officine Universelle Buly was built on a no microplastic policy. Microplastic is one of the most insidious environmental polluters produced by the beauty industry. They are minuscule plastic particles, less than five millimeters in diameter, which are used in beauty products like toothpaste, soap, shower-gel, and cleansing masks as abrasives or exfoliants. Water-filtering systems aren't designed to sift out particles this small so they enter into the water system, contaminating lakes, rivers, and oceans, and then enter into the human food chain, first consumed by fish who are in turn consumed by us. Shockingly, microplastics have been found in drinking water and bottled water and even in the air we breath and in our bodies. According to Global Citizen and the UN Environment Programme, a single shower can result in 100,000 plastic particles entering the water system. Known for their meticulous research and commitment to responsible entrepreneurship, Victoire de Taillac and Ramdane Touhami researched old and new solutions to the microplastic problem. They discovered a multitude of natural alternatives such as sand, beeswax, and honey, realizing that if we want to live in a plastic-free world we must turn to the past.

The 2020 #noplastic campaign.

AT THE BEGINNING THERE WAS NO PLASTIC—HOW DID WE CREATE THIS POLYMERE WORLD?

The first plastic was called Parkesine and created in 1856 by the English chemist Alexander Parkes. In 1867, at the Exposition Universelle of Paris, Parkes presented his invention to the public and won an award. Parkes was not commercially successful with his invention but the idea was developed further by American businessman John Wesley Hyatt, who founded the Celluloid Manufacturing Company, most famous for its contribution to the film industry. Today it seems ironic, but at first plastic was a discovery that promised to save the environment. For example, celluloid could imitate and replace ivory, a natural resource which was becoming increasingly scarce and pushing elephants to the brink of extinction. Plastic was hailed as the savior of the elephant. For the first time human manufacturing was not constrained by the limits of nature. Natural materials like wood, metal, stone, bone, tusk, and horn could be preserved and replaced by plastic substitutes. Plastics could protect the natural world from the destructive forces of human need.

The beginning of the 20th century was an exciting time for chemists. There were many breakthroughs that would lead to the development of plastics as we know them today. In 2019 the Science Museum in London published *The Age of Plastic: From Parkesine to Pollution*, showcasing the stories of pioneers like Alexander Parkes and the Belgian chemist Leo Hendrick Baekeland, who in 1907 invented Bakelite, the first fully synthetic plastic, meaning it contained no molecules found in nature.

THERE WAS A WORLD BEFORE PLASTIC, BEFORE INDUSTRIALIZATION, BEFORE MASS-PRODUCTION, BEFORE THE FALSE PROMISE OF CAPITALISM LED US TO BELIEVE THAT WE CAN CONSUME WITHOUT LIMIT OR CONSEQUENCE.

This was the first thermosetting plastic, which when heated could be moulded into any shape and when it hardened again would maintain that shape permanently. And it could be colored. It was used everywhere for toys, tools, furniture, cars, jewellery. Or Swissman Jacques Edwin Brandenberger who in 1913 invented cellophane. Produced in thin and flexible sheets, this transparent and waterproof material was soon discovered and adopted by the packaging industry. In 1935 American chemist Wallace Carothers developed nylon, marking the rise of synthetic fabrics, used in the textile industry for everything from tights, sweaters, and shirts to parachutes. In 1973 Nathaniel Wyeth developed a way to replace glass bottles with plastic bottles. Light, transparent, and cheap, his invention is the standard for mineral water and drinks packaging today.

THE AGE OF PLASTIC

During the economic miracle in the 1960s, plastic invaded people's home en masse, because it was affordable. It was no longer the need to preserve scarce natural resources that made the production of synthetic alternatives a priority, it was the desire for booming business. According to author Susan Freinkel (Plastic, a Toxic Love Story), "plastics challenged traditional materials and won, taking the place of steel in cars, paper and glass in packaging, and wood in furniture. The possibilities of plastics gave an almost utopian vision of a future with abundant material wealth thanks to an inexpensive, safe, sanitary substance that could be shaped by humans to their every whim." Nobody imagined the damage it would do. The durability of plastic, once its crowning success, has become a dark shadow across the natural world. About 79% of plastics remain in our environment, piling up in landfill sites, filling up rivers, lakes, oceans and killing our wildlife. According to Rex Wyler, co-founder of Greenpeace International, globally over 330 million tonnes of plastic are produced annually. As of today, some 9 billion metric tons of plastic have been produced and spread around the world: "To the plastics industry, this is a global success story. Plastics helped create a throwaway culture. Several generations have now grown up believing that tossing out a drink container is completely normal, reasonable behaviour. Ecology teaches us, however, that there is no away. Everything that passes through our hands ends up somewhere."

Greenpeace calculated that if current production and waste management trends continue, by 2050, there will be 12 billion tonnes of plastic in natural environments.

THE POSSIBILITIES OF PLASTICS GAVE AN ALMOST UTOPIAN VISION OF A FUTURE WITH ABUNDANT MATERIAL WEALTH THANKS TO AN INEXPENSIVE, SAFE, SANITARY SUBSTANCE THAT COULD BE SHAPED BY HUMANS TO THEIR EVERY WHIM. NOBODY IMAGINED THE DAMAGE IT WOULD DO.

Better to end up at a flea market than at the bottom of the ocean.*

*since 1803 our bottles have been made mainly out of glass

#noplastic

THE NO PLASTIC
CHALLENGE

Today the glowing reputation of plastic is lost, but it is difficult to replace. An estimated 120 billion units of packaging are produced every year by the global cosmetics industry, most of which are not recyclable. In her essay, "How the Beauty Industry is Feeding Plastic to you and the Planet," environmentalist Annija Erdmane describes how packaging is the number one contributor to plastic production in the world. In 2015, research found that packaging accounted for 146 million tonnes of plastic every year. The difficult challenge for Victoire de Taillac and Ramdane Touhami was to build a world of beauty products without using any plastic. That meant developing packaging-solutions for each product. De Taillac and Touhami looked back at pre-plastic days of production and consumption and found ideas for sustainable solutions. Two years of research went into creating Officine's plastic-free characterful soap oil dispenser. Inspired by an old faucet element discovered at an antique dealer, the refillable Buly soap oil dispenser is made from solid brass gilded with fine gold

THERE IS ONLY ONE THORN LEFT
NOBODY IN THE WORLD HAS YE
BUT VICTOIRE DE TAILLAC AN

and set on a marble slab which allows it to be attached to the wall. All of Officine's creams and toothpastes come in aluminium tubes, a material used by pharmacists for centuries because it is impermeable to air, so the products last longer. Scented candles are packaged in marble and glass, which becomes as much of a feature as the candle itself. Ramdane Touhami designed signature glass bottles for all of their liquid products, like the water-based perfumes and body oils. They are presented in beautiful clear, amber or milk-white opaline glass bottles. The latter was first made in Venice in the 16th century as a competitor to porcelain. It is sturdy and resistant enough to calm customers' concerns that the glass could shatter in the bathroom. All Buly screw caps are made from Zamac, an alloy composed primarily of zinc, containing 4% aluminum, 3% copper, and less than 1% magnesium. All pipettes are made of glass. Officine's toothbrush handle is made out of acetate, a manmade fiber derived from cellulose. Acetate plastics are environmentally friendly because they are biodegradable. The brush is made either from Italian badger hair, for sensitive gums, or natural silk, for those who prefer more strength. The scented alabaster stone sits in a specially designed porcelain box. Officine's soaps are first wrapped in a fine sheet of paper and then packed up in their signature cardboard box. All nude products, like combs, body brushes, and hair brushes are sold in cloth bags, while sponges and stones are wrapped in kraft paper. Those who order online receive a package that is lined with wood wool. In addition to Buly's sustainability commitment, de Taillac and Touhami implemented a recycling system, offering its customers the opportunity to return glass containers, which are then sterilized and reused. There is only one thorn left: the liquid dispenser pumps. Nobody in the world has yet found an alternative, but Victoire de Taillac and Ramdane Touhami are on it.

THE LIQUID DISPENSER PUMPS. FOUND AN ALTERNATIVE, RAMDANE TOUHAMI ARE ON IT.

Next page: There was a life before plastic. The proof... For the packaging of its powders, soaps, perfumes, etc., Officine Universelle Buly uses paper without ever sacrificing either the quality or the beauty of the object.

INNOVATE WITHOUT DENYING ITS HISTORY

The will to create

Scented matches invented by Officine Universelle Buly.

Still-life featuring alabaster and comb, by Officine Universelle Buly.

When Ramdane Touhami starts working on a new project, his first goal is to break all the rules: "I can't imagine not adding anything new, not innovating. This was the case with Cire Trudon, where I made improvements to the candlewax and the wicks, and for which I designed the bell jars. And this is also what we did for Officine Universelle Buly. The first challenge we gave ourselves was to get rid of all the unpleasant olfactory elements of a perfume, such as the plastic, the alcohol, and even the saponification. And we succeeded in preserving our best fragrances without denaturing them." As one of the 20th century's greatest inventors, Nikola Tesla, once wrote, "Instinct is something which transcends knowledge." Very early on in their design of Officine Universelle Buly's catalog of perfumes and beauty care products, Ramdane Touhami and Victoire de Taillac, trusting their intuition, decided to expand the historic perfumer-vinegar maker's heritage, pushing it to its outermost limits, ultimately to obtain an incredibly high level of quality. Innovation lay at the heart of the production, and it was essential for Ramdane Touhami to do more than just reproduce what was already there: "To have a brand also means creating the unexpected and being where no one expects you to be. You can't get stuck on history. Buly is faithful to the work of Jean-Vincent Bully, but it's also fairly unorthodox. With his introduction of perfumed vinegar into the realm of beauty products in the 19th century, Bully was truly ahead of his time. Officine Universelle Buly tries to capture Bully's innovative spirit and harness it for the 21st century. I envisioned something that doesn't exist in the market for beauty products today, but which at the same time feels very familiar to people."

"To have a brand also means creating the unexpected and being where no one expects you to be. You can't get stuck on history."

Ramdane Touhami

THE CHALLENGE OF A WATER-BASED PERFUME

The most astonishing example of this innovative spirit in Buly's catalog is Eau Triple, a revolutionary, water-based, alcohol-free perfume, a veritable chemical feat that took years of research and testing to achieve. In the world of perfumery, where alcohol is a standard component, a water-based perfume seemed an impossibility, an anomaly, and the exception. Creating this type of perfume takes a lot of time and effort for the perfumer, the chemist researchers, and the suppliers of the raw materials. The floral and other essences and their chemical compositions are much harder to balance than simply adding more powerful artificial additives or ingredients. Using water as a base and following the principle of microemulsion was a considerable challenge to overcome, but it was one that Ramdane Touhami accepted without hesitation: "A perfume without any alcohol or ethanol was our way of resolving the paradox of a brand that relied on both the past and the future. We created the first water-based perfume in the world, Eau Triple, which evokes a number of places and landscapes, and it has become our signature. I've always thought it odd that perfume could be such a manifesto, such a signature; after all, it leaves its trace everywhere, even after the person wearing it has left the room. In the past, perfume was perhaps worn mainly as a way to attract or seduce others, but I think that we should just wear it for ourselves, as a way to feel better about everything. We worked very hard on creating this water-based perfume. There are several beauty brands that now make alcohol-free fragrances, but when we first had this idea in 2014, all the perfumes on the market contained alcohol. We asked ourselves the very simple question, what's better for your skin, water or alcohol? The choice is obvious. And our innovations are not limited to water-based perfume. Cosmetics research is so much more advanced now than when Bully started his company. We want Officine Universelle Buly to be relevant for the 21st century. We honor the forward-thinking mindset of our founder with the cutting-edge research we conduct in our own laboratory here in France. Always keeping one foot in the past, we have updated formulas with scientific discoveries and results that Jean-Vincent Bully himself would have used if given the opportunity, and we package everything with Officine Universelle Buly's signature artistic designs. This is what makes our product much more than just an object; it's ultimately a succession of complex challenges that we ultimately manage to overcome." And the resolution of this technical challenge led to a catalog of 12, sensational perfumes, created with the greatest rigor in terms of their quality and their sophistication. These alcohol-free perfumes can be worn on one's skin as well as in one's hair; they're not intrusive, but they do hold throughout the day. Here too Buly sought the perfect balance between not too much and not too little, in observance of the prescription from another century that: "A good perfume adjusts to both the person and their personality. It should not precede nor follow the person wearing it too strongly; it should not emanate imperiously. It pleases everyone and is never bothersome."

A prototype for the first
Eau Triple bottle in 2013.

"A PERFUME WITHOUT ANY ALCOHOL OR ETHANOL WAS OUR WAY OF RESOLVING THE PARADOX OF A BRAND THAT RELIED ON BOTH THE PAST AND THE FUTURE."

Ramdane Touhami

Officine Universelle Buly is deeply committed to using cutting-edge technological research to create the most extraordinary and beneficial products possible, but the brand describes them in a very 19th-century manner. Ramdane Touhami maintains that, "Buly is committed to innovation in beauty care, but instead of using a vocabulary burdened by science and technology with phrases like, 'This facial lotion, the culmination of our research in molecular biology, will revitalize your stem cells,' we define our Eau Superfine, for example, as a 'Floral lotion with rose distillate that will soothe your face and make it more beautiful; it softens and consoles your skin.' Here, the past is married to the future, without compromise, but instead with a unique sense of aesthetic harmony."

Next page: Still-life featuring a scented candle, scented matches, and an Eau Triple bottle, by Officine Universelle Buly.

OLFACTORY INVENTIONS:
NEW OBJECTS
TO SCENT YOUR SPACE

After revolutionizing how perfume is made, Officine Universelle Buly created home fragrances in forms that had never existed before. As Victoire de Taillac explains: "We wanted to find new ways to perfume spaces by playing with different sensations and new mediums. The products we created were totally new and had never been seen before; they represent innovations both in terms of their use and the object itself."

For example, Alabaster is composed of a porcelain box with a blue decoration, a small piece of an exceptionally porous sedimentary stone, and a bottle of a very perfumed oil. After you put one or two drops of the oil on the stone, you put the stone in the box, which you leave open for the time it takes to scent the room. The alabaster diffuses any one of Buly's eight fragrances quite effectively, but without any heat or vapors. It can be used to scent bathrooms, hallways, studies, closets, and wardrobes. Ramdane Touhami's inspiration for the alabaster came from a unique object he discovered in Japan, but the name comes from the Greek vases used to store scented oils for one's skin, the very first perfumes, whose terracotta retained their scent. The perfumed match is another creation that has considerable deodorizing properties. Cut out of long pieces of a soft wood and soaked in a perfumed solution, they envelop a room with the simple gesture of being lit. They come in the same eight fragrances as Buly's alabsters and candles. They are an unusual way of quickly and elegantly scenting a room, with just a spark. As surprising are the perfumed ceramic pencils that one dips into a vial of any of the eight home fragrances. They rest nicely on one's desk or anywhere else, scenting the air with their trompe-l'oeil design.

In 2020, while the beauty industry focused intently on producing antibacterial gel, Ramdane Touhami was thinking of new ways of freshening the air for people wearing masks to fight against the Covid-19 epidemic. He ultimately designed a patch to attach to the outside of one's mask that releases a refreshing scent: the Autocollant Odoriférant, or Scented Sticker. The refreshing notes of peppermint, eucalyptus, and lemon make the air within one's mask that much more tolerable. The year 2021 sees another two new creations, the first of which is the perfumed lamp, a beautifully designed desk lamp that diffuses its fragrance when the light is turned on. Officine Universelle Buly created this lamp to resolve a specific problem: consumers in Asia are often uneasy about using scented candles because of the very frequent earthquakes that occur in this part of the world, as the open flame of a tipped candle could start a fire. With the alabaster and the perfumed lamp, there is no fire and, therefore, no danger.

The Robinet Cap of Officine Universelle Buly allows your well-closed tubes to stand straight, just ready, and at your service. This cap is sold individually and independently of the tubes it accessorizes.

To coincide with the Olympic Games scheduled for the summer of 2021, Ramdane Touhami has created another surprising product: Eau Gymnastique, a refreshing olfactory solution for sports shoes that make sneakers smell brand new with just one spray. Eau Gymnastique scents your shoes immediately, but the micro-encapsulation of its ingredients ensures that the fragrance will continue to emanate as one wears the shoes. The idea had been growing in Ramdane Touhami's mind for a long time. A fervent collector of sneakers since time immemorial, he knows better than most how attractive the notion of newness is in this domain. Having one's shoes always smell clean had been an impossible dream for sneaker collectors (who are increasing in number because of the dominance of streetwear). And now this dream has become a reality, because of Officine Universelle Buly. In search of new challenges, Buly is now bringing its inventive spirit to a revolutionary new makeup line.

Above: Scented decorative pencils, a brand new way to perfume an interior, 2020.
Below: Scent patches for masks created during the Covid-19 epidemic, 2021.

Electronics projects scheduled for 2022: Beauty accessories with some specific technologies to clean the face.

Two years of research were necessary to create the Officine soap dispenser, entirely handmade in France from solid brass gilded with fine gold.
Its marble plate, which allows it to be fixed to the wall, is engraved with gold leaf with the name of the restaurant or house for which it is intended.
It is currently deployed in prestigious restaurants.
Right page: The scented lantern, where the light heat induces the scent, by Officine Universelle Buly, 2021.

HOW TO AVOID "LAS VEGAS" SYNDROME?

Every ritual deserves a temple: Buly's world

Sign outside the Aoyama'store, Tokyo.

IN PRAISE
OF THE
ORNAMENT

Officine's world of rituals and beauty is deeply rooted in the 19th century. It has the power to turn every product into a beacon of tradition and history. Perfumes, oils, powders, accessories can be taken home... Unlike stores! Customers should be overcome as soon as they set foot in one, for the store goes beyond a mere scenic role: it rounds off a trinity, together with the product and the Buly staff, completing an opus akin to a *Gesamtkunstwerk*, a total work of art assumed by Ramdane Touhami: "When Victoire and I launched Buly in 2014, we only intended to have one store, a store that would transport the visitor back to the atmosphere of a 19th-century apothecary. How things have changed! These spaces have become a window onto centuries-old artisanal know-how, offering nature's most beautiful materials. These techniques deserve to be perpetuated, and bring aesthetic relevance to a world in need of it, all this in a Paris lacking historical stores dedicated to perfume. The City of Light is the world's epicenter of perfumery, and yet all the places that bore testimony to this heritage have disappeared. Elsewhere, the Santa Maria Novella perfume store in Florence, or 1920s store Knize in Vienna—designed by Adolf Loos—bring their old-fashioned grace to the city. In Paris, there was a market to be imagined and developed. This thought was the foundation stone I brought to the rue Bonaparte adventure.

My first move was to hire a carpenter with a strong vision. As we progressed on our journey through the woodland, it became clear that centuries-old French oak would be an ideal companion for the interior design and for our windows and cabinets. A rare walnut burl wood veneer would do wonders for frames and ornaments, precious marble from the Pyrenees would lend its spectacular luster to the counter. In order to be more precise, more engaged, I took a course at the Ecole Boulle, a famous applied arts school named after André Boulle, Louis XIV's Master Cabinet-Maker. The cabinets are topped with doucine[1] moldings; window frames and rich imperial velvet curtains have been designed and made by knowledgeable craftspeople.

Through technical prowess, the store turned into a master painting! But having a 'Made in France' seal wasn't enough to create a coherent ensemble. I had Italian earthenware tiles shipped over to include their artisanal, irregular finish. Each piece of furniture was carefully shellacked[2] to give it a particular shine and color. Not all my design sources come from the same era. They are more of a tapestry of various styles woven together. Some of the items are antiques—like the Roman metal numbers fixed to the cabinets, bronze statuettes, clocks, or old portraits found, dusty and hidden, in my wife's family château. Others come from my own interpretation of the 18th and 19th centuries. I find it enchanting not to be exact when it comes to the era that inspired me: at a time when you can find anything online, it is necessary to keep certain things shrouded in mystery, to maintain a mist to soften the edges. Jean-Louis Dumas, the visionary man behind Hermès, asked Japanese *mangaka* to write the story of the firm in manga form. 'There are many secrets in the house of Hermès. These secrets are the best kept there are.' Atmospheres bearing traces of different eras, without being exact representations of a specific style give a space a feeling of passing, multidimensional time. Whatever the place, whatever the constraints, custodians of French know-how were sent on-site and brought their skill to local materials and techniques. Isn't Officine Universelle Buly an ode to universality, even in its name? Experience prompts us to rethink our own

1. A doucine, or cyma, is a molding that is convex and concave in a continuous curve.

2. Shellac is a resinous substance (obtained from the lac insect) melted into thin flakes and used for making varnish.

rules, our architectural dogmas. Woodwork, cabinet-making, and painting are our elite arts, on a par with fine jewellery and goldsmithery, they have the power to sublimate a material and turn it into an artistic piece."

For Ramdane Touhami, "The ornament is a stepping stone, with the power to transport the visitor to another era. Nowadays, so many of the interiors presented in magazines convey a bare minimalism. I don't really object to that. But can you be sincerely thrilled in such a space? In a castle, in a cathedral, my breath is taken away at the sight of their richly crafted interiors; by the sheer amount of work and patience displayed, allowed by the transmission of craft through generations. The architectural ornament had a meaning, it was not just a splendid decor attached to the structure. Minimalist spaces as we know them are devoid of any ornament and are deemed timeless. They do not refer to any specific era of the past. They may be immutable, but they're historically neutral. It's a choice. It's not mine, though."

BULY'S WORLD OF RITUALS AND BEAUTY IS DEEPLY ROOTED IN THE 19TH CENTURY. IT HAS THE POWER TO TURN EVERY PRODUCT INTO A BEACON OF TRADITION AND HISTORY.

Store entrance and its burl walnut cabinet, Officine Universelle Buly, rue Bonaparte, Paris.

6 RUE BONAPARTE
THE PARISIAN CAMPAIGN

Opening your first store is like planning a conquest, akin to Emperor Napoleon Bonaparte's campaigns towards victory. And yet, the first shop, on rue Bonaparte, almost never saw the light! Ramdane Touhami and Victoire de Taillac had first set their minds on the rue Dauphine, a stone's throws away. Two requirements had to be fulfilled for the project to have proper substance: moving into a historical place—a building with an architecture contemporary to Jean-Vincent Bully, and in a relatively quiet street. "I perambulated the streets of the 6th arrondissement with a manual counting machine, calculating the flow of pedestrians from certain angles. I had to cross out some of the major roads: if the street was too busy, people would just have exclaimed, 'Oh, here is a new one!' This couldn't happen, it would mean our process had failed," says Ramdane Touhami. The future Officine had to blend in with its surroundings and, like a jewel box, pique one's curiosity from the outside without being overly present. "A first stone in our shoe appeared when the sellers from rue Dauphine backed out." The store was ideally placed, neither too concealed nor too exposed, with the added merit of having the buses from two important lines stop just in front of our windows, when the very Parisian traffic light—i.e., very long—turns red just a few meters away. The real-estate deal started to take on a deliciously Romanesque, Balzacian flavor: for the second time, the rue Bonaparte was slipping through Ramdane Touhami's fingers; the project was at a dead end: "As this acquisition was the cornerstone of the whole montage, Victoire went to visit Mme de Montbrison to try and persuade her." During the conversation, it appeared that this well-established family from the Rothschild dynasty had received protection from Nazi persecutions from Victoire de Taillac's grandfather himself. This unbelievable, serendipitous coincidence recreated the link between the two families and the deal was soon sealed, in 2013. Significant renovation work followed: we had to faithfully recreate the codes of an ancient apothecary that could have been Bully's family's, whose last store closed in the 1930s. Ramdane Touhami had a very precise vision of that shop: "The architectural elements could absolutely not be trifled with! We needed to instill the feeling that the store had been taken over as it was, in an immaculate state." The original atmosphere, where accumulation was key, was summoned from the past: drawers by the dozen, longitudinal wooden cabinets, shelves, pharmaceutical glassware—pots, vases, bottles. He took inspiration from the apothecaries of the Hôtel de Dieu in Troyes and in Tournus to reconstitute the scenic elements of the time and borrowed the design of the ornamental molding from the framework of beams in the Ingres Museum in Montauban, under the supervision of an expert who works with the Château de Versailles. Friezes of vine rinceaux[3], these leafy arabesques, combine with anthemia[4], rosettes, while a fine cerulean-blue edging highlights beams cured with acid to give them the patina of age. As a homage to Paris, the shelves were designed like passageways running under arcatures[5] reminiscent of the rue de Rivoli's iconic perspective and punctuated by acorns at their point. On the shelves, parallel glass jars look like a perfect alignment of buildings on a street—or sweet jars. They bear labels with Louis XIV-style interlacing—crowns, baskets, ribbons, and hand-written calligraphy. Pharmaceutical glassware is everywhere in furnishing. These jars were carefully designed in the Middle Ages, both for their ease of handling and for ensuring the perfect metrology of the precious products—the 'dosage know-how,' for pharmacy is the exact science of proportions. The impressive wood cabinets were chiselled by the craft of a woodworker historian, made of entablatures topped with anthemia and Louis XV-style shells, and flanked by doucines." The floor is a bi-color, checked pattern made of varnished earthenware tiles from Umbria in Italy, fired in 5,000-year-old Etruscan kilns at a low temperature. With this exceptional Italian know-how, the tiled floor bears subtle nuances of color from one tile to the next. Furthermore, Ramdane Touhami thought about the floor on the long term: "The very fragile nature of the tile would inevitably acquire a patina with the constant stepping. It was a safe bet that after just a few months, the whole floor would have aged like it had been installed two centuries ago." As a masterpiece, the commanding counter sits under windows framed with moldings, a homage to the decorum of master perfumers of the 19th century. Ramdane Touhami also has an obsessive hatred of self-service: "I abhor the idea that the clients could help themselves. They ought to be a spectator and touch with their eyes only. That is also why I had a water fixture installed to allow customers to try out our pomades, soaps, and oils... Of course, the tap is made of mother-of-pearl, its mascaron[6], a swan head acquired at the sale of a Loire Valley château. The counter presides over every attention and exchange: it is the interface between the clients and the salespeople and is topped with so-called "Brèche de Bénou" marble. This distinctive ornamental material is incredibly rare; from its quarry came the superb stone whose luster graces the corridors of the Louvre Museum, Versailles, and the Opéra Garnier. No extravagance is off-limits for me. None."

3. A rinceau is an ornamental motif consisting essentially of a sinuous and branching scroll elaborated with leaves and other natural forms (as derived from the acanthus).

4. Anthemia, or palmettes, are ornamental moldings carved to look like a palm leaf surrounding an axis, often following an ogival curve and bearing a rinceau in their inferior part. They have been used since antiquity.

5. An arcade of small dimensions, such as a balustrade, formed by a series of little arches. It can be a blind arcade, decorative rather than structural.

6. In architecture, a mascaron ornament is a face, animal or human, sometimes frightening or chimeric, whose alleged apotropaic function was originally to ward off evil spirits so that they would not enter the building.

Sales counter, Officine Universelle Buly, rue Bonaparte, Paris.
Next page: Store overview, Officine Universelle Buly, rue Bonaparte, Paris.

"THE VERY FRAGILE NATURE OF THE TILE WOULD INEVITABLY ACQUIRE A PATINA WITH THE CONSTANT STEPPING. IT WAS A SAFE BET THAT AFTER JUST A FEW MONTHS, THE WHOLE FLOOR WOULD HAVE AGED LIKE IT HAD BEEN INSTALLED TWO CENTURIES AGO."

Ramdane Touhami

Sketch for the Bonaparte store.

Buly's coat of arms logo on glazed terracotta, Officine Universelle Buly, rue Bonaparte, Paris.

OFFICINE UNIVERSELLE BULY IN TAIPEI
A FRENCH WOMAN IN TAIWAN

To celebrate the opening of the second Buly store, and the first outside France, Touhami refrained from reusing the codes defined for the rue Bonaparte in their entirety. "We need to innovate! The space does display French ornamental elements such as a mural inspired by a medieval pharmacy in Burgundy, which took a specifically mandated decorative painter weeks to design. On the ceiling, a rib vault, reminiscent of the strict Gothic architecture, frames a grid pattern filled with odalisques, floral compositions and crests. The architectural metaphor is extended with a succession of round wood arches and alcoves alternating with spandrels[7] and a Louis XVI button ornament. Arched blind dormer windows display eloquent 18th-century portraits in engravings by Broc or Lemire Aîné, drawing teacher at the École Royale de Polytechnique." These treasures, found in the cellars of Victoire's family château, represent the main human emotions and feelings through eloquent, almost mystic, engraved effigies. Officine in Taïwan plays with a light-and-dark contrast, a play on light here echoing a shadow there. An olive-green panel brings nuance to a brighter spot, oak frames lighten the wooden path drawn by burr walnut. The French-style flooring is made of travertine[8] with cabochons—in Burgundy stone—with a touch of exoticism brought by a combination of orange and gray tones. The Carrara white marble counter sits like an emblematic throne, streaked with green, gray, and orange veins, atop fluted[9] wooden jambs[10] embracing delicate molded friezes. Further down, a passage lined with concave oak panels conceals a discreet door that may or may not lead to other worlds... Ramdane Touhami crossed influences: "This far-from-home store is in line with the American and Japanese trend to translate a local space into an international setting, without adapting it. Come to think of it, this space does have, although timidly, components from the local culture—beside the colonial-style canework on the casement windows. Taipei marks the premises of my aesthetic deglobalisation philosophy, which is to consider a necessary adaptation to local decorum."*

7. A spandrel is the almost triangular space between one side of the outer curve of an arch, a wall, and the ceiling or framework.

8. Travertine is a type of limestone that is formed by mineral deposits from natural springs. Other minerals mix together with the calcite to create unique swirls and movement that give travertine its distinctive character.

9. In architectural decoration, fluting or reeding is a surface worked into a regular series of (vertical) concave grooves or convex ridges, frequently used on columns.

10. In architecture, a jamb is the vertical part of a door, a window or an opening.

19ᵗʰ-century prints by Lemire the Eldest above the marble counter in the Taipei store in Taiwan.
Next page: Overview of the Taipei Officine.

View outside the store in the Cheong Dam district.

SEOUL
L'AMOUR EST BLEU

11. Strip of wood or metal used for support between panes of glass, as in a window. A technique used at a time when it was difficult to make window glass in large dimensions.

12. A Solomonic column, also known as a barley-sugar column or a spiral column, is a column with a twisting or spiraling shaft.

The title was borrowed from Claudine Longuet's 1960 song and is an ode to blue-toned emotions. For the first time, Officine was moving into a contemporary space. This building in the upscale area of Cheong Dam had to be decorated. Giving it a welcoming look implied creating a bubble with an ultramarine chromatic scale. Ramdane Touhami summoned an almost Mediterranean atmosphere by adding arched windows, with plaited cast-iron muntins[11] and a sun on the crowns: "We mixed up the historical timeline with a store sign written in a new typeface inspired by Jakob Erbar's first geometric sans serif—Erbar Grotesk Schmalhalbfett—and Paul Renner's illustrious Futura. A small garden with a terracotta pavement graces the entry and gives it a majestic appearance. Note that this composition outlines the two hand-painted logotypes. As soon as I open the door, I aspire to a complete change of atmosphere. The contrast between a soft, luminous exterior and the interior in chiaroscuro brings exactly that. I am particularly fond of religious architecture, and I wanted to get the mystical presence of the apse of a church." To that end, the space is filled with wood cabinets made of arcades, arched openings, and small columns. The latter, commonly used since the Baroque era, ornate cabinets and woodwork. Their twisted, helicoidal shape is inspired by the majestic columns supporting St Peter's baldaquins in Rome—Solomonic[12] columns. He explains: "The sculpture work went as far as surrounding the room with lines of arched niches punctuated by small columns, whose execution is a vibrant witness to the incredible technicality of traditional woodwork. The decorative painter made the trip to Seoul to paint the 50-odd drawers bearing the name of natural ingredients, as is the custom in French apothecaries." Adding a spot of color to the scene, the counter is topped with a Guatemala Green marble, whose stone comes from Rajasthan in India. As a nod to Korea, we used painted bamboo on the mirrors' muntins, a homage to the lush Damyang Juknokwon garden in Seoul. French-style pharmacy and naturalism practises were transferred to Korean ground with 30-odd herbaria artfully mounted on wooden frames, alongside Broc and Lemire Aîné engravings. They are a historic reminder of the watercolors on vellum kept in the Museum d'Histoire Naturelle in Paris. The botanical specimens lead the eye to the second floor, where a ballet of Buly staff lends its rhythm to the store experience. The store becomes an intimate home with a remarkable reception room.

Sketch for the
Seoul Officine.

Next pages: The herbaria in their burr walnut frames, in the Cheong Dam district Officine.
Overview of the Cheong Dam district store.

TOKYO
KINTSUGI AND
RETRO-FUTURISM

Officine Universelle Buly's shop in Tokyo represents an architectural extravagance—a space that embodies the bridges built by Buly between eras and cultures. This audacity was rewarded with two prizes at the 2018 Frame Awards. One half of this bisected store is straight out of 19th-century France: marvellously refined wooden ornaments—pillars with helicoidal engaged columns, candelabras with their bobeches[13], dentil[14] frieze, cornice, and coffered ceiling—are on display, like a Haussmanian facade. At the top, sculpted mascarons represent Greek deities, reminiscent of the effigies on the sides of Paris bridges. The space is structured by the arcatures formed by the glass cabinets, akin to Romanesque transverse arches[15], while apothecary jars and a swan neck double faucet represent typical features of apothecary furnishings. Officine's entire team of French craftspeople came to Japan for several weeks for the sole purpose of building this slice of history in accordance with the best practices of the 19th century. The store's other half, like a mirror reflection, was crafted by Japanese artisans. It emanates from the most contemporary aspects of Japan: waxed concrete, lit up by a Barrisol ceiling. For Ramdane Touhami, it was essential to integrate local and contemporary elements in this ultramodern building: "I wanted to sneak concrete inside the place. The light springs from the arched alcoves made of herbaria, like stained glass. The herbaria have been trapped in resin, the beauty of the plant immortalized. Four tonnes of the mixture were used for this floral glass wall. There are no display windows here, as they call for short decoration cycles when Officine opted for a diffuse space-time continuum, modeled on the rhythm of the 19th century." Located on a mezzanine floor, the store literally represents the meeting of two worlds, connected by a thin golden line reminiscent of the ancient art of kintsugi. As in a piece of ceramics whose cracks are sublimated by gold rather than concealed, the true nature of the company is made brightly apparent: a genuinely Universal Officine—both temporally and spatially—which, emboldened by its glorious past, does not shy away from any creation or combination.

13. A metal or wood cup or ring around the socket of a candlestick, intended to catch dripping wax.

14. In classical architecture, a dentil is one of a number of small rectangular blocks resembling teeth, used as a decoration under the molding of a cornice.

15. A supporting arch which runs across the vault from side to side, dividing the bays. it usually projects down from the surface of the vault.

THE STORE LITERALLY REPRESENTS THE MEETING OF TWO WORLDS. CONNECTED BY A THIN GOLDEN LINE REMINISCENT OF THE ANCIENT ART OF KINTSUGI.

Exterior view of the Tokyo
Daikanyama store in Japan.

Sketch for the
Daikanyama store.

Next pages: View of Daikanyama store, the 19th-century side.
Opposite view of Daikanyama store, the 21st-century side.

The two worlds of the shop are connected by a thin golden line, reminiscent of the ancient art of kintsugi.

Right, Victoire de Taillac and, left, Ramdane Touhami in the Daikanyama store, April, 2017.

Front store, Officine Universelle Buly, Hong Kong.

A FRENCH OFFICINE IN THE HEART OF HONG KONG

In the middle of Wyndham Street in Central, the space sports an impressive 5.5-meter-high ceiling. For Ramdane Touhami, the place is obviously perfect for developing an ecclesiastical metaphor: "In its layout, it looks like a small abbey, where one could easily create a transept and high ogival arches. Looking at this oblong space, I thought of boudoirs, these long, crunchy French biscuits used to make strawberry Charlotte. It inspired me to design a woody Charlotte. In the oval shape, the floor is more than just a feature. The vintage pavement, marked with solid-blue tiles, contrasts with the amber and chocolate tones of the rest of the store. It's actually a mix-up. The patterned tiles were originally meant for the Paris store, while Hong Kong was supposed to inherit the ones that are now flooring the rue de Saintonge. It was such a beautiful mistake, we had to keep it that way. After all, didn't such a blunder result in another mythical dessert, the tarte Tatin, in 1899?" The glass window at the entrance being hard to conceal, it necessitated the creation of a fake window display behind—large stretched-fabric cartouches bearing text, remind the visitor of the Victorian era, when the flamboyant queen reigned over the city-state. The front facade received a marine varnish, a symbol of the bustling activity of the harbour city, and a way to protect the surface from humidity. The arched windows are wood replicas of the aforementioned boudoirs, with bobeches on top. The signature drawers look like they're floating 10 centimetres above the ground, while accessories are suspended on long red velvet panels, as characteristically displayed by 19th-century haberdashery merchants. Is it an invitation to self-service here? Absolutely not. The impression conveyed is subtle. The visitor walks into a ceremonial space where protocol ought to be duly followed.

Next page: Overview of the store in Central, Hong Kong.

NEW YORK
THE ART DECO LINER

Officine Universelle Buly returns to a resolutely Art Deco atmosphere, with the promise to look like it set up shop around the opening of the Bergdorf Goodman department store in 1899. The richness of details produces an immersive reality inspired by the Golden Age of New York architecture. The lacquered wood panels are patterned with brass lines, the charcoal or ivory cracks, typical of this glorious style, blend with the surrounding chromatic harmony. For Ramdane Touhami, the Art Deco approach here didn't stop at the designing stage: "There, the Ruhlmann chromed mirror sits, a triumphant aesthetic symbol like every mirror in the Buly officines. The homage to this architectural style is completed with authentic shagreen cabinets, made by a cabinetmaker from star designer Emile Ruhlmann's atelier." The windows turned octagonal; the central cabinet, hexagonal. The latter's entablature[16] echoes Art Deco buildings' windowsills and its niches are adorned with similarly cracked-looking Florentine vases. The cupboards are entirely fluted, and their handles bear an exclusive design, created for the store. An inscription in 1930s typeface, hand-painted in golden letters, says "Officine Universelle Buly chez Bergdorf Goodmann." Ramdane Touhami remembers: "And to think store management cried bloody murder for alleged misuse of the name... It was a work of art! Destroying these letters was out of the question. We kept them preciously." The right flank shows, mounted on a large frame, a genuine advertising poster from the 1920s sent to New York by Officine and taken from its private collection. Its delightfully outdated message says: "Les modes ont changé, mais le vinaigre de Bully embellit toujours." ("Fashions may change, but Bully vinegar always beautifies.") A successful bet for Ramdane Touhami: "This store is an aesthetic manifesto against the contemporary trend, where all spaces are a variation of the same architecture. We did so well that visitors thought that the store was as old as the emblematic flagship store of 5th avenue."

Sketch of the project at Bergdorf Goodman.

16. In architecture, the upper part of a classical building supported by columns or a colonnade, comprising the architrave, frieze, and cornice. It can also be above or around doors, windows or furniture.

"THERE. THE RUHLMANN CHROMED MIRROR SITS. A TRIUMPHANT AESTHETIC SYMBOL LIKE EVERY MIRROR IN THE BULY OFFICINES."

Lacquered wood and brass cabinet in Art Deco style for Officine Universelle Buly at Bergdorf Goodman, New York.
Next pages: Art Deco counter, at Bergdorf Goodman.
Combs display cases, at Bergdorf Goodman.

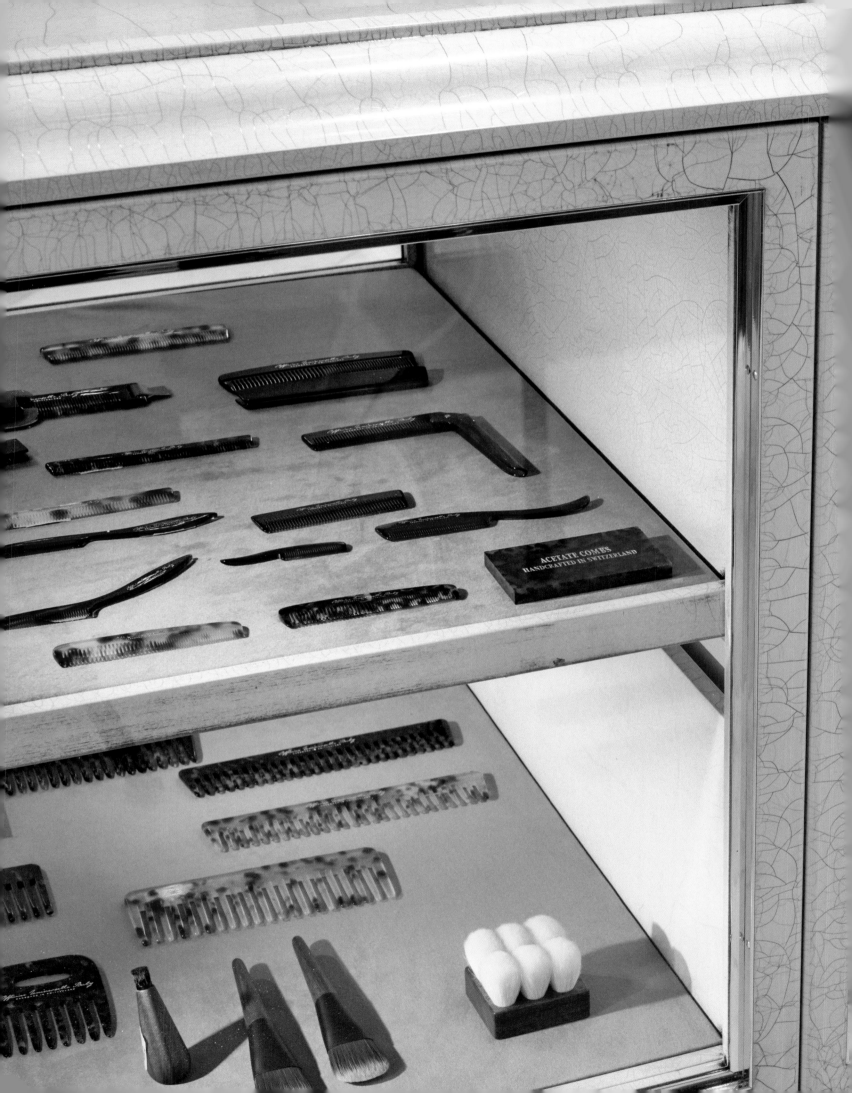

ACETATE COMBS
HANDCRAFTED IN SWITZERLAND

Wall lights by Pierre Chareau circa 1930s, Officine Universelle Buly at Bergdorf Goodman, New York.

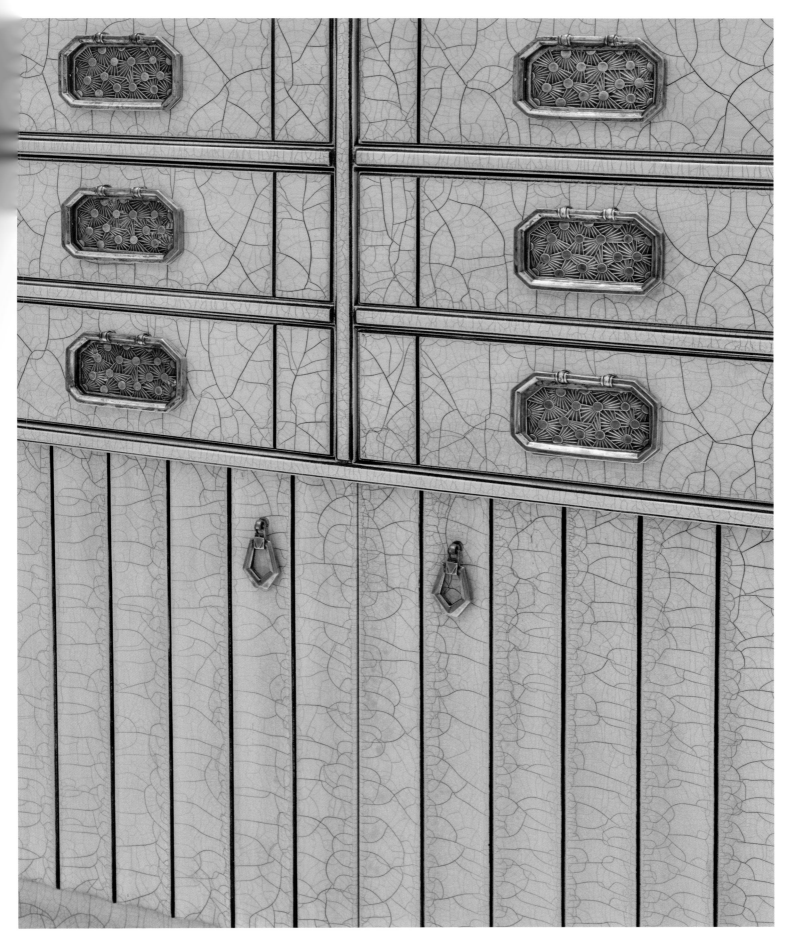

Detail of the drawer handles of Officine Universelle Buly, Bergdorf Goodman, New York.

The Officine rue de Saintonge store, view from the interior courtyard.

SAINTONGE
THE DAEDALUS STORE

Officine Universelle Buly Rive-Droite is a place with a strong history, as it took over the premises of a former foundry, the Ateliers Rudier. Established in 1874, the foundry created masterful works of art for Bourdelle and Maillol, and even Rodin's famous Thinker. The huge space had seen many changes and had lost its former glory, a perfect challenge for Ramdane Touhami: "What a shame, when this place has seen the works of so many geniuses! When we got the keys to Saintonge, we walked into a former electrical equipment store. Everything was gray and dusty. We had to break everything and start again from scratch. The cabinetmakers undertook a Herculean task to recreate an atmosphere in a place that was just long and narrow, and quite unexciting. Its decent surface area was an invitation to create adjacent, but isolated, spaces, lined up in sequence to awaken curiosity and a desire to see more. This new adventure started in 2017." After walking through a door under two spherical crystal pendant lights, the visitor notices drawers, shelves, and displays running up the walls almost absurdly to be embedded in the narrow coffers on the ceiling. He assumes this surrealistic effect: "I took great pleasure in playing with this disruptive, humoristic note. I played with the wall, folding it in half and enhancing the realistic effect with extra drawers and replicas of Buly bottles, adapted to be suspended." Long glass windows with torus[17] moldings compose a line of small arcades, large wheels holding a candelabra hang from the entablatures, and cartouches bearing the names of Officine's products act as marble pediments. A counter, stretched into an "L" shape, and made of Sarrancolin Opera marble, brings out, with its many colors, the plethora of items artfully presented to the eye of the visitor. Bringing a theatrical flourish to the scene, a vintage brass mast from a ticket booth from an opera house segments the room. The arched moldings frame verdigris bronze medallions and parading nymphs straight out of Pompei. Just below, printed on fabric, goddesses follow the codes of 19th-century aristocratic perfumery. Fifty-odd drawers—a signature feature of Officine along with the perfumes—surround a large (and supposedly secret) door, as simple as it is discreet. Such is the parallelism of the cherry burr's veins that they form lozenges and ornamental patterns and evoke 3-D moldings. The wood is varnished with a technique called "padding." On the right-hand side, an emerald-like handle was inspired by an absolutely splendid Venetian palace. From another angle, two alcoves in the front and the back of the store display to the curious eye antique vases and a strange portable fountain, meant to be attached to a carriage and found in an antique shop. The floor is made of Umbria stone and spreads out like a honeycomb.

17. A bold convex molding generally semi-circular in cross-section.

Next page: Retail counter at the Officine rue de Saintonge, Paris.

Detail of the folding counter, Officine rue de Saintonge, Paris.

One of the Buly logos in enamel on the front door of Officine rue de Saintonge, Paris.

CAFÉ TORTONI
THE TASTE
OF OFFICINE

From the Saintonge street, two rows of glass globes punctuate the ceiling and catch the eye of the passerby. Le Grand Café Tortoni, yesterday a highlight of the Chaussée d'Antin neighborhood, is now adorned with a Flanders marble counter. Set like a Parthenon with a marble pediment lined with cartouches and framed between two pilasters, the back counter is covered with antique tableware, coffee equipment, and various delicacies encased in 19th-century brass and glass displays. The Saintonge store staff is in full uniform here. White tuxedo jacket, bow tie or black crocheted tie, orange apron. The quality of the contact with the client, the service, are key to Buly's total architecture. On the walls, the long, vertical, flat-arched frames with moldings are made of Breccia marble and punctuated with brass rosettes. The inscriptions bear the name of illustrious customers, immortalized alongside the specialties of the house. The teas, coffees, and ice-creams are at arm's length from the outside as well: an ingenious small sliding window was set in the front window to serve takeaway aficionados. On the counter, a genuine, bulging chocolate maker divides the space to provide the absolute privilege of an intimate conversation to customers in search of discretion. On the way to the back of the cafe, there used to be a sloped display presenting a range of "onigiris"—small Japanese rice-based sandwiches with a filling—set in a Japanese atmosphere, under a remarkable work of art by colorful artist Mami Sato. After online and phone orders started booming, the display gave way to a counter dedicated to the art of "pliage," or folding. The store was then graced with a new gray and alabaster ceruse patina and a multitude of convex mirrors and plasters. The dark door, inspired by Jean Prouvé, studded with six portholes and bearing an elegant vertical brass handle, leads to a bucolic courtyard.

ON THE COUNTER, A GENUINE, BULGING CHOCOLATE MAKER DIVIDES THE SPACE TO PROVIDE THE ABSOLUTE PRIVILEGE OF AN INTIMATE CONVERSATION TO CUSTOMERS IN SEARCH OF DISCRETION.

Grand Café Tortoni counter, rue de Saintonge, Paris.
Next page: Exterior view of Officine Universelle Buly and Grand Café Tortoni.

OFFICI

1803

Fermé le lundi

GRAND CAFÉ TORTONI

❖ CAFETIER ❖ LIMONADIER ❖ GLACIER ❖

fondé à Paris rue Taitbout en 1798

VEND SES PLÂTRES

Exposition :

du 27 Février au 17 Juin .

HORAIRES OUVERTURE
DU LUNDI AU DIMANCHE
DE 11 heures À 19 heures

NIVERSELLE BULY

CAFÉ TORTONI

AU COMPTOIR

CAFÉ CHAUD ET GLACÉ
FEUILLES DE GLACES AUX FRUITS DE SAISON
GLACES ET SORBET MAISON
JUS DE FRUIT (AU KILO)
MADELEINE

HORS SAISON
LA GALERIE

GLACES ET CAFÉS
A Emporter de 8 h à 19 h

A EMPORTER

CAFÉ MINUTE .	3 .	EUROS
CAFÉ ALLONGÉ .	4 .	
THÉ .	5 .	
SODA AUX OLIVES .	5 .	
CHOCOLAT CHAUD DOUX .	6 .	
CHOCOLAT CHAUD CORSÉ .	6 .	
MADELEINE "GENOUX DE TORTONI" .	3 .	

PRESERVEES:
PICKING FLOWERS
FROM THE SKY

On the way to this floral cabinet, the visitor needs to walk through one of the Saintonge Officine's cupboards with a hidden door. For Ramdane Touhami, this room "en enfilade" brings a slight fantasy atmosphere. Like the wardrobe in Narnia, it is a frontier between two worlds. After a short journey, a majestic—yet intimate—office presents its outdated walls to the eye: casts, frames, and plaster busts bring their company to the preserved beauty of thousands of herbs suspended in a sky of flowers. The accumulation of objects was proportional to the time spent there. In this space, the number of curiosities quadrupled... From the outside, the Japanese robin's song—a familiar bird nicknamed Jean-François—could make you feel a hundred miles away, dazzled by the beauty of dried flowers.

FROM THE OUTSIDE, THE JAPANESE ROBIN'S SONG — A FAMILIAR BIRD NICKNAMED JEAN-FRANÇOIS—COULD MAKE YOU FEEL A HUNDRED MILES AWAY, DAZZLED BY THE BEAUTY OF DRIED FLOWERS.

The "Préservées" floral cabinet, accessible from the Saintonge store through a hidden door.

Sky of flowers, detail of the "Préservées" floral cabinet, rue de Saintonge, Paris.

The "Préservées" floral cabinet.

View of the massage room at Officine rue de Saintonge, which replaced the "Préservées" floral cabinet in November 2019.

MASSAGE
AND
TREATMENT ROOM
ZELLIGE
AND ATLAS

Lying on a dense leather mattress bought from a collection of 19th-century furniture, the visitor lets their gaze meander along the dense floral vault. The zellige tiles, a homage to the ones adorning Moroccan bath houses, cascade down the sides of a blue-rimmed 1930s basin. The padded doors buffer the merry effervescence of the Officine, while a thick and heavy night-colored curtain shelters the senses in a space turned completely serene.

Left and right, details of the treatment and massage room.

HORS SAISON, THE SERVICE COUNTER:
A PERPETUAL SPACE

The configuration under the glass roof was a clear invitation to let ideas evolve naturally. First, it was a place to stage the capsule streetwear collections Ramdane Touhami designed for Korean brand Hazzys. At the time, the main feature was the micro-garden in the pit at Saintonge, alongside genuine 1930s window displays, an army of 30 mannequins and waxed concrete on the floor. Since 2019, inspired by typesetter's cabinets and their myriad of sorting drawers, it has been home to Officine's Services Counter. Sheltered from the excitement of the Marais by a discreet courtyard, the counter displays rare and precious papers on brass rods, like a kiosk offering monograms, damask prints, brocatelle or tilapia leather. On the counter, embossed leather frames were inserted to cushion the calligrapher's writing movements and preserve their fluidity. Ramdane Touhami kept the garden pit between this double wooden cabinet: cactus and palm trees harmonize with the tan color of the space.

The plasters room, an ephemeral Hors Saison space at Officine rue de Saintonge, Paris.

Japanese gift papers from the service counter, at Officine rue de Saintonge, Paris.

Overview of the plasters room, an ephemeral Hors Saison exhibition at Officine rue de Saintonge, Paris.
Next page: The wrapping service counter, Officine rue de Saintonge, established June 2019.

SELFRIDGES
A PIECE OF FRANCE
IN LONDON

It's one of the biggest counters outside France. Ramdane Touhami imagined Officine Universelle Buly in Selfridges as an islet of Frenchness in the heart of bubbly London: "I set up the Neoclassical interior design as an homage to famous 18th-century British architect Robert Adam." This store, situated amidst impressive columns with volutes on the capitals displays obvious Victorian inspirations. A massive beech cabinet boasts windows decorated at the top with Gothic corbels with ogival quintifoils[18]. Orichalcum medallions—a copper, zinc, and brass alloy used by Romans in Antiquity—are juxtaposed with black square marble tiles. The enfilade is completed by fluted pilasters. On the entablature, marble cartouches with inscriptions, bobeches, and dentil frieze are nested under a full cornice. Wood and glass surfaces mingle in shapes reminiscent of Dalí's melting clocks and their subversive optical effect as if wood and glass had been melted, in a symbiotic Dalí-Gaudí visual, where torus moldings dislocate to form unusual shapes. The Flanders marble counter and the upholstered velvet in the windows stand out with their brighter shade against the dominant white color. In the central alcove, under a shell, stands a bronze clock with a statue, seemingly there to crystallize time. An absurd note, twinkling with humor, within a Chipperfieldian institution.

18. Bearing five foils or lobes.

WOOD AND GLASS SURFACES MINGLE IN SHAPES REMINISCENT OF DALI'S MELTING CLOCKS AND THEIR SUBVERSIVE OPTICAL EFFECT AS IF WOOD AND GLASS HAD BEEN MELTED, IN A SYMBIOTIC DALI GAUDI VISUAL, WHERE TORUS MOLDINGS DISLOCATE TO FORM UNUSUAL SHAPES.

Next page: Overview of the Officine Universelle Buly store at Selfridges, London.

COPENHAGEN
THE MEDITERRANEAN
ON THE
NORTH SEA

Officine Universelle Buly at Holly Golightly in Copenhagen bears zellige tiles with navy or ultramarine blue hues. Ramdane Touhami wanted to bring something as disruptive as "a Mediterranean atmosphere into the Danish temple of minimalism and wood. This store is a first humoristic-aesthetic manifesto against local standards!" Directly on the faience, the decorative painter drew high, round arches decorated with laurel wreaths and long drapery punctuated with naturalistic rosettes. The design was also inspired by the prizes won by Bully, the perfumer, at the Paris World Expositions of 1867 and 1878.

"THIS STORE IS A FIRST HUMORISTIC-AESTHETIC MANIFESTO AGAINST LOCAL STANDARDS."

Ramdane Touhami

Counter for Officine Universelle Buly in Copenhagen.

Outside the store, Officine Universelle Buly in BAL, Kyoto. "Perfumes" is written in Japanese on the light.

KYOTO
A REAL PRETEND TEA HOUSE

Kyoto's Officine final sketches, 2018.

Kyoto gives the beginning of an answer to the existential question: how to integrate a store into a luxurious shopping mall? For Ramdane Touhami: "The competition, the variety of stores, the crowds: you have to strike hard, and fast. We recreated the look of a street to catch people's attention. The front of the store captures the minimalist essence of Kyoto's tea houses—"sukiya zukuri." From the outside, straight wood beams, light whitewashed walls, rice paper windows let nothing on of the eclectic adventure inside. The only clue comes from the inscription on the small lamp: "kosui" or perfumes. As soon as the visitor passes the braided rope curtain, they shift into the atmosphere of a 1920s pharmacy." Inside the store, the painted ceiling stands 4-meters high and displays the famous 18th-century Broc and Lemire Ainé engravings and their eloquent portraits. They're hung in an unconventional way: suspended from the ceiling on brass cross-braces—the faces of the characters looking at the Versailles wood flooring. On the wall, the light oak cabinets are alternatively warmed up by burr elm and awakened by the dense, damask, pleated dark duck-blue velvet upholstery. Alterning convex and concave shapes play around the sides of the window cabinets. The central cabinet snakes down towards the adjacent ones in a very Art Deco whip movement. In the middle of the wooden central island, a porthole reveals the blue velvet displays laid out behind. The pomades and soaps are presented in pyramids for a precise, repetitive geometric effect, offsetting the round shape of the 50-odd alabaster vases from a traditional pharmacy. Here, the differences between French and Japanese worlds collide in a paroxysm: for Japan, light hues and neat, smooth surfaces; for France, the richness of the ornaments.

KYOTO GIVES THE BEGINNING OF AN ANSWER TO THE EXISTENTIAL QUESTION: HOW TO INTEGRATE A STORE INTO A LUXURIOUS SHOPPING MALL?

Next pages: Outside the store, Officine Universelle Buly in BAL, Kyoto.
Overview of the store, in BAL, Kyoto.
Detail of the retail counter, store in BAL, Kyoto.

TOMORROWLAND
THE FUTURE
WITH A TOUCH OF THE PAST

The tiny space in Shibuya, Tokyo, plays with the glass's transparency around a Neoclassical cabinet. Round openings in the glass windows bring a retro-futuristic touch to the strictness of the antique medical and administrative furniture. The drawers and hatches bear Roman numerals and are decorated with rich wood moldings. The centerpiece is a sculpted wood chest on high feet ornate with small columns, an invitation to be curious with its glass top revealing hidden treasures in its transparency.

Skylight details in the Nihombashi store, Tokyo.

NIHOMBASHI
A POCKET STORE

At the crossroad of timelines, the Officine in Nihombashi, Tokyo, brings the strength of the past to the inventiveness of the future, all this in a tiny space. This compact store is situated on a pedestrian street in a shopping mall, with a large glass front. It produces an optical effect, as if one passed through a mirror. In this doll's house-sized replica of an Officine Universelle, imperial green contrasts with dark orange, Japanese minimalism faces French-style accumulation. An imposing diagonal segments the central arched wood cabinet, whose transverse arch evokes the nave of a Romanesque chapel, lending the ensemble its futuristic, pure, smooth lines. The counter is topped by a chevron-shaped display; the round openings of the niches, like modern hagioscopes[19], are lined with a delicate double listel molding.[20]

19. A narrow oblique opening in a wall or pillar of a church to permit a view of the main altar from a side aisle or transepts.

20. A listel is a small flat face interposed between moldings to divide them.

IN THIS DOLL'S HOUSE-SIZED REPLICA OF AN OFFICINE UNIVERSELLE, IMPERIAL GREEN CONSTRATS WITH DARK ORANGE, JAPANESE MINIMALISM FACES FRENCH-STYLE ACCUMULATION.

Next page: Overview of the Nihombashi store divided into two sections, Tokyo.

NEWOMAN
THE
ANTIQUE NYMPH

For Ramdane Touhami, the space for this store was constrained: "It was in the middle of an alley of the NeWoMan store in Tokyo. We had to catch the attention and the eyes to attract the flow of people. To this end, I organized a meeting between a Japanese master glassmaker and Officine's cabinetmaker so that they could design an imposing central cabinet while being very clear. The "whip" line and the commanding baroque look extends into a cornice with a double molding." The abundant light, a crucial attention catcher, doesn't come from the outside but from a double glass wall. The top shelves are castellated [21] to display bottles and pomades. The wood tones, the Versailles wood flooring and a Pierre Garriche stool warm up the immaculate atmosphere. A majestic Italian mosaic pictures a straight-out-of-a-book goddess, as "a symbolic ode to Officine's Huile Antique." The inferior part of the cabinet is made of Kerala cherry wood, fluted horizontally and vertically in the style of Mies van der Rohe. A leather pad has been inserted on its top to make the calligraphy work as smooth and comfortable as possible.

21. With crenels.

THE WOOD TONES, THE VERSAILLES WOOD FLOORING, AND A PIERRE GARRICHE STOOL WARM UP THE IMMACULATE ATMOSPHERE.

Contrast between wood and bright white in Officine Universelle Buly, NeWoMan store, Tokyo.

Left and right: Calligraphy counter in the NeWoMan Store, Tokyo.

THE OFFICINE AT LE BON MARCHE
BECOMING PART OF A LEGENDARY PARIS DEPARTMENT STORE

Ensconsed in the Bon Marché Rive Gauche, Officine embraces the architectural lines designed by Louis-Charles Boileau and Armand Moisan, builders of this Paris institution. Mixed with Art Deco elements, the store doesn't shy away from Officines' customary rich ornaments. Hand-painted capital letters run on the pediment of the wide entablature. It is one of the rare Officines without any molding on the walls. The ornament mostly comes from the nature of the cherry wood, its cut defining perfectly symmetrical patterns. The brass and glass showcases bring back the aesthetic look of the hotel reception desks of yore. A water feature was not forgotten. On the right-hand side of the counter, a niche hides the strangest vintage piece of furniture: a wooden washstand whose basin moves in and out as needed, just like the movable panel of a secretary's desk. This allows the visitor to wash their hands elegantly and in the most old-fashioned way.

A typical piece of Parisian street furniture, the Morris column, was the inspiration for this display for the collaboration with the Louvre Museum, Le Bon Marché, 2020.

View of the niche hiding in its retractable door a sink, Bon Marché store, 2020.
Next page: View of the counter of the Officine au Bon Marché, ground floor, 2020.

L'OFFICINE UNIVERSELLE BULY

TOKYO

LONDRES

PARIS

HONG KONG

LE BON MARCHÉ RIVE GAUCHE | BU

SÉOUL | SAN FRANCISCO | TAIPEI | OFFICINE UNIVERSELLE BULY

YOKOHAMA
A STUDY
IN BRICK WORK

The brick cabinet with its perfectly lined niches is an answer to the peculiar location of the store, in an industrial hallway. The wide counter—with a breadth of more than 10 meters—brings together local materials and French history. The architectural composition includes a wave movement, the central focus being a cash booth door that seems to be literally breaking out of the brickwork in a big crash: a frontier between the sales space and the rest of the Yokohama shopping mall. Forty-odd niches and oculi[22] encased in wood bring a playful tone to the decor.

22. A circular opening in the center of a dome or in a wall.

Detailed view of the junction between wood and bricks at Officine in Yokohama, Japan.
Next page: General view of the Yokohama store, Japan.

Detail of the exterior sign featuring a backlit Pommade Concrète, Kotto Dori store in Tokyo, Japan.

KOTTO DORI
BRICK
AND
VELVET

An imposing neon Pommade Concrète tube brightens the alleyway. The new store is set in a building built in 1982. It had a special meaning for Ramdane Touhami: "It reminded me of my hometown Montauban's old red-brick buildings. I was eager to conquer the Aoyama neighborhood, as I really loved the atmosphere when I first came here in 1990. Having a store there was a long-time dream: the space is a true invitation to a "present nostalgia," and Buly share the building with Japanese brand Comme des Garçons. In a single space, Ramdane Touhami rolls out three different types of brickwork, reminiscent of the street pavement: "We wanted to design a dual space, where passersby cannot distinguish the store from street elements. The exterior ought to step into the interior. A complete camouflage. The masonry creates a bridge between the two worlds, reminiscent of the beauty of old Japanese baths. Inside, the store is an ode to retro-futurism; it was even repartitioned to get this effect." On the right-hand side, two backlit niches create a big halo of light. The first one is a homage to the art of perfume distillery. The visitor can observe a profusion of tubes and glass pipes, worthy of the cinematic imagination of the greatest laboratories. The transparent, borosilicate glass canals, manufactured by Kiriyama, are playfully irrigated by our own Huiles Antiques. The second window shows a rigorous alignment of body oils, whose bottles' sober tones resonate against the orange hues of the brickwork. Notably, the grouting echoes the gray tone of the brushed metal ceiling—and it is not by chance: the ashy hues are another expression of Buly's presence in the modern world. On the left-hand side, it's another story entirely. The contrasting ambiance is brought by the massive use of coralline velvet upholstered in "bird's beak"[23] molding woodwork around dozens of stucco cameos. Seventy-two rosettes were necessary to create the concave shapes on the angles of the panels. French magnificence is displayed through rich ornaments: fluted columns, studded with diamond shapes[24], arched compartments on the side, marble cartouches on the entablature, and a bread-oven-shaped niche. At the water point, a narrow stainless-steel basin sits under an automatic tap, the soaps available in a metal frame.

23. A pendant fillet with a channel behind it on the edge of a corona, a stringcourse, etc., so called because in profile it resembles a bird's beak.

24. The diamond shape is a flat-pyramid design used on stone or wood.

Next pages: Interior of the Kotto Dori Officine in Tokyo, Japan. On the left: The retail counter and its ornate niche.
Right: The stills and laboratory glassware Details, Kotto Dori store, Japan.
View of the laboratory glassware and its tangled tubes, at the Kotto Dori store.

FUTAKO-TAMAGAWA
THE REGENCE
IN TOKYO

Futako-Tamagawa is the Tokyoite equivalent of Parisian Neuilly, a place where architectural certainties shouldn't be disturbed, of course. The space prompted us to keep a very Parisian angle, rather conservative and bourgeois. It's one of the rare stores set in a shopping mall with an opening towards the outside. Metal jambs prolong the effect of the display counter and cabinets' material. The dark wood is inspired by Régence panels used in woodwork, a classic feature of Paris apartments. Here, instead of fabric, we put up photographs, framed in wood. The bright atmosphere brought by the Barrisol ceiling is softened by Versailles wood flooring. The store is a practical manifesto, an answer to the question: "How to sell perfume?" As Ramdane Touhami was designing the special project for the Louvre, he created a new scent diffusion process, a glass system with an atomizer bulb that allows the customer to be as close as possible to the aromatic components, without even having to apply it to the skin.

THE BRIGHT ATMOSPHERE BROUGHT BY THE BARRISOL CEILING IS SOFTENED BY VERSAILLES WOOD FLOORING.

OFFICINE UNIVERSELLE BULY À FUTAKO TAMAGAWA
fondée à Paris en 1803

Entrance, Futako-Tamagawa store, Tokyo.
Next pages: Side window of the store, this window to the mall was created especially for the occasion.
Detail of an accessories display case in the Futako-Tamagawa store, Tokyo.

KO TAMAGAWA

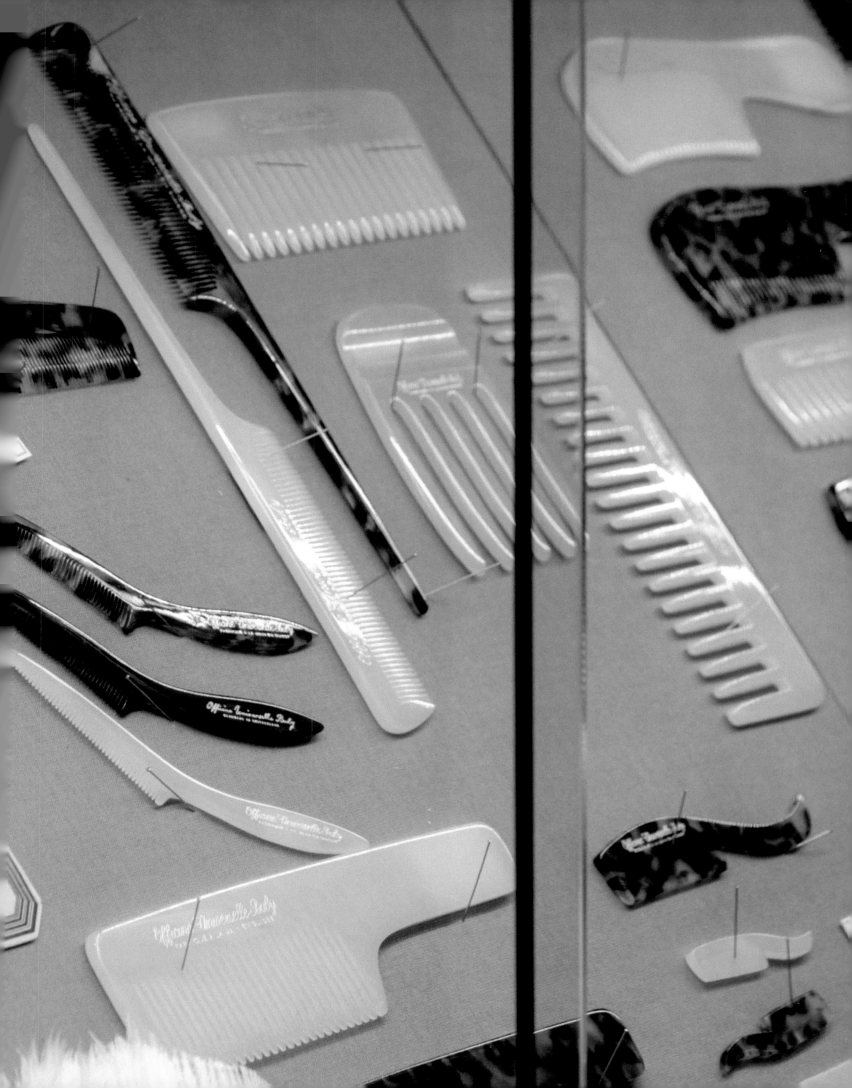

OFFICINE UNIVERSELLE BULY FONDÉ A

Detail of a display case in the Sapporo store.

SAPPORO
THE REGENCE
IN JAPAN

Officine in Saporo, the largest Japanese city north of Tokyo, was in-spired by the Tokyo Post Museum, where the purity of large windows contrasts with the ornamental richness of the statuettes and plasters displayed in opaline shelves. On the ground, the cabochon flagstone floor in black and white creates geometric patterns. Chocolate-colored wooden cabinets, with backlit frames, display green velvet compart-ments and brass jambs. Imposing golden letters engraved by a stonema-son underline the ceiling with the words "Officine Universelle Buly."

Next page: Overview of the Sapporo store.

Detail of the marble counter in Le Bon Marché, Paris.

LE BON MARCHE
PARIS
REACHING FOR
THE FIRST FLOOR

"When Le Bon Marché offers you a spacious spot on the much sought-after first floor, simplicity would suggest just moving the existing ground-floor store up one level. I don't do simple. It was too good an opportunity to rethink and redesign the whole concept. This oblong counter is like a big dinner table, where customers are treated as guests and invited to join," said Ramdane Touhami. Three layers of Rosso Levanto marble display the stone's spectacular black, gray, blood-red, and white veins. The mahogany cabinet brings its deep, rich palette to the general composition, flanked by two medallions bearing Officine's name. The same marble as the counter is used for the plinth. On the sides, long alabaster-colored windows display Officine Universelle Buly's curiosities.

Marble counter in Le Bon Marché, Paris.

OFFICINE
CROSSES THE CHANNEL

Entirely made by a French craftsman, Officine Universelle Buly's counter was inaugurated at the distinguished institution of Dover Street Market. The ambitious cabinet is covered in pink faience tiles, reminiscent of the ornamentation of Prussian fireplaces. An incredible technical prowess allowed it to raise to a serious height of more than three meters. The powdery-pink hue is eye-catching and sparks curiosity with its extraordinary volume and bright color, playing with the counter's with mirror- and luster-like effects. The irregular edges, typical of these ceramic tiles, bring a unique relief.

Detail of the matches display on the Officine faience counter, in Dover Street Market, London.

The Officine pink faience counter, in Dover Street Market, London.

Detail of the display, in Officine Universelle Buly, Osaka store, Japan.

A FRENCH CORNER
IN OSAKA

Officine Universelle Buly in Osaka brings its iconic wood arches to the Hankyu Umeda flagship store. With its eye-catching coralline hues, the Flanders marble stands out in the middle of an ultramodern institution. Bobeches and cartouches bearing gilt letters drawn by a master engraver underline the distinctiveness of French architecture.

Overview of Officine Universelle Buly, Osaka store, Japan.

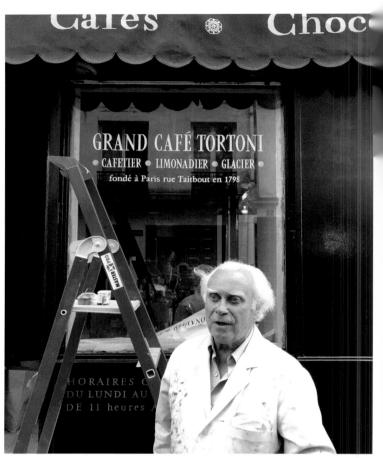

Above, left: Jacky ornemental painter, drawing golden letters in 1970s.
Above, right: Jacky finishing the Saintonge store, 2017.
Above: The Tomorowland counter workshop, where craftsmen make final finishing touches before painting, 2018.

OFFICINE'S CRAFTSMEN

Designing stores means, of course, thinking about how you're going to decorate and furnish them, and who is going to bring their craft to implement this vision. Ramdane Touhami brought together the best in their business, extraordinary craftspeople whose skills can transform any material into a precious artefact. Jean-François is an enthusiastic specialist of ornamental history. His knowledge brings the insight necessary to choose the type of molding, the faces that will be featured on the mascarons, etc. depending on the chosen ornamental style. Through his expertise, any piece of wood can become an element of a majestic stage. Jean-François is based in the French Burgundy region, and mainly works on precious wood species: elm and walnut burr, cherry wood, pear wood, mahogany, amaranth. Jacky, Officine's decorative painter, brings the decor and the moldings to life not through wood, but through painting. He worked at the Château de Versailles as an art restorer and created the gracious text painted on the stores' drawers and windows. Each letter is hand-drawn and hand-painted, exquisitely rendering the refinement of French culture.

Left: Ramdane Touhami in a working session with his cabinetmaker, 2017.
Right: Self-portrait of Ramdane and Jacky, ornamentalist painter for Officine, 2017.

THE ART
OF
DISPLAYING

Marble plaque for display engraved with golden letters by Offcine.

Even the brass price display was carefully thought out by Officine.

Graphic variation of the packaging specially designed for wholesale, 2020.

L'ARMOIRE OFFICINALE

The window display cabinet is characteristic of Parisian officines and is inspired by "Comtoise" armoire wardrobes and their crafted cornices. On the pediment, an engraved frame can be customized for each location.

IMPLEMENTING WHOLESALE

OFFICINE AT THE GALERIES

The ephemeral space set within the Galeries Lafayette department store is designed like an anteroom: small, intimate, and confidential. Thin, twisted columns flank the numerous niches here and there. In a couple of them, antique vase flaunt their rich copper ornaments. Classic French magnificence is highlighted by 30-odd porcelain apothecary vases and "verre églomisé" mirrors. Sitting atop "vert de mer" green marble, perfectly aligned bottles and boxes overlook the delicate canework—the star of this space. The prices are indicated in brass cartouches. Above the cashier window, a gold-rimmed mascaron playfully oversees the operations. A small, free-standing Art Deco vanity mirror plays with the light around, the decor and its coppery hues. On the bottom half of the cabinets, arched frames display inspiring 18th-century portrait engravings..

ST JOSEPH IN SAN FRANCISCO

Officine Universelle Buly in San Francisco was a surprising journey. A former Neo-Gothic church was chosen to house the shining chapel of the Officine in an antiques store. There a selection of beauty and fragrance essentials is displayed alongside decorative objects found by Ramdane Touhami, as if it was the back room of a Parisian antique dealer: under the partitioned arches, a French spirit reigns under a vast drape of painted curtains.

OFFICINE AT LOTTE

To design this space, Ramdane Touhami drew inspiration from Paris' newspaper kiosks, their wood reflected and warmed up by the golden lights. Each counter showcases a so-called "Crema Marfil" marble top, the feature harmoniously matching the existing floor. The main cabinet's 80 drawers are an ode to the ostentatious accumulation displayed in 19th-century officines. Inside the arched display windows, the backlit shelves exhibit the various items with a contemporary touch.

A LITTLE PIECE OF OFFICINE IN OHIO

A replica of the main cabinet of the rue Bonaparte, complete with its emblematic doucine moldings and burr walnut, crossed the Atlantic to set store in Ohio. "We sent our ambassador to the United States of America, in order to be duly represented…" says Ramdane Touhami.

THE COSMETIC WORKSHOP

Hyundai's counter honors the sobriety of a 1930s typesetter's cabinet. The granite pillars and jambs bring a welcome contrast to the warm look of the wood.

THE GANGNAM COUNTER

The beauty counter, set in the elegant Seoul neighborhood, is in line with Ramdane Touhami's retro-futuristic approach. Despite its small size, the counter manages to present all the traditional elements of Paris' apothecary shops: mirrors, molded octagonal display windows, apothecary jars. A bespoke lighting system and minimalist glass surfaces bring a modern, contemporary touch to the 19th-century atmosphere.

GABRIELLE HEARST

Within the Carlyle Hotel on the Upper East Side, Officine offers the essentials of French beauty. The richly molded high cabinet looks like it was spirited away from a luxurious paneled Paris apartment.

SOUTHERN TERRITORIES

The wooden cabinets were designed to blend perfectly with the architecture of Australian department stores. About a dozen counters were set up with richly ornamented furniture, in tune with Ramdane Touhami's retro-futuristic vision. Round glass openings stand next to the light-colored woodwork. The displays are a homage to 19th-century cutlery shops.

THE SOCIAL COMPANY OR THE INVERTED SOCIAL PYRAMID

When sellers take power

Ramdane Touhami's office in the Akasaka neighborhood, Tokyo, 2020.

Work in progress in the office, rue Bonaparte in 2014. The large central table was conceived to gather ideas and people.

When Ramdane Touhami embarked on his journey to build Officine Universelle Buly, one of his founding goals was to create a company in which everyone involved would be happy and proud. For him, this meant that Officine would use only the highest quality products. His quest to find the best materials in the world often led him to Japan. A great admirer of Japanese culture, especially its behaviour-codes, Touhami came across the Shinto philosophy "honmono," a concept of genuineness.

THE PHILOSOPHY OF BEING HONEST

Shinto is a religion that originated in Japan. Alongside Buddhism, it is the largest form of religion there. Purity, one of the main Shinto beliefs, guides their approach to life. In Shinto teaching, purity means to be truthful and to cultivate authenticity and a sense of the beautiful. Another important Shinto belief is *Makoto*. This means "sincerity in the heart" and underpins the Shinto approach to the world. Out of these core Shinto sensibilities comes *honmono*. It translates directly as "the real thing" but the full meaning is more complex, encapsulating notions of craft, culture, and heritage. *Honmono* is used to describe objects that are made by master craftsmen using skills that are passed down from one generation to the next. This transmission of wisdom guarantees an exceptional final product that is honmono, the real thing. It is a seal of quality. When you buy something in Japan which is labeled *honmono* you can be sure that it is premium quality, the best in every respect. Another important part of *honmono* is the community that builds up around the object. The passion and dedication of the craftsman is felt by those who buy it. They value the object and when they use it become part of a long chain of tradition which has been perfected over hundreds of years.

This poetic notion of *honmono* resonated with Touhami's vision of Buly. "Japanese culture has influenced me throughout my entire career. When I learned about *honmono*, I had found Buly's path. The philosophy of *honmono* is all about carefully creating genuine products that make everyone involved happy. In creating Buly, I very much wanted all the people committed to Buly to be proud of what we do here: from the creator who imagines a new product to the craftsmen who brings their passion to the task of producing it, the salesperson who is proud to transmit their know-how, the builders and manufactures who lend their hands in creating Buly stores, the typographer who designs our catalogs, my wife and myself and, of course, the customer," says Ramdane Touhami. Holding the elegant Buly catalog in his hand, engraved with gold cover-lettering on blue-gray recycled paper, he explains: "You can open it on any page, stop at any item and find a genuine product. Take page 22, for example: Palo Santo wood from Ecuador, known in the Amazonian shamanic tradition to cleanse the soul and drive out negative energies when it is burnt. Or incense which has for centuries been made by the monks of Mount Athos." And obviously, that incense, so special and sold in several scents by Officine, is a perfect example of a product made with pride in an unbelievably grueling and long process.

"THE PHILOSOPHY OF 'HONMONO' IS ALL ABOUT CAREFULLY CREATING GENUINE PRODUCTS THAT MAKE EVERYONE INVOLVED HAPPY."

Ramdane Touhami

A wooden chair in Ramdane Touhami's office, rue de Saintonge (left), and a green one in Asakasa (right).

Next pages: Ramdane Touhami's office in Asakasa, Tokyo, 2020.
E-shop preparation room, Officine Universelle Buly's office in the Akasaka neighborhood, Tokyo, 2020.

WHEN THE PRODUCT IS AN INCREDIBLE ACT OF FAITH

Mount Athos is an autonomous monastic state, a mountainous peninsula, situated in north-eastern Greece. Legend says that the Greek god Athos threw a giant rock at Poseidon which fell into the Aegean sea and became Mount Athos. The peninsula is accessible only by boat and only to men. Women are strictly forbidden to ensure that the monks remain celibate. It is probably the only place on earth inhabited solely by men. The locals call its territory "The Garden of Virgin Mary." Tradition says that as the Virgin Mary sailed to Cyprus, her boat was blown off course and she landed on Mount Athos. When she walked ashore she fell in love with the nature and beauty of Athos and blessed the mountain.

Mount Athos is referred to as a Holy Mountain where over 2,000 monks live an ascetic life. The everyday lives of the monks are divided into three eight-hour rhythms. Eight hours of praying, eight hours of resting, and eight hours of working, during which the famous Mount Athos incense is made. The burning of incense is a vital part of Orthodox tradition, so the monks use only the best practices to produce the highest quality product because incense is something that will be offered to God. Known as teardrops because of their shape, Mount Athos incense is made by hand the same way it has been made for hundreds of years. Its main ingredient is pure frankincense resin, taken from the trunk of the Boswellia tree. The monks then mix the frankincense powder with essential oil, patiently working it into a paste. It is a very laborious task, requiring strong arms to knead the sticky resins. The right amount of essential oil naturally creates an elastic quality in the frankincense powder. To create high-quality incense, it must be soft, almost like clay. After the essential oil and frankincense are mixed together, it is placed onto a table. The monks roll out the mixture like a bread dough over the entire table and then cut it into small pieces, which are placed into a bowl of talcum powder so they don't stick together. The incense is left out to cure for at least 24 hours. It is then packaged into boxes before heading to Officine Universelle Buly's headquarters in Paris, France.

KNOWN AS TEARDROPS BECAUSE OF THEIR SHAPE. MOUNT ATHOS INCENSE IS MADE BY HAND THE SAME WAY IT HAS BEEN MADE FOR HUNDREDS OF YEARS.

The Mount Athos Church, 2017.

Rida, a member of the Officine's family from 2017, wearing the staff's blue jacket.

A MANAGEMENT ANCHORED IN THE 19TH-CENTURY'S MOST PROGRESSIVE SOCIAL THEORIES

Incense made by the monks of Mount Athos, since the 10th century, is *honmono*. When you burn it, you appreciate 1,000 years of tradition and the dedication of its craftsmen. "It's about what you want to be known for," says Ramdane Touhami. "Striving for *honmono* is beautiful and rewarding. We welcome challenges and are relentless until we find solutions. It's an unconditional commitment to quality. We invest not only all our skills and knowledge, but our pride and love too."

But Touhami expands the idea of *honmono* even further, beyond the tradition-craftsman-buyer relationship, applying it to the entire ambience of the company. Buly is a family-run business and every member is respected and promoted equally. For example, it is part of Buly's corporate concept to provide further training for all employees: the sales staff are trained in calligraphy, embossing and engraving objects, and in the art of Japanese gift wrapping, all techniques that have been practiced for centuries, know-how that Touhami would like to preserve. Touhami was also inspired by the business practices and innovations of Aristide Boucicaut, who established career path advancement for all employees in his Paris department store Le Bon Marché in 1857. Like Boucicaut, he believes the dignity of the worker is the most important requirement for a healthy and happy working environment: "The more you involve people in your philosophy and the more passionate and proud they are about their work-environment and the products they sell, the happier they are. Their happiness gives value to the company. That for me is *honmono*: working with dignity."

"The more you involve people in your philosophy and the more passionate and proud they are about their work-environment and the products they sell, the happier they are. Their happiness gives value to the company. That for me is 'honmono': working with dignity."

Ramdane Touhami

Video broadcasted on social networks showing Officine's master-calligrapher giving a lesson to form the letter "A," 2019.

Video series *Our Top-30*: About 30 Officine employees talked about their favorite product, 2020.

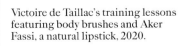

Victoire de Taillac's training lessons featuring body brushes and Aker Fassi, a natural lipstick, 2020.

Victoire de Taillac's training lessons featuring hyaluronic acid, 2020.

Victoire de Taillac's training lessons featuring the Officine's dental care products, 2020.

THE CUSTOMER IS KING

Take the idea of service seriously

Eau Superfine on a 19th century lithography.

Let us quickly consider the incredible sim[...]
life as depicted on stage. In the 1970s in [...]
Spectacle," Guy Debord highlighted the [...]
corollary: the image. The same issues that [...]
today's niche perfumeries: how can we consu[...]
buying? To consume better requires, above [...]
verselle Buly, Ramdane invites us to retu[...]
its habits, its organizing principles. Creatin[...]
quasi-theatrical process, in which countles[...]
sidered. The stage design, the actors, the stor[...]
vice of reality, along with a desire to never [...]
a question of creating a simulacrum, but of [...]
past centuries, in line with the concept of h[...]
losopher Jean Baudrillard. The image tak[...]
real image of our world... Isn't this the task[...]
or she has to faithfully transcribe the ambiti[...]
comes a marketing tool, wherein the perceiv[...]
No. 6 rue Bonaparte hopes to become one of [...]
delightfully antiquated customs—all in the [...]

ty between imagined life, real life, and
enow-famous book "The Society of the
sses of consumption and its omnipresent
ccupied Debord 50 years ago persist in
better and how can we rethink the act of
, a return to things. At Officine Uni-
o the 19th century in an ode to its customs,
faithful and authentic time capsule is a
details and technical aspects must be con-
he plot, the ending, these are all at the ser-
fake or superficial. Nevertheless, it is not
turing a legitimate, authentic essence from
nerrealism formulated by the French phi-
from our world appears more real than the
that falls on every theatre director when he
ns of an author or an era? The theatre be-
d illusion becomes reality. The boutique at
those scenes of old-fashioned life with its
idst of a decidedly 21st-century Paris.

Ivone, a member of the Buly family since March 2019.

SETTING
THE
SCENE

In 1959, the sociologist Erving Goffman observed that social life is structured like a stage and its various elements: the actors, the audience, the backstage area. The more impactful the show, the more it gives rise to awareness and emotions. As Claude Maffesoli put it, we are involved in the "re-enchantment of the ordinary," where goods and services are oriented towards hedonistic, symbolic, and interpersonal values. The staging of commerce and the writing of its script require the participation of the spectator (customer) in order to form exceptional memories. In this theater of sales, the shop has gradually become the place of enchanted consumption, with an atmosphere that lends itself to making purchases, and in the process, giving customers that special, extra touch. Buying fragrance or cosmetics is no longer a banal task, but rather a ticket of admission to a tailored experience.

"THINGS HAPPEN ON STAGE AS THOUGH THEY WERE REAL."
Paul Claudel

TELLING
THE
STORY

Before "putting on a show," you need to establish the story. The formal rules dictating what makes up a play's opening scene are comparable to the opening lines of a novel. According to "Manuscript 559" of the Bibliothèque Nationale de France, "A good opening scene, in classical playwriting, must inform the audience of what the play is about as well as the circumstances surrounding the action. It must inform the audience of where the action is set, and even of the time that the action begins. It must state the name, position, temperament, and interests of all the main characters. It must be complete, short, clear, interesting and plausible." This provides the backdrop for the play's inciting event and, indeed, the story that follows. No one will pay attention if the story does not hold up. Firmly established, clearly structured, the story unfolds seamlessly and becomes embedded in people's minds and lives. On the stage that is Parisian life—fragrant, refined—the plot is molded into a unity of place (Paris), and whose unity of time (the 19th century) stands in exquisite contrast to the marketing and sales techniques of the present era. The spectator peers into the lives of Claude and Jean-Vincent Bully, and is encouraged to understand the link between these men's discoveries and the innovative techniques we use today. Here we see the concept of "one eye on the past, one on the future."

"CUSTOMERS ARE NOT WAITING, THEY ARE WATCHING. THIS IS A CEREMONY, IT'S LIKE A PLAY."

The Financial Times, 2016

Girls in Officine Universelle Buly uniforms reading *An Atlas of Natural Beauty*
by Victoire de Taillac & Ramdane Touhami, in the Palais Royal Gardens, Paris. Photographer, Arthur Oscar.

BUILDING THE SET THE STAGE, FOOTLIGHTS, SCENERY, AND RED CURTAINS

Unlike a creative agency whose approach relies solely on products and the appearance of its shops, Ramdane Touhami proposed a new take, one that uses theater as its metaphor. In doing this, he hoped to create an immersive atmosphere, as if one were pushing open the doors of time itself. The desire to use centuries-old carpentry techniques (made obsolete by a 1983 law meant to reduce work-related injuries by prohibiting craftsmen from creating their own tools) required extremely precise workmanship. This was done in the manner of those builders of grandiose opera sets, only here the work was on a more human scale where every nuance, every aspect of the set could be easily discerned. Reproducing the look of a master perfumer's and apothecary's counter down to the very last detail required a wealth of materials and know-how. The drawers were arranged in blocks of 50, with enamelled plates in Roman numerals taken from an old clock. The aesthetic codes specific to the Industrial Revolution dictated the use of a specific marble for the sales counter (Brèche de Bénou), the ever-present glassware on shelves adorned with arches and finials, and the walnut burl cabinets whose distinctiveness is such that the glass paneling is held in place not by screws, but by bands of silk. Cast-iron radiators were brought in, thick satin curtains were installed on the doors, along with so much more. Specialists with a trained eye will be able to appreciate these details as they browse the store.

OFFICINE DE LA RUE BONAPARTE CONVEYS THE ILLUSION OF AN UNINTERRUPTED PRESENCE IN THIS SPACE, PERSISTING THROUGH THE CENTURIES DESPITE THE TWISTS AND TURNS OF HISTORY.

A space is more than just the decor on the walls—it includes the floor and ceiling too. At 6 rue Bonaparte these have both been carefully thought out, with the antiqued beams, hand-painted with decorative motifs: intricate compositions of flowers, braids, and palmettes. The floor, made of glazed terracotta, was fired in 1,000-year-old Etruscan kilns. To give the illusion that time has left its mark on the scene, the paintings have been aged and the wood polished; more importantly, though, the scene needed to include decorative elements that weren't in keeping with the chosen time period. And, so, we find a checkout counter with Art Nouveau accents, spot lighting from 1950s lamps and a logo with a 1930s flair. Only the light rail, the sole survivor of a former art gallery, has a 1980s feel. Officine de la rue Bonaparte conveys the illusion of an uninterrupted presence in this space, persisting through the centuries despite the twists and turns of history. "By establishing a distinctive dramatization, notably through suggestive decorations, the new shops emphasize the social element of making a purchase."[1]

1. Isabelle Calvar-Madec, Fabien Ohl, Gary Tribou, *Management et avenir*, p. 139.

Flora, a member of the Buly family since June 2016, performing specific wrapping for an online order.

THE ACTORS, THEIR ROLES, AND THEIR INNER LIFE

The staff must be in unison, with no step out of place in this delicate ballet of making a sale. In this respect, they are as much ambassadors with an established protocol as they are actors serving the text (the narrative), the subtext (emotions), and the brand. The narrative must be truly and fully embodied: in addition to learning the wealth of cultural references, the staff at Officine Universelle Buly must have a working knowledge of the 800 products on offer. The properties of every product, be it cosmetics, fragrance, or their base ingredients, are recorded in a thick 500-page tome. This bewilderingly dense volume requires considerable diligence and patience to memorize, like a work by Chekhov. An authentic experience is achieved by serving the customer, through the connection established by the employee-actor. It is therefore essential to make the salesperson central again, since he or she animates the scene, arouses the attention of the spectator-customer, and becomes the beating heart of the commercial battlefield. Salespeople are the elite force of the boutique, for they alone bring about the final denouement: the act of making a purchase. In order to beat the competition, each salesperson must be trained and made aware of the wide variety of items for sale. This way they can become a master of an impeccable ritual of advice and support. It is through this that the romance and fantasy behind the brand are conveyed to the customer. The sales staff have to use courtesy and eloquence to tell and transmit stories, an essential element of sales. Through their choice of words, their tactfulness, the appropriate tone, their sense of propriety, their gaze and gestures, the actor-salesperson puts the customer-spectator in a state of receptiveness. Officine Universelle Buly is above all a celebration of a love of words and a passion for a forgotten form of etiquette. Conversation is an art defined by poise and politeness, as Louise Foulon-Lefranc wrote in her treatise *La femme au foyer* (*The Housewife*).[2] The Baroness of Staffe, in her book *The Rules of Etiquette in Modern Society*, professes that "everything changes with time, but much more in appearance than in reality, more in form than in substance. Things based on one principle are the same, in all centuries and in all places. There

2. Louise Foulon-Lefranc,
La femme au foyer
(*The Housewife*), 1941.

SALESPEOPLE ARE THE ELITE FORCE OF THE BOUTIQUE, FOR THEY ALONE BRING ABOUT THE FINAL DENOUEMENT: THE ACT OF MAKING A PURCHASE.

are only superficial differences... We are accused of having cut down the tree of propriety. Said tree—to extend this excellent, almost tangible analogy—has not even been pruned. It has kept its main branches; we have hardly trimmed it, limiting ourselves to cutting off the most cumbersome branches. Is it a crime, then, to have done away with the tiresome and useless rituals,

Halimata, a member of the Buly family since January 2018.

Eri, a member of the Buly family since Febuary 2017.

Rei, a member of the Buly family since June 2018.

3. Baronne Staff,
*Usages du monde, règles
de savoir-vivre dans la
société moderne,*
(*The Rules of Etiquette
in Modern Society*)
1891

4. *Ibid.*

the overblown formalities, the customs that have become irrelevant? All this, it must be admitted, was as troublesome, in our busy age, as a full-length dress was for trudging about on foot."[3] Aside from the inevitable modernisations that she highlights here, the Baroness endorsed the notion of perpetuating social customs and restoring the ceremonial traditions epitomized by a sales staff. Good manners, or the art of etiquette, had its golden age from 1800 to 1914, when bourgeois etiquette reasserted the art of *savoir-vivre* and reinvented the rules of civility. "That is why Paris is the moral compass of the world. An elegant nation never falls into certain base offenses. It can commit follies, but not indignities. On its worst days, its chic remains."[4] Elegance is intrinsically Parisian and the world looks to Paris for guidance. The brand's ambassadors must make this reality central to how they imagine themselves in the space. This historical approach and the embodiment of it is reminiscent of "the art of experiencing," a process promoted by the theater practitioner Konstantin Stanislavski. The actor, here, is a kind of onion composed of different layers, where each layer must be worked through and fully embodied in order for the actor to truthfully bring their role to life. If, in acting, we depend on the virtues of memory to achieve sincerity, we must first search for sincerity within ourselves, to fuse in ourselves the person (us) and the persona (the character in the play). Officine operates like the vocational world of old, where the employer distinguishes itself by offering a comprehensive apprenticeship to the staff. It is a place of education where one learns of beauty, social conventions, the etiquette of a time past, etc. Where one learns that the way words are represented on the page is just as important as the choice of the words themselves. To this effect, calligraphy lessons are given by a master in the field and are a mandatory rite of passage before completing a sale.

Calligraphy lessons bring distinction to that act in which we signal our personality: writing. Japanese origata, a technique that allows any paper to be transformed into a subtle casing for a gift, is elevated to an artform. The training demands that practitioners transcend the self, and it contributes to *honmono*. When the actor-employee learns and communicates his or her joy, the entire scene is better for it. When measured in terms of theatrical performance, the burden of responsibility on the salesperson is considerable. In the theater world, they say there are no bad actors, only actors who haven't been fortunate to be directed properly; the same is true for the store. The salesperson-actor is there to guarantee that the potential customer has not made a mistake in coming. If the salesperson is mediocre, they can spoil the tremendous amount of work done by the entire team behind the scenes—the factory workers, product designers, the PR team, and the editorial and regulatory departments. The salesperson is the last and by far the most important link in a long chain of processes.

THE ACTOR, HERE, IS A KIND OF ONION COMPOSED OF DIFFERENT LAYERS, WHERE EACH LAYER MUST BE WORKED THROUGH AND FULLY EMBODIED IN ORDER FOR THE ACTOR TO TRUTHFULLY BRING THEIR ROLE TO LIFE.

Details of the mirror at the Paris rue Bonaparte store.

THE MISE-EN-SCENE

5. Solomon, 1983.

6. Dominique Le Jean Savreux, *Mise en scène du point de vente et comportement du consommateur : une approche expérientielle par l'imagerie mentale*, 2009.

Sacha Guitry reminds us that "Theater can never be considered a pleasurable art... because what is at stake is not the pleasure of the performer, but rather the pleasure of the spectator." More than simply giving the illusion of attending a show, the distinctive staging must equally fulfill certain marketing criteria. And so, before opening to the public, the space is fine-tuned backstage: the staff adjust the lights, dust off their clothes, shine their shoes... The troupe tends to the hyper-reality of things. In order to combine so many unique details into a perfectly orchestrated whole, a keen director's eye is necessary before the spotlight can be switched on. We are talking about an experience here, a spectacle for the senses, where the spectacular dimension must create a euphoric sensation for those who attend, a "retail experience as theater,"[5] a communication tool at the service of the brand and not as an end in itself.[6]

REHEARSAL MAKES IT PERFECT

With lots of hard work and many rehearsals, the movements of the staff must be carefully calibrated, much like a ballet, where the gestures have been thought out with a goldsmith's precision. The illusion must be pulled off! The costume, ie. the uniform, contributes to this visual effect: sober lines with a refinement that has been lost over time. Sometimes a blouse with a detachable Claudine collar, or a slim fit in thick denim dyed a midnight blue. Sometimes the uniforms are fashioned after the housekeeping schools of the previous century: pleated skirts, a collared leotard or a ruffled shirt. The costume even includes the aesthetic rigor of every individual: the staff's shoes must be smart, polished, and discreet. And let's not forget the hands, so essential to graceful movement and central in preparing our products. Our hands reflect how we take care of ourselves—not to mention the effectiveness of Buly's products! The staff's hands, then, act as ambassadors, and, as such, they must be perfectly moisturized, their nails scrubbed, minimally adorned. The ladies' hair is to be styled in a bun, pulled back in a method that was chosen by a specialist. The gentlemen's beards should be full, clean, combed, and lustrous. The painstaking propriety that marked the glory days of past centuries has a charming effect today. The staff's faces represent the care and wisdom professed by Officine Universelle Buly, and a salesperson's radiant face will instantly convince the clients of the effectiveness of the products on offer.

THE COSTUME, IE. THE UNIFORM, CONTRIBUTES TO THIS VISUAL EFFECT: SOBER LINES WITH A REFINEMENT THAT HAS BEEN LOST OVER TIME.

Mina, a member of the Buly's family since 2018.

SILENCE...
THE CURTAIN GOES UP!

As they wait for the stage curtains to lift, many an actor has pondered who is in the audience, where they were before this. The opening of a store requires a similar train of thought: "When a customer enters, I ask myself where he or she is coming from. What brought them here? Is it on the advice of a friend? Have they come to prepare for a romantic night out? Or was it simply pure chance?" asks Ramdane Touhami. We turn on the lights. They glow in soft, coppery halos that reflect off the wooden cabinets. We make sure music (opera, French romanticism) is playing—but not too loud. Conversations need to be audible, and music, when played at the wrong level, takes on an aggressive and irritating quality. A scented candle is placed on a desk and lit to awaken the customer's sense of smell. We cultivate an atmosphere that appeals to all five senses: researchers have found that the absence of music reduces the time shoppers spend in stores. The tempo sets the pace for purchases and the musical style is an effective means of targeting customers and defining the brand.[7] We evoke the importance of various stimuli such as music, colors, smells, or proximity to others, in order to give the store a distinctive image.[8] A visit to the store must be associated with pleasure and emotion, mediated by a multi-sensory experience.[9]

7. Rieunier et Daucé, quoted by Émilie Hoëllard, "La mise en scène du point de vente : une démarche pour renforcer l'appropriation de l'enseigne par la cible visée," PhD thesis completed at Caen University, 2013.

8. Émilie Hoëllard, "La mise en scène du point de vente : une démarche pour renforcer l'appropriation de l'enseigne par la cible visée," 2013.

9. *Ibid.*

"APPROACHING THE CUSTOMER IS ABOUT CONVEYING A PASSION, ABOUT GRASPING YOUR SCRIPT WITH FERVOR AND COMMUNICATING A STORY." *Ramdame Touhami*

The first line to be delivered is, above all, a "Bonjour madame, Bonjour monsieur." The voice is calm, warm, reassuring, but full of respect. It is this art of greeting that sets the mood for the customer. You can forget those horrible phrases such as "What can I do for you?" or "Let me know if there's anything I can help you with." They lead to a tragic and one-sided conversation that quickly peters out. "Approaching the customer is about conveying a passion, about grasping your script with fervor and communicating a story. It is through history that everything passes, through this precious medium of the spoken word. The decor captures the spirit,

Cake trompe l'œil of an Officine Universelle Buly product
at the opening of the Saintonge store.

the history keeps it truthful, and etiquette lends it magic," insists Ramdane Touhami who has even crowned one of his employees with the title of "Head of Decorum." The peak hours in the store are closely studied, analyzed and audited. They cause upheavals that must be strictly managed: all roles need to be redistributed and specialized. Each person is assigned a task in order to speed things along: during peak moments, the cash register, the wrapping counter and the calligraphy station are all manned by a designated person. A smile and a "we'll be right with you" helps to keep the customers patiently and gracefully waiting. Meanwhile the staff shows no signs of rushing or stress. On the contrary—you have to slow down the pace when the mood starts to feel frantic and the store gets packed. It is in these moments that the Officine Universelle Buly demonstrates its power in escaping the constraints of time: the admiring clientele is ready to wait 45 minutes to acquire a simple hand cream. As soon as their turn comes, many of the spectators applaud the vintage atmosphere and its striking realism. The counter is illuminated with a thousand lights, trained on the middle of the stage like spotlights, as if it were the center of action. On the staff-actor side, we play to the whole room, performing for the front row, but also—or especially—for the last. Attention and courtesy must be consistent, and taking the time to converse is standard practice. When it comes time to chat with a customer, we watch our fellow workers from the corner of our eye, gauging how much space we and the others in the store have, like squares on a chessboard. We ring the concierge bell if backup is needed. The customer is invited to proceed to the checkout counter where their items can be tallied up and where payment is handled discreetly, away from prying eyes. Taking our time is an essential quality at Officine Universelle Buly, it's our way of pushing back on quick consumption and rushed processes. Time stands still, and the Officine time takes its place: the time of attentiveness, of folding, of the candlelit calligraphy desk, where a master of calligraphic arts, dressed in a suit, creates sumptuous knots and arabesques as a way of personalizing the gifts. The customer suddenly becomes a spectator-actor, where they themselves participate in the making of the plot.

INTRIGUE, THE DENOUEMENT, AND THE CLOSING SCENE

From the second they lay eyes on the store to the moment they exit it, the public must be won over—not by means of seduction, but by force of persuasion. The persuasiveness, as mentioned above, comes from the story, the actors, the staging. It forms the core of intrigue, where the product becomes a symbol of its own story, its history, its origins, its longevity, and its effectiveness. Will the customer choose it? If the answer is yes, then both parties have a happy ending—that is to say, the purchase, but also a relationship built on trust, and a customer who has been won over, convinced to come back and benefit from the brand's expertise. A perfectly folded receipt, a bag from Officine Universelle Buly swinging in the streets, and this image, the most flamboyant finale of them all: an elegant item dancing across that larger, infinitely more impressive backdrop: the elegance of Paris itself.

Example of a Buly's uniform, in situ on the Paris banks.

THE ART OBJECTS
The offering ceremony

E TURNING NTO GIFTS

Initials are embossed on the elegantly textured,
color-of-time wrapping paper. The old-fashioned
gilt initials are emphasized with a velvet ribbon.

When we speak of beauty, we search for an essence, a definition, a criterion, but beauty is sensorial, the result of a direct, unanimous experience. This distinction, which does not in any way assert itself, more or less corresponds to our current usage."[1] For the philosopher Etienne Souriau, beauty was to be found along the path of experience, to be exalted and enacted through our own actions. According to André Comte-Sponville, the beautiful is even a "concept," and beauty, "a pleasure and an opportunity." A boutique becomes a showcase for excellence that sets beauty into movement for the visitor to experience; it promises happiness and aestheticism. The intent is entirely ceremonial. "The protocol assigns everyone their place, in a ceremony"[2] that leads to a sense of subjugation and enchantment at the hands of a hyperreality... to which we are accustomed. The many small details in this process constitute signifiers that speak volumes about our intentions. This network of signs that Roland Barthes described represents a non-verbal vector that reveals our deepest feelings and anxieties. So it was necessary to think about the whole of these means of expression.

1. Etienne Souriau, *Vocabulaire d'esthétique.*

2. André Comte-Sponville, *Dictionnaire philosophique.*

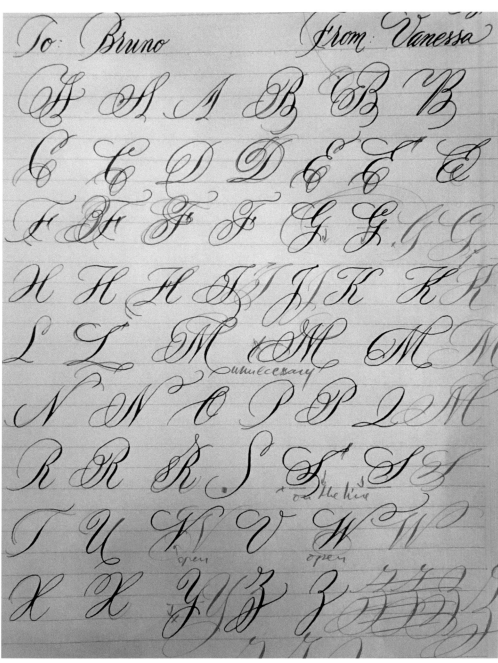

Calligraphy exercise board.

A HIDDEN COMBAT

The advent of a digital, screen-based society will irrevocably lead to the death of cursive scripts. The use of pen and ink is a subtle form of resistance that seeks to make people aware of the art of writing well and properly forming one's letters. It is a considerable challenge to train our international associates, whose penmanship reflects a great cultural diversity, not to mention that the discipline of handling a calligraphic pen doesn't come naturally to anyone… but ultimately, celebrating the old means celebrating its most beautiful customs. Handwriting has the power to render speech mute. It is "a process that we currently use to immobilize, to fix the language we articulate, which is fleeting by its very nature."[3] This extension of our personalities, with its studied gestures and codification, has the virtue of being a vector of communication and personalization in relation to a recipient.

3. Charles Higounet, *L'Écriture*, PUF, coll. "Que sais-je?", 1964.

THE ADVENT OF A DIGITAL, SCREEN-BASED SOCIETY WILL IRREVOCABLY LEAD TO THE DEATH OF CURSIVE SCRIPTS. THE USE OF PEN AND INK IS A SUBTLE FORM OF RESISTANCE THAT SEEKS TO MAKE PEOPLE AWARE OF THE ART OF WRITING WELL AND PROPERLY FORMING ONE'S LETTERS.

Left: The process of embossing consists of pressing typographic blocks onto golden sheets.
Right: Personalization at Officine Universelle Buly takes all possible forms. Here, initials embossed in gold letters on exquisite wrapping papers.
Next page: Bookplates collection conceived for the book *An Atlas of Natural Beauty*.

A few words suffice for the most loving declarations or the
merriest wishes. A Master Calligrapher from Officine uses
his best quill to compose a telegraphic message.

At its founding, Officine Universelle Buly had to respond to an essential question: how to exalt beauty… at a very affordable price? To avoid using labels that were too expensive for a new business, it was important to rely on inventiveness. The team began by handwriting with simple pencils and felt-tip pens. This showed that nature endows some human efforts considerably more than others, disconcertingly so; some of the renditions were beautifully done, while others could disappoint. Officine had to create a system to harmonize everything. Ramdane Touhami decided to focus on the writing arts to achieve a certain standard in our presentation. Since the rise of printing and moving characters in the 15th century, the art of writing well has become a skill that requires a compass, a ruler, and a square. Carefully forming one's letters creates a sense of delight, and it leaves an indelible impression, and so, in 2015, a calligraphy machine appeared in the boutique. The names of the cosmetics and their recipient were elegantly executed on a neutrally tinted cardboard box, but this act of prowess had one unpleasant side-effect: the machine was so hard to configure, that it took 20 minutes to print a single label. And worse yet, its slowness was rivalled only by its noisiness (which was drowned out with the voice of Maria Callas in the background). Its nevertheless exceptional yield convinced Ramdane Touhami to bring in a professional master calligrapher, who was put in charge of deciding on beautiful, individual letters.

"IT IS A KIND OF CHOREOGRAPHY OF WRITING. THE BOUTIQUE STAFF WRITES THE NAME OF EACH CLIENT ON THEIR PURCHASE, WHICH GIVES RISE TO A KIND OF PERFORMANCE FOR THE CLIENT. THE EXPERIENCE IS PRESSED INTO THE PAPER SO THAT THE MEMORY WON'T FADE AWAY."

Ramdane Touhami

It was decided to settle on an English style of cursive script from the 18th century known as Roundhand derived from the Cancellaresca (or Chancery) and Italian Bastarda scripts from the 15th century. It is the high-brow descendant of Dutch master calligraphers such as Jan van den Velde and Ambrosius Perling. Roundhand was appreciated for its professional applications in the world of business and generally for its both utilitarian and refined aspect. The script was written differently, with a square-tipped quill instead of the pointed-tipped goose feathers that had been used until then. This style used both pressure and a special calibration of the quill to readily yield a long, slender line with the lightest touch on the paper and to make a full stroke by pressing harder. Roundhand possesses highly aesthetic qualities, a sense of dreamy romanticism in its arabesques and delicate tracery.

A growing demand over time led to a reshuffling of all the pieces on the chessboard, and the master calligrapher began to train the staff at Officine, to help them save time and be more independent when making a sale. From that moment on, everyone learned how to fold gift paper properly, write a short message, and affix a label for any recipient coming to the boutique. Transforming a gift into a figuration of its intended recipient is irrefutable proof of one's love and consideration for that person. Calligraphy represents a trace of otherness that Buly has sought to promote, and Ramdane Touhami emphasizes that this technique is a key part of this dramatic ensemble: "It is a kind of choreography of writing. The boutique staff writes the name of each client on their purchase, which gives rise to a kind of performance for the client. The experience is pressed into the paper so that the memory won't fade away."

Mme/M. *Super Maman*

Produit: *Huile Antique Miel d'Angleterre*

Date: *Le 6 Décembre 2014*

BULY

A name or a message could be artfully laid out on the product's box at Officine.
The very first cardbox in gray color.

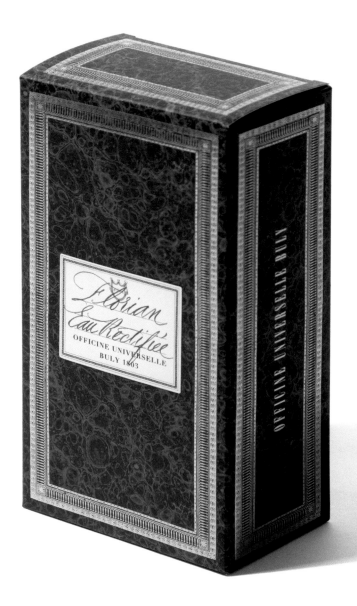

The 2019 cardbox with green marble print.

SAVOIR-RECEVOIR, OR THE ART OF HOSPITALITY

Any establishment that aspires to a sense of excellence must possess its own army of signifiers. Hotels have their imperial-style sheets, fabrics, and furnishings. Restaurants use personalized cutlery, flamboyant silver, embroidered table linens, perfectly symmetrical china, maîtres d'hôtel of the greatest professionalism, gueridons for serving meats... just as the service à la Française instituted under the Ancien Regime demanded. It is Versailles that gave us this ceremony, which became the standard for *savoir-recevoir* across Europe. If there is any magic in this world, "it is often at a meal, in that constant tension between the necessity of a meal and the sumptuousness of its spectacle."[4]

4. Patrick Rambourg, *L'art et la table.*

A boutique must adopt a service-based approach where splendor and spectacle are the norm, where perfection and a sense of mastery permeate every detail of a sale. The objects must wear their costumes: the gift paper and its folding must rival the French art of table service. Once again, Officine strives for elegance, but at the lowest possible cost. Which is why "one should not confuse plush and elegant," as instructed by the 1892 edition of the *Illustrated Encyclopedia of Female Elegance.* "A dress made with velvet costing twenty-five francs per meter may be perfectly grotesque and inelegant, while a sense of imagination can turn fabric costing one franc per meter into an exquisite dress, provided that one understands the nature of the fabric and how to shape it."[5] Officine also strives for simplicity, but it must express a sense of refinement. To embellish our various items (creams, candles, and flasks, among others) in their different sizes, Ramdane Touhami opted for simplicity and standardization in the paper. He took his inspiration from a monogrammed checkered floor, like the emblematic travertine stone pattern. By attaching sheets of paper with an adhesive ribbon (whose secret to success lies in being double-sided!) any form becomes ennobled with ease and an incredible sense of simplicity.

5. Valdès, *Encyclopédie illustrée des élégances féminines,* 1892.

A BOUTIQUE MUST ADOPT A SERVICE-BASED APPROACH WHERE SPLENDOR AND SPECTACLE ARE THE NORM. WHERE PERFECTION AND A SENSE OF MASTERY PERMEATE EVERY DETAIL OF A SALE.

Another way to personalize: to choose the image that will adorn the box of Officine Universelle Buly's Savon Superfin.

Gift packaging with the emblematic paper of *Officine Journal de l'Empire*.

This checkerboard pattern was taken from an illustration in the *Journal of the Napoleonic Empire* (a kind of official gazette that published the minutes of the legislature's sessions) from 1803, the same year in which Officine Universelle Buly was created. There are four kinds of packaging: the paper is deftly folded and counter-folded to yield patterns of braids, V-shapes, bellows, even machicolations, all of which recall the allure of origami. A hand cream is adorned with a berlingot, while candles and glass cloches are elegantly wrapped with paper braids. The cornerstone of this system is a series of self-adhesives that hold everything together and even cover any mistakes when folding the paper (accidental rips or bumps in the paper that require a little something extra to be held together). It borrows much from the look of old-fashioned perfumes from the 19th century (curtain folds, scroll patterns, rich colors) to produce a uniform ensemble which works very well. On the condition that almost all edges are smooth and the paper as taut as a full sail in the wind. Dexterity is everything, and success is taken for granted. To get there, the team takes its time, and this becomes an opportunity to talk, as if everyone is in a salon. "Some people work in the back-office of the E-shop while others are at the counter helping clients in person. Officine has some 900 products, and all our employees are required to know each one well, whether it's an oil, a powder, or a comb. We expect everyone to master the various packaging protocols," Ramdane Touhami insists.

DEXTERITY IS EVERYTHING. AND SUCCESS IS TAKEN FOR GRANTED.

INTO THE
STYLISH FOLD

As an enthusiastic devotee of Japanese philosophy, Ramdane Touhami has created a cultural syncretism between many of this culture's key traits and a French sense of rigor. Two virtues are thus combined: the French art of folding rests on the same principles as origata, the packaging technique of artistic paper folding. This art of presentation markedly expresses the very essence of a present in Japanese society, in which the culture of giving is omnipresent, and where everyone systematically acknowledges and rewards the good actions of others. In his *Empire of the Signs*, Roland Barthes devotes considerable attention to those signifying elements that are as important as the object itself. "In this country (Japan), the empire of signifiers is so vast that it exceeds the word and results in an exchange of signs. Modern Japan, a country of unexpected subtlety, derives its strength from a muted language, from a codification that is all too evident to the Japanese. This silent game, which is at first glance inaccessible to foreigners, reveals a rich, traditional culture that is totally integrated into the modern Japanese lifestyle."[6] "The *origata* etiquette of paper folding is a universal language transmitted with a sense of sacredness by one of the female descendants of the family of the Shogun, Japan's former military governor, that Officine has especially requested as a consultant. I love this Japanese attitude of paying so much attention to the external packaging of a gift, and I have integrated this into Buly. Whether online or in the boutique, the staff engages in this ceremony of the gift, similarly to the one performed for tea, by using the different folds of *origata*," Ramdane Touhami observes.

6. Roland Barthes, *L'Empire des signes.*

> *"I love this Japanese attitude of paying so much attention to the external packaging of a gift, and I have integrated this into Buly."*
>
> *Ramdane Touhami*

Origata was reserved to the Emperor's family as a way to embellish and protect poems, objects, coins, and even messages. It is an art down to the milimeter, using traditional washi fiber paper that is handled according to a precise geometry worthy of a Vasarely or a De Stijl painting. Every package must be signed with a ribbon and a specific fold, so that the packaging becomes an object in itself and "no longer is the passing accessory to the transported object; it instead becomes the object itself," as Barthes mused. This is emblematic of this veritable culture of giving, in which every object can become a gift, where the commonplace becomes exceptional, and where the ineffable manages to express itself. The arrival of our Japanese gift paper in 2019 illustrates the archetype very well. Rare, precious papers hang from brass rods. French motifs such as monograms and damask, brocatelle, and tilapia patterns go hand in hand with the precision of Japanese folding.

Eau Triple Damask Rose surrounded by gifts in embossed papers.

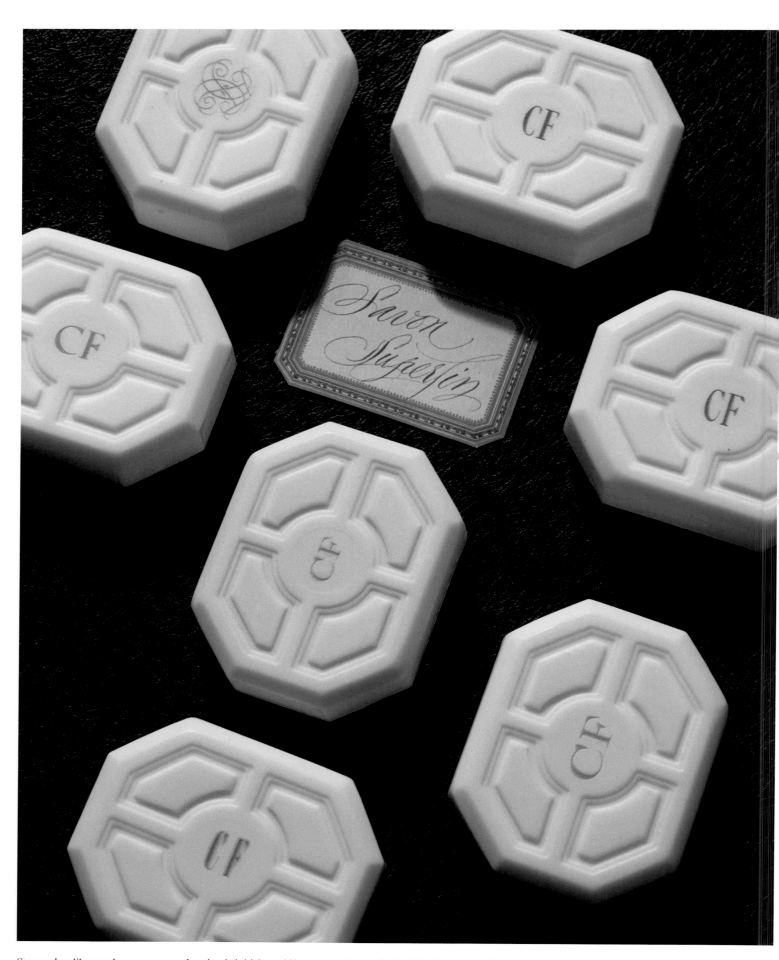

Stamped on like a seal, monogrammed or simple initials could be engraved on the back of the Savon Superfin.

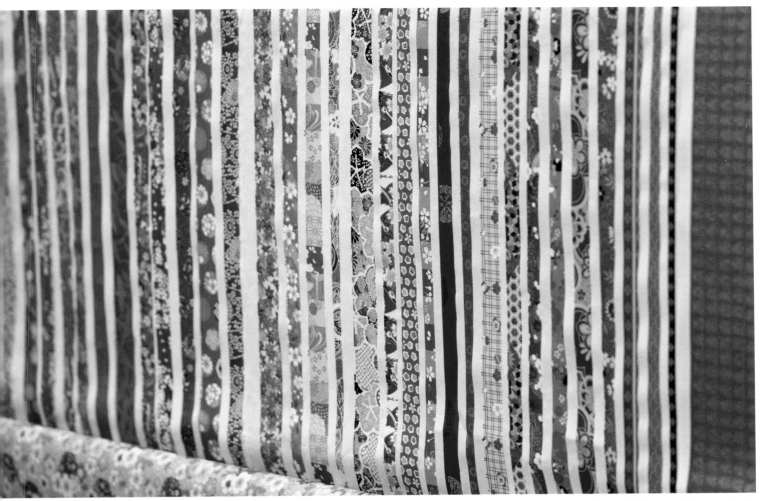

Precious Japanese wrapping papers on show at Officine, rue Saintonge, Paris.

Next page: Collection of labels created for the soap Savon Superfin boxes.

BULY

FABRIQUÉ EN
FRANCE

Savon Superfin
DE
L'OFFICINE UNIVERSELLE BULY

FABRIQUÉ EN
FRANCE

Savon Superfin
DE
L'OFFICINE UNIVERSELLE BULY

LE MOINEAU FRANC

Savon Superfin
DE
L'OFFICINE UNIVERSELLE BULY

FABRIQUÉ EN
FRANCE

Savon Superfin
DE
L'OFFICINE UNIVERSELLE BULY

Examples of gift packaging made with Japanese papers.

WHEN AN OBJECT METAMORPHOSES INTO A GIFT

Transforming an object into a gift means personalizing it and noting its destination. In this way, everyone feels they have a stake in the object being given. Since the Renaissance, people have decorated their wooden cabinets and the front faces of drawers with engravings. And since the Enlightenment, people have decorated the covers of knickknacks such as snuff boxes, candy boxes, and drageoirs, as well as coats of arms, mirrors, and china in the same way. Artisans in Bohemia used a technique known as *Zwischengoldglas*, literally "gold between glass." Jean-Baptiste Glomy, artist and framer to the King of France, revived this gold glass technique that dates back to antiquity. A scene is created under glass using a gold leaf that is engraved. Exorbitant in cost, this technique was reserved for royalty and its daily living requirements, but it gradually spread as such objects came to be resold to merchants and private citizens. This process, with its unique luster, marks an object's possession and destination profoundly. The glass and its surface become, in French, *glomisés* or *églomisés*, meaning that they are gilded. The trend spread all the way to Parisian shop signs and their well-known gold letters on black backgrounds, even to the sphere of Der Blaue Reiter, the Expressionist movement founded by Kandinsky, Macke, Klee, and others. This imaginary world of elegance inspired Ramdane Touhami to develop a technique using laser machinery that yields a similar result. The beam innervates the material, engraving and sculpting it, and it is then slowly gilded to produce the final result, the person's surname.

THIS IS EMBLEMATIC OF THIS VERITABLE CULTURE OF GIVING, IN WHICH EVERY OBJECT CAN BECOME A GIFT, WHERE THE COMMONPLACE BECOMES EXCEPTIONAL, AND WHERE THE INEFFABLE MANAGES TO EXPRESS ITSELF.

ENGRAVING AS AN IMPRESSION ON BOTH MIND AND MATERIAL

Mavelot, the talented engraver of coats of arms to her Royal Highness Anne-Marie-Louise d'Orléans, known as La Grande Mademoiselle, dedicated a book of drop cap initials to the crown prince in which each letter of the alphabet became a composition unto itself that melded a number of interwoven patterns. "Painting and sculpture gave their most beautiful expressions for this noble design, but their zeal undid them; they outdid themselves without achieving their purpose,"[7] Mavelot said with excessive modesty in his epistle. The extraordinary result of his work is an inventory of initials, ranging from collections of two to four letters, that are executed with the most sumptuous arabesques. Having eventually fallen into the public domain, these treasures have been digitally recreated and are now used to decorate soaps and other items at Officine Universelle Buly using the aforementioned engraving technique. Embossing and *foulage* debossing are standards of traditional printing. Every aspect of the paper's grain and texture is highlighted as impressions and reliefs are delicately made on the paper's surface. Typographic characters are embossed or textured, stamped like the papal bulls and seals from the Middle Ages used to certify signatures on documents. Using a heat technique, the initials are set onto any surface with rolls of extra-fine, golden sheets. "Oh, how happy he will be!" The happy customer could exclaim seeing the name in gold letters.

7. Charles Mavelot, *Nouveau livre de chiffres*, an important book for painters, sculptors, engravers and others, invented and engraved by Charles Mavelot, 1680.

TYPOGRAPHIC CHARACTERS ARE EMBOSSED OR TEXTURED, STAMPED LIKE THE PAPAL BULLS AND SEALS FROM THE MIDDLE AGES USED TO CERTIFY SIGNATURES ON DOCUMENTS.

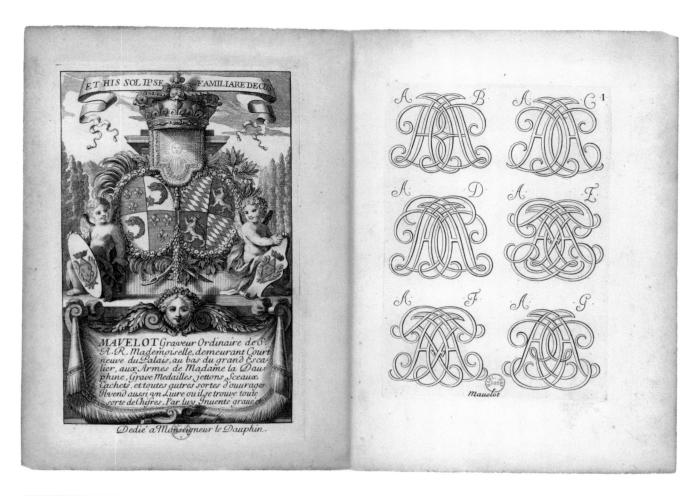

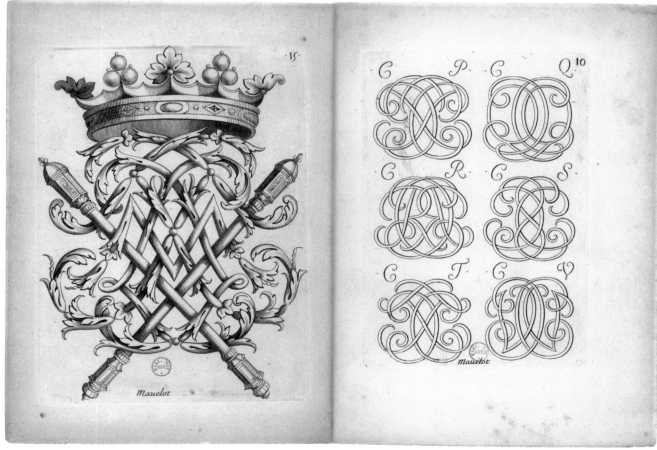

Designed by French engraver Charles Mavelot in the 18th century, these large capitalized alphabet letters, also called monograms, have doubled strokes and interlacing, inspired by the gracious curves of handwriting.

337

The 2021 model features embossed prints in gold, historic medals won by Bully at the World Expositions. The logo has been redesigned for this occasion.
Next page: Christmas box, release Fall 2021.

Officine
Unive

FONDÉE   À PAR

selle

Buly

S EN 1803

THE LOUVRE COLLECTION

Giving museums an extra sense

Ramdane Touhami and Victoire de Taillac
at Officine Universelle Buly inauguration
in the Louvre in 2019.

When we speak of the senses, what do
es as faculties of perception, forming a s
one of five pathways through which we
of smell in particular that could change
At its core, a museum is purely visual:
and we are even surprised if there are an
of sounding too bold, we'd like to believe
incorporated into museums. This way, w
forms an artistic whole. If we could sme
of art, it would inject new life into the st
anyone better qualified than Ramdane
in the real word. And it was the phrase,
Touhami used as a guiding principle for

TION ADVENTURE

ve mean? Aristotle defined the sens-
called external sensoriality. Smell is
perceive the world, and it is our sense
the way we think about museums.
e can neither touch nor taste the art,
works that make sound. At the risk
another sense – that of smell – could be
hen combined with the sense of sight, it
l a perfume that was inspired by a work
ictly codified world of art. There isn't
Touhami to bring these concepts to life
"Adding Meaning with Scent," that
his art project at the Louvre.

HIT OR MISS!

Welcome to the Louvre. It is impossible to ignore its sumptuous galleries, which impart on anyone who passes through them a sense of majesty and power. This former royal residence was occupied until the 18th century before being abandoned, in favor of the Château de Versailles and the Palais des Tuileries. In 1793, following the French Revolution, the Palais du Louvre was declared the Central Museum of Art. Both Napoleons (I and III) tirelessly pursued two goals: to increase the size of the museum and to expand its foreign collections. On a beautiful day in 2019, the scent of perfume wafted through this lofty expanse of cut stone, fragrances trailing through the sprawl of galleries and corridors. It was Tuesday, the day the museum is closed to the public, and Ramdane's signature orange cap could be seen weaving between the sculptures.

THE PROJECT RAISED A SECOND PHILOSOPHICAL, IF NOT SYNAESTHETIC, QUESTION: IF YOU APPROACH A WORK OF ART, WHAT DOES IT SMELL LIKE?

1. Chantal Jaquet, *Philosophie de l'odorat* (*The Philosophy of Smell*), Chapter IV "The Art of Scent", PUF, 2010.

2. Erika Wicky, Lecture at the Collegium de Lyon—Institute for Advanced Study, 2019.

3. "Wild Statistics about the Louvre," *Challenges*, April 3, 2013.

As Ramdane Touhami roamed the collections testing his *aisthetikos* (senses of perception in ancient Greek), he had to answer an essential problem of perfume: can fragrance "in its own right, give birth to olfactory beauty?"[1] The mysterious project he was working on would have to combine the intangible power of scent to the towering tradition of art—and for the first time in the history of French perfumery no less. The perfume he was seeking to create would have to unite an aesthetic of beauty with an aesthetic of pleasure—two concepts that are all too often opposed. The project raised a second philosophical, if not synaesthetic, question: if you approach a work of art, what does it smell like? As soon as you are close, it loses its evocative nature and gives off a purely material odor. The meadow of flowers flees, suddenly miles away; the carefully arranged fruits of a still-life evaporate. "A painting is not meant to be smelled; keep your distance: the smell of paint is not healthy!" This warning, attributed to Rembrandt[2], signals the disappointment of our sense of smell, and Officine Universelle Buly had to respond to this pitiful state of affairs by launching a large-scale experiment. And in doing so they paved the way for the famous French institution to license what was immaterial. In a building comprising 243,000 m² of exhibition space, 14.5 km of corridors, 10,000 steps, 410 windows, and 3,000 locks[3], this was the first time scent would join the ranks of the museum's countless selling points. In the early stages of the project (February

Winged Victory of Samothrace photographed by the Neurdein Brothers at the Louvre in 1891.
Next page: *Galleries of the Museum*, two photographs by the Neurdein Brothers, 1891.

2019), the institution had in mind a temporary installation featuring an Officine Universelle Buly in one of the galleries. It would be nothing more than a commercial project that would combine the French know-how and refinement promoted by Ramdane Touhami and Victoire de Taillac with the museum's marketing objectives—a perfect synergy. During a preliminary meeting, though, Ramdane Touhami laid the foundations for a sweeping vision, and suddenly a simple space rental suddenly became a project of epic proportions. A bold and brazen vision was the driving force behind this project: can cultural goods be licensed, like brands? "How can one legally and commercially establish an extension of a work of art? How can we build on top of an artistic work while staying artistically faithful; how can we add meaning to what exists already? The idea was revolutionary. The task, then, was to build a veritable franchise on top of a 500-year-old work, integrating a commercial dimension into a work that must not be desecrated in any way—all this by using a new artwork whose medium is solely perfume," says Ramdane Touhami. In order to develop this large-scale project, it was agreed over the course of several meetings to trademark any accumulated knowledge, as well as the standards and procedures. "The Louvre must think differently, it must acquire the snobbery that is by all means entitled to."

DARING TO BLEND PERFUME IN THE SLIPSTREAM OF PAINTING

The idea was simple: choose the most distinguished French perfume houses and commission their best noses. They will then be given an exciting challenge: to create a fragrance for one of the museum's iconic works, bringing it to life through perfume. This special collection would then be marketed in a pop-up boutique, imbued with its own distinct narrative. The constraints: none. After the perfumers had chosen a work of art that spoke to them, they could use whatever fragrances they desired, freely imagining the work's olfactory expression. This was in the vein of Marcel Duchamp and Andy Warhol as well as the Symbolist, Futurist, Dadaist and Surrealist movements, all of which paid special attention to the sense of smell. For so long scent had been sorely neglected by museums[4]; and so Ramdane Touhami wished to reintegrate fragrance into the cultural continuum, rescuing it from the fringes of history and artistic creation. "The need for museums to represent visual or auditory art through smell seems less urgent, as there does not seem to be any apparent olfactory value added to these exhibited works,"[5] argues the historian Anne Nieuwhof. She proposes a legitimate appropriation of culture by the senses, for example with the exhibit at the Tate Modern where the cold surfaces of Umberto Boccioni's sculptures were meant to be understood through touch. Or in 2013, when you could experience the softness and voluptuousness of René Magritte's clouds in a dish served at MoMa. Or the way visitors are enveloped in Van Gogh's vibrant colors at the "Van Gogh Alive"[6] exhibition. Similarly, since 1960, the Viennese-inspired Café Sabarsky and Café Fledermaus have become olfactory and culinary oases inside New York museums. "In these cafes, customers sit on chairs designed by the Austrian modernist architect Adolf Loos, and… in the restaurants other period objects can be found…

4. Anne Nieuwhof, "Olfactory Experiences in Museums of Modern and Contemporary Art", PhD thesis completed at Leiden University, 2017.

5. *Ibid.*

6. *Ibid.*

7. *Ibid.*

light fixtures by Josef Hoffmann and benches covered with Otto Wagner's fabric from 1912."[7] Beauty, elegance, and design incorporate new modalities of sensory experience in order to play with the culture surrounding the museum. This theory echoes the sensuality required for any sales experience, in which a seductive spectacle is played out. In this project, aesthetics and intense reflection replace strict codes and conventions. The aim of this is to heighten the experience of visiting the museum and to work towards a polysensoriality. Towards a realism that is fragrant, authentic, and bold.

THE LOUVRE MUST THINK DIFFERENTLY, IT MUST ACQUIRE THE SNOBBERY THAT IS BY ALL MEANS ENTITLED TO."

Ramdane Touhami

By joining forces with a renowned museum for this project, Officine Universelle Buly, whose dedication to perfume is unwavering, became a beacon of French elegance and distinction. If Paris seduces, then perfume magnifies those passions. And thus, at the onset of this monumental project the Louvre assumed an almost bewitching aspect. Although Rembrandt thought that "a painting is not made to be smelled," it can nevertheless carry the scents of what it depicts.

Galleries of the Museum photograph by the Neurdein Brothers, 1891.
Next page: The eight fragrances from the Louvre collection by Officine Universelle Buly.

351

OFFICINE UNIVERSELLE BULY
MAISON FONDÉE À PARIS EN 1803
en collaboration avec
LE MUSÉE DU LOUVRE

Le Verrou
DE FRAGONARD

par le parfumeur
DELPHINE LEBEAU

LES PLUS HAUTES RÉCOMPENSES
ont été obtenues
À TOUTES LES EXPOSITIONS

FABRIQUÉ
EN FRANCE

MARQUE
DÉPOSÉE

OFFICINE UNIVERSELLE BULY
N°6 RUE BONAPARTE PARIS
DÉPÔT EXCEPTIONNEL AU MUSÉE DU LOUVRE

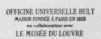

OFFICINE UNIVERSELLE BULY
MAISON FONDÉE À PARIS EN 1803
en collaboration avec
LE MUSÉE DU LOUVRE

La Victoire de Samothrace

par le parfumeur
ALIÉNOR MASSENET

LES PLUS HAUTES RÉCOMPENSES
ont été obtenues
À TOUTES LES EXPOSITIONS

FABRIQUÉ
EN FRANCE

MARQUE
DÉPOSÉE

OFFICINE UNIVERSELLE BULY
N°6 RUE BONAPARTE PARIS
DÉPÔT EXCEPTIONNEL AU MUSÉE DU LOUVRE

OFFICINE UNIVERSELLE BULY
MAISON FONDÉE À PARIS EN 1803
en collaboration avec
LE MUSÉE DU LOUVRE

La Nymphe au Scorpion
DE BARTOLINI

par le parfumeur
ANNICK MÉNARDO

LES PLUS HAUTES RÉCOMPENSES
ont été obtenues
À TOUTES LES EXPOSITIONS

FABRIQUÉ
EN FRANCE

MARQUE
DÉPOSÉE

OFFICINE UNIVERSELLE BULY
N°6 RUE BONAPARTE PARIS
DÉPÔT EXCEPTIONNEL AU MUSÉE DU LOUVRE

AND PERFUME BECOMES A BRUSH, AND IT PAINTS WITH SCENT

Eight perfumers were handpicked and invited to reflect on a work. They were the backbone of the project and essential to the process of creating the fragrances. These noses had the task of immersing the spectator in the work, its time period, and its atmosphere. Incidentally, their work brought up an ontological question: what are we as we stand before a masterpiece? Does perfume intrinsically possess a transcendental value, "another beginning" in the words of Heidegger? With perfume we can be brought safely into port, or left lost and adrift, or even plunged into a mystical abyss. More often, though, perfume simply initiates a conversation between a master's work and it's newly dreamed-up fragrance.

INCIDENTALLY, THEIR WORK BROUGHT UP AN ONTOLOGICAL QUESTION: WHAT ARE WE AS WE STAND BEFORE A MASTERPIECE? MORE OFTEN, THOUGH, PERFUME SIMPLY INITIATES A CONVERSATION BETWEEN A MASTER'S WORK AND IT'S NEWLY DREAMED-UP FRAGRANCE.

However, this total freedom frightened more than a couple of people: for one, there was the difficulty of choosing a work from amongst the dizzying abundance. And that, despite the extraordinary atmosphere of concentration and contemplation created by the lack of the public. Bartolini's *Nymph with a Scorpion*, Ingres's Bather, also known as *The Bather of Valpinçon*, Gainsborough's *Conversation in the Park*, Georges de La Tour's *Joseph the Carpenter*, Ingres's *The Grande Odalisque*, Fragonard's *The Lock*, the *Victory of Samothrace* and the *Venus de Milo* were all included in the project.

A worried look, a candle, a sweep of the hand or a wisp of smoke are enough to launch the master perfumer on a creative and aromatic journey. "The soft and comforting notes of amber are enriched by the woody notes of cedar and vetiver. They make up the raw atmosphere of a workshop worthy of *Joseph the Carpenter*," says Sidonie Lancesseur. Then there's the relaxing, deliciously hygienic atmosphere of *The Bather* by Ingres: "A supple, milky skin, trickling water, the scent of the linen underneath her. These pictorial elements are extremely concrete in terms of scent. Perfumers are like interpreters, able to transform a color, a light or a texture into a note. For example, the green velvet curtain (on the left) reminded me of lavender absolute, rich and dark. Notes of orange blossom and neroli pay homage to sun-dried sheets, symbolizing the perfect beauty of bathing," explains perfumer Daniela Andrier. Myrrh, an aromatic compound, has been considered sacred since biblical times, and it adds a seventh heaven to the *Victory of*

Antique postcards and art books create a vintage atmosphere around three products from
The Louvre Collection: Eau Triple Saint Joseph the Carpenter,
scented candle The Lock and scented postcard The Valpinçon Bather.

Samothrace: the prow of the boat sails in Mediterranean winds infused with jasmine, orange blossom, rose, and magnolia, as described by the artist Aliénor Massenet. Dorothée Piot chose to bring *Conversation in the Park* to life with an olfactory ode to Eaux de Cologne, very much in vogue at the time. Roses, citrus notes, and galbanum pay homage to both the garden and the woman's very elegant attire in the painting. For Annick Menardohe, *Nymph with a Scorpion* was an evocation of youth, revealed in aldehydic notes (mandarine). "To simulate the scorpion's venom, I used a hint of bitter almond, which contains traces of cyanide, to convey this subtle toxicity." In the eyes of Jean-Christophe Hérault, the perfumer for the *Venus de Milo*, it was more amber and woody notes that symbolized the sculpture's restraint, followed up with a bouquet of contrasting floral notes, owing to their heightened femininity. Last but not least, *The Lock*, reinterpreted by Delphine Lebeau, sent a coded message through scent—a scandalous fragrance where the forbidden mingles with the enigmatic. Lebeau used lily for its heady finish, sweet as it is voluptuous, and then for contrast, she used chestnut, evoking those darkened shadows where drapes and sheets appear obscured in paint. As for Domitille Michalon-Bertier, she lent Ingres's *La Grande Odalisque* a veil of sensuality, using pepper, cinnamon, cumin, and cardamom. Meanwhile, notes of incense paid homage to the perfume burner at her feet. To complete the trip to the Orient, powdery notes and rice embodied the Odalisque's makeup while myrrh brought the mystical atmosphere to new heights.

THESE PICTORIAL ELEMENTS ARE EXTREMELY CONCRETE IN TERMS OF SCENT. PERFUMERS ARE LIKE INTERPRETERS, ABLE TO TRANSFORM A COLOR, A LIGHT OR A TEXTURE INTO A NOTE.

Perfumer Sidonie Lancesseur during a conversation with Ramdane Touhami at the Louvre in 2019.

Next page: Scented postcards from The Louvre Collection by Officine Universelle Buly.

D... de
Thomas Gainsboro...

CARTE POSTALE PARFUMÉE

Officine Universelle Buly, N°6, rue Bonaparte, Paris.
Dépôt exceptionnel au musée du Louvre

LA VÉNUS
DE
MILO

LA GRANDE ODALISQUE
de
Jean-Auguste-Dominique Ingres

CARTE POSTALE PARFUMÉE

Officine Universelle Buly, N°6, rue Bonaparte, Paris. Dépôt exceptionnel au musée du Louvre.

SAINT JOSEPH
CHARPENTIER
de
Georges de La Tour

THE BEAUTY
OF MUSEUMS

The special collaboration featured a visual identity whose distinctiveness was cherished by both Officine Universelle Buly and the museum. Exciting new elements were developed for the project: typographers at Art Recherche Industrie developed a typeface inspired by 19th-century encyclopedias; the scented candles were sold in holders made of Venetian terrazzo, a refined aggregate of cement, stone, and marble powder; and the labels, which included medals from the World's Fairs and old-timey phrasing, were a natural extension of the Buly style. The sales space had to be on par with the ambitions of the project. True to his philosophy of "aesthetic deglobalization," Ramdane Touhami took over the space by incorporating a necessary historical dimension. Rather than an apothecary's counter, Touhami envisioned a mix between a sculpture studio and a museum souvenir shop. This majestic store was an extension of the museum's collections. The design played with time conventions: the traces left by frames were easily visible, along with their nails and hanging wires stretched with studied negligence. A coating of artificial dust (from plaster powder) was sprinkled on the shelves and architectural motifs, restoring an old-fashioned atmosphere. Officine's customary theatricality was on full display, with elements like a thick velvet curtain, made by a theater upholsterer, and a cashier's booth fashioned after sales counters of days past. The store abandoned its role as a sales space and took on the aura of the museum—a room where souvenirs had defied the ravages of time.

RATHER THAN AN APOTHECARY'S COUNTER, TOUHAMI ENVISIONED A MIX BETWEEN A SCULPTURE STUDIO AND A MUSEUM SOUVENIR SHOP.

The sales staff donned traditional uniform: large painters' smocks made of washed linen, always reflecting the unity of time and place. Intense attention to detail sustained the hyperreality of the space: antique and second-hand objects, such as a postcard display from the 1900s, vitrines, and statuettes adorned the shop. Archivists from the Louvre—those custodians of ancient *savoir-faire*—rediscovered old photographic prints of the Neurdein brothers dating from 1891, reproductions of which adorned the shelves. Calligraphers were brought in to create informational posters, while a master stonecutter made the price lists and displays. A painter who'd worked for the Palace of Versailles decorated the huge window with sumptuous golden letters. On the mirror, the exhibit text for visitors appeared in seven languages, conveying a sense of universality and posterity. "For the first time, eight great perfumers interpret eight masterpieces from the Louvre's collections." Officine Universelle Buly at the Louvre freezes a 19th-century museum souvenir shop in time. The style is that of a sculpture studio where masters and apprentices might have worked side by side, surrounded on all sides by a shade of sun-bleached blue. The leaves of the Versailles-style parquet flooring, with its rhombuses and diagonal woodwork, follow the strict codes of traditional cabinet-making. Sales staff enact enchanting rituals and offer French-style service from behind an exquisite cashier's booth. Like a small theater, this little shop becomes a fully fledged sales counter where every desire is fulfilled with poise and finesse."

Officine Universelle Buly at the Louvre, 2019.

A detailed view of the perfume alembics with some alabasters, and a calligraphy display on the wall for the Louvre's Officine.

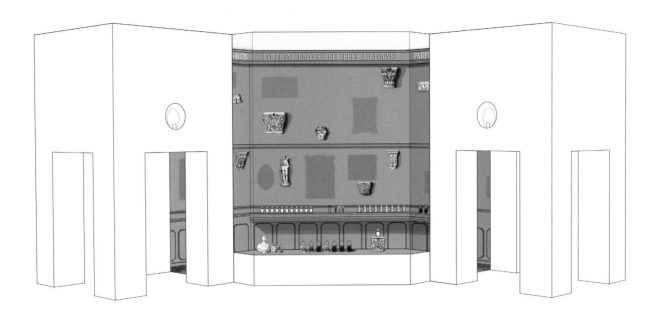

First digital sketch of the store, front view, 2019.

First digital sketch of the store, transverse view.
Next page: Replica sculptures from the museum collection, perfumes display, and register box in the Louvre's Officine, 2015.

CAISSE

FROM THE ACT OF CREATING TO THE WORLD OF MEDIA

Creating a thing of beauty requires considerable resources. Working with a National Institution meant accepting the associated administrative complications and a whole host of departments getting involved in the process. Like government ministries, some signed off on briefs and ideas while others vetoed them. Hidden from most, the creative process involves all manner of diplomatic maneuvers and compromises—and yet one must take care not to lose sight of the initial creative spark, or you risk extinguishing it entirely. What was meant to be a single press day at a closed museum evolved into, well, three days, given the level of interest. This proved to be the project's trickiest negotiation. A first challenge was getting approval for visitors on a day when the museum was closed. Another was deciding how to bring the scents to life in the galleries. Resolving this issue was a lengthy undertaking. Ramdane Touhami wanted to install perfume diffusers near the artworks. The museum refused categorically! A museum is not a theater or a reception hall: it must comply with a number of legal constraints. To get around this, the team had to develop a dry diffusion method inspired by old alembic distillers. This innovation proved to be so effective that it is gradually being deployed in shops worldwide as it faithfully transmits the essence of a given fragrance. This breathtaking event, with its incredible sophistication and unprecedented offerings, was hailed as a success by a small army of journalists. The opportunity to discover the Louvre with nobody else around is a unique experience, to say the least. The media coverage reflected this excitement: 50 prestigious titles (*The Financial Times' How to Spend It, The New York Times, Paris Match, Le Figaro, Travel + Leisure, Vanity Fair, Architectural Digest, WWD, The Times, The Wall Street Journal, Wallpaper, The Telegraph,* ZDF, SVT, etc.) published headline stories on the event. The press coverage allowed 150 newspapers to show the world how France reigns supreme in the world of perfume.

The eight perfumers who worked on the Louvre x Buly 1803 Collection.
From left to right: Delphine Lebeau, Domitile Michalon-Bertier, Dorothée Piot, Sidonie Lancesseur, Aliénore Massenet, Daniela Andrier, Annick Ménardo, and Jean-Christophe Hérault.

New ways to communicate or do DON'T without BECOME marketing A CARICATURE

For the scholar Dominique Wolton, communicating means including others within one's sphere of intentions. Officine Universelle Buly incorporates this approach into the wording of its texts and more generally, its very strong attachment to the French language. This forms the cornerstone of the strategy behind all of Buly's external communications. It reveals each time a love of text and a knowledge of the world of beauty care, which is at times expressed with a poetic turn of phrase.

The first home page design for the Officine website in 2014.

BULY'S VOICE,
LIVE ON THE INTERNET

Victoire de Taillac reminds us that Buly applies the same tone everywhere: "A literary style on social media has to be more concise. You have to adapt the target to the channel. As a brand, we like to express ourselves, and we basically write like writers. We do this to create a special bond with our customers. That doesn't mean using words seductively in the negative sense of the expression, nor does it involve some game of smoke and mirrors to hide anything. Words instead express a passion we share with each other and which we want to share with others. Our communication obeys a Kantian morality; a merchant must act loyally towards his or her clients, in accordance with a higher sense of duty. Buly has more than just its reputation or its own interests in mind; loyalty to our customers is one of our core values.

We write to our customers in the same way that we address them in our boutiques. It's a point of pride for us. A healthy dose of cheekiness, being catchy, and a flair for clever ripostes are essential to both our oral and written communications. Buly is light years away from using the current vocabulary in vogue that is replete with anglicized neologisms. Our newsletters and Facebook or Instagram posts also obey this same logic. A newsletter often adopts the tone of a magazine, where the story focuses on something intangible, on a concept rather than a product. The secret lies in promoting the idea of the brand without ever getting the customer "to buy our laundry detergent at any cost," as advertising dogma would have it. Online, our posts take the form of a funny drawing or a riddle to tickle people's curiosity and enrich their knowledge with any number of references. Wordplay abounds, and we hardly ever hold back on this front. Our translators are able to translate the emotion of a message with impeccable faithfulness. People often tell us that our tone "resembles that of a book," and this never fails to make us smile. This is why we are called Buly Universelle, or "universal;" we are always navigating across many cultures.

"People often tell us that our tone 'resembles that of a book,' and this never fails to make us smile. This is why we are called Buly Universelle, or 'universal;' we are always navigating across many cultures."

Victoire de Taillac

We explore the repertory that language offers, but images also play a role, a primary one at that. Ramdane directs our visual communications as part of the overall artistic direction, which consists of giving meaning to the photographs. There are a number of artistic references: the baroque is used for country scenes, Dadaism for some seasons, and Cubism, Figurative art, and Fractal art are all used at different instances to embellish the imagery. Photographs are carefully reviewed and tested before being disseminated to the public. At that point, the conjunction of words and visuals generates an immersive experience in digital art; the image captures people's attention, but the words charm them.

Our goal is to give viewers the sensation of digitally opening a window onto our world for a brief moment in time. The internet allows us to measure how much our customers like and appropriate our universe by massively reposting homemade still-lifes, pictures of our boutiques or of architectural elements that form part of our identity. Through these attentive and affectionate testimonials, social media shines an exceptional spotlight on what we do."

Next page: Still-life in a dollhouse set with bathroom products, 2018.

WHAT THE WORLD DESCRIBES AS "PRINT"

First getting started is often the source of lovely memories. Victoire de Taillac reminisces: "When Buly was still just a project in the making, we wanted to produce a magazine. This was one of my and Ramdane's passions. We wanted to fill a void we saw in the market for beauty magazines by publishing something that also invoked literature and the arts, that engaged in a scientific but nevertheless refined level of discourse, but which was never forbidding or off-putting. Our fascination with literature, which took the form of very dense, highly documented texts, came to its first fruition with our publication of *Parfumerie Générale*, even though the style was fairly comical, if not abrasive. The birth in 2013 of *Corpus*, which saw the publication of two additional issues, was a source of inspiration for Buly's editorial content. Together with a friend of mine, the head of communications for a museum in Paris, we undertook the immense task of compiling the first catalog for Officine Universelle Buly. Talk about writer's block! This initial publication, which we dedicated to Claude and Jean-Vincent Bully, became an initial lexical foundation, a crucial step in the creation of the brand. The catalog's style absolutely had to be in sync with the lexical sphere we had chosen for the names of Buly's products. For example, the words we used to describe Eau Superfine, Huile Antique, or Lait Virginal had to further the evocation of the historical, almost dreamlike universe suggested by the product names. This exercise in meticulousness helped establish our core texts, which still anchor our editorial teams to a shared base today. We often think of the voice that a public institution has, which is steady and unchanging. Buly exercises this same sense of constancy to render beauty as something intelligent and serious."

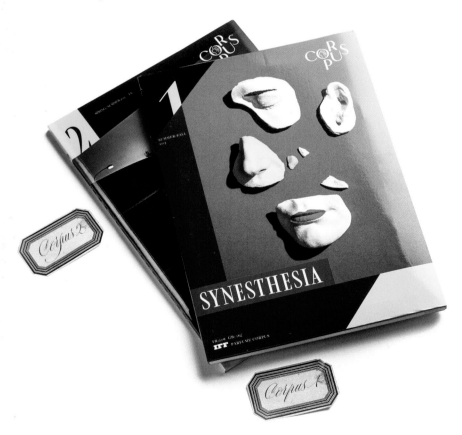

The two *Corpus* issues, the first about "Synesthesia" in 2014 and the second about "Evolution" in 2015.
Right: A pile of *Atlas of Natural Beauty* published in 2018.

"The birth in 2013 of 'Corpus', which saw the
publication of two additional issues, was a source
of inspiration for Buly's editorial content."

Victoire de Taillac

AN ATLAS
OF
NATURAL BEAUTY

BOTANICAL INGREDIENTS
FOR RETAINING AND ENHANCING BEAUTY

In the *10 Steps of Manufacturing Combs*, Officine honors ancient and preserved technical know-how, where the importance of the gesture and the artist's experience is essential, Italia, 2019.

In its *Beauty Adventures* saga, Officine travels to the countries with ancestral beauty customs, and meets the actors who strive for natural daily care. Here, a journey to Kalymnos in Greece for the discovery of natural sponges, 2019.

IMAGES IN WORDS AND OTHER VIDEOS

Iconoclastic and experimental, Buly's videos use disruptive techniques pleasant for their visual qualities, and soundtracks with the definitively 1950s deep-voiced intonation. Beauty care traditions from countries all over the world are featured in documentary-style shorts. Video content is also produced for special occasions for social media (the advent calendar, New Year's greetings, promotional videos, among others).

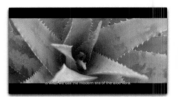

The *Beauty Adventures* series episode about camellia oil from the Goto Islands in Japan, 2017.

The *Beauty Adventures* series interview with a Geisha in Nara, Japan, 2019.

The *Beauty Adventures* series the amazing story of the shungite magical stone, Russia, 2019.

The *Beauty Adventures* series interview of the eldest barber in the world, Shitsui Hakoishi, aged 105, Japan, 2018.

The *Beauty Adventures* series interview with the natural argan oil producer, Morocco, 2017.

The *Beauty Adventures* series the quest for aloe vera, Mexico, 2019.

The *Beauty Adventures* series how
to create the long-lasting Japanese
minebari combs, Japan, 2018.

Promotional video, conceived as an echo of the French presidential discourse about the Covid battle. Officine supported the Abbé Pierre charity foundation during the pandemic, 2020.

The *Pause Parisienne* series shows an enjoyable tour of Paris, 2019.

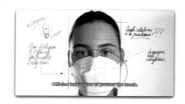

Video made by Officine for scented patches conceived to refresh masks with a Sacha Guitry-style voiceover, 2021.

Commercial for Pommade Concrète, 2018.

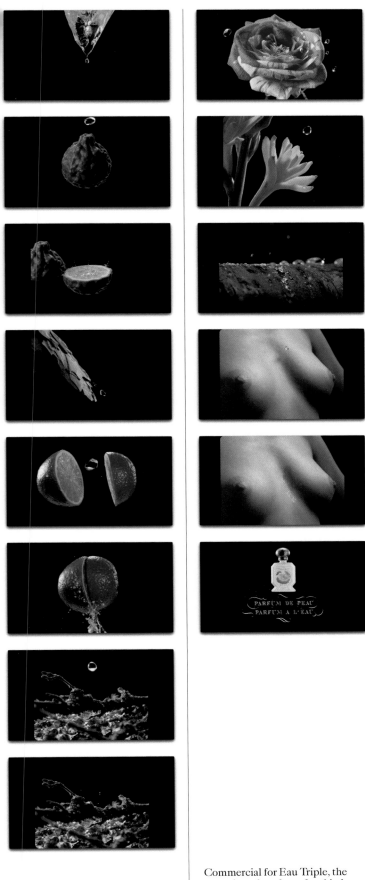

Commercial for Eau Triple, the
water-based perfume for skin by
Officine Universelle Buly.

THE PRESS

Officine Universelle Buly is a hive of innovation. Every year, dozens of new products land on the wooden shelves of its beauty counters. To spread the word about its creations among as many people as possible, Buly is in constant touch with prominent journalists and press outlets. The expertise that Victoire de Taillac has accrued in this area (as the former head of PR for the concept store Colette and as the founder of a media relations bureau of the same name) helps ensure that Buly's repertoire is well distilled into traditional journalist writing. These "old school" techniques remain effective and reliable. Buly is able to stand out because it uses very direct titles and catchy headings, to which it adds just a dash of lyricism. Isn't this the best way to avoid the norm and to make an impression?

Advertising published in the *The New York Times* for Officine Universelle Buly at Bergdof Goodman in 2017.

L'OFFICINE UNIVERSELLE BULY OUVRE
SON COMPTOIR CHEZ SMETS LUXEMBOURG

***

**

« The Most Chic Beauty Emporium of the World »
THE NEW YORK TIMES

UNE PREMIÈRE LUXEMBOURGEOISE

Entièrement réalisé par un artisan français, le comptoir de l'Officine Universelle Buly au Luxembourg s'inaugure au sein de la très distinguée institution Smets.

Ce cabinet d'envergure, composé de faïences roses, n'est pas sans rappeler le raffinement des cheminées prussiennes. Dans un volume hors du commun aux teintes rose poudré, le comptoir joue de ses surbrillances et d'effets de miroir. Le devers propre aux céramiques, promènent la main au gré d'un toucher agréable.

Rétro-futuriste, de la conception de ses protocoles de soins jusqu'aux traits de ses boutiques, l'Officine Universelle Buly s'oppose à l'uniformisation de l'esthétisme et ses standards internationaux. Chaque boutique possède son identité esthétique et ses codes propres.

Press release for the opening of an Officine store, 2019.

Still-life with natural sponge.

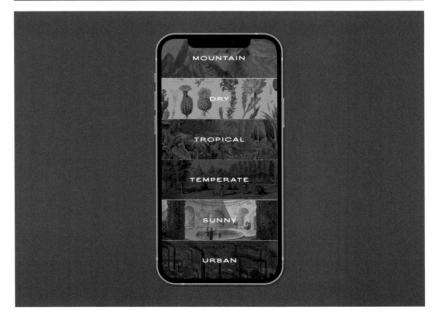

Screen images of the new Officine Universelle Buly application named Skin Concierge.

Baume des Muses highlight.

Bath time tools focus, easter 2017.

Advent Calendar, 2018.

No plastic obsession, aluminium tubes highlight.

Natural beauty focus.

Engraving service highlight.

Officine Universelle Buly in a nutshell.

Japan's finest accessories.

Eau de la Belle Haleine focus.

Officine Universelle Buly curiosities selection.

Minebari combs highlight.

A fine selection of the Officine's wide range.

Scented products highlight.

Accessories focus.

Officine Universelle Buly makes noise!

Collaboration with T-Site Tokyo main visual.

Airplane magazine advertisement.

Oral care complete routine.

EVOLUTION OF THE WEBSITES

Circa November 2014.

Circa May 2017.

Circa January 2018.

Circa April 2019.

Circa June 2021.

Screen captures of the mail-order selling video made by Officine Universelle Buly, September 2018.

THE OTHER KINGDOM: THE WEBSITE AND CUSTOMER RELATIONS

Ramdane Touhami has always thought of the officiers-préparateurs—the sales-people—as Buly's elite corps, unlike most major conglomerates, who tend to prize their marketing departments above everything else. To this end, management of the website and customer relations are key to people's perception of the brand. Customer communications follow the same rules as the service provided to physical customers in the boutiques. The people in charge of customer relations have to use the same lexicon as what is routinely distributed to the press and used in the stores, on the internet, and on the website. The art and manner of our communication requires that the customer always leaves a boutique satisfied, with a smile on his or her face. The staff must be perfectly diplomatic in providing information and assistance on a daily basis, as a way to reassure and comfort customers. Email messages are never standardized and there is no preset form. The only requirement for staff is the one stated as part of their job when they are hired: "Impeccable language and penmanship." Ramdane Touhami states: "It's a question of politeness. The website is a boutique unto itself, and the photographs use the same aesthetic codes developed for the other platforms. Buly is not just a beauty products store where you can buy carefully selected items from the world over. Buly is a kind of medium that invites you to experience the expertise and intelligence that our predecessors have brought to the world of beauty–through our products, our boutiques, our illustrated catalog, our self-published magazine, and our website."

WHEN BULY MAKES PEOPLE SMILE

Winning our customers' trust definitely involves laughter. Underneath its stuffy appearance, Buly engages in constant jest and humor, French-style. Some product names are meant to provoke a smile: Vide Poche, which is for treating wrinkles, is a play on words between a trinket bowl and "emptying your pockets," Eau de la Belle Haleine, which is a play on words between Belle Haleine for good breath and Belle Helène, used to describe a pear dessert, for example, is a body gel, while Eau Gymnastique is a perfumed spray for your sneakers. Buly has definitely been around for a while, but it is not at all mired in tradition.

Sex Shop Animal: The upcoming opening of the new Officine Universelle Buly on rue Vieille du Temple in Paris will be made in the visual and aesthetic style of a true-fake sex toy boutique for dogs, before the actual Officine Universelle Buly opens! This hoax makes us stand out against the competition, and it dispels the notion that Buly is irretrievably stuck in some sort of historicizing continuum.

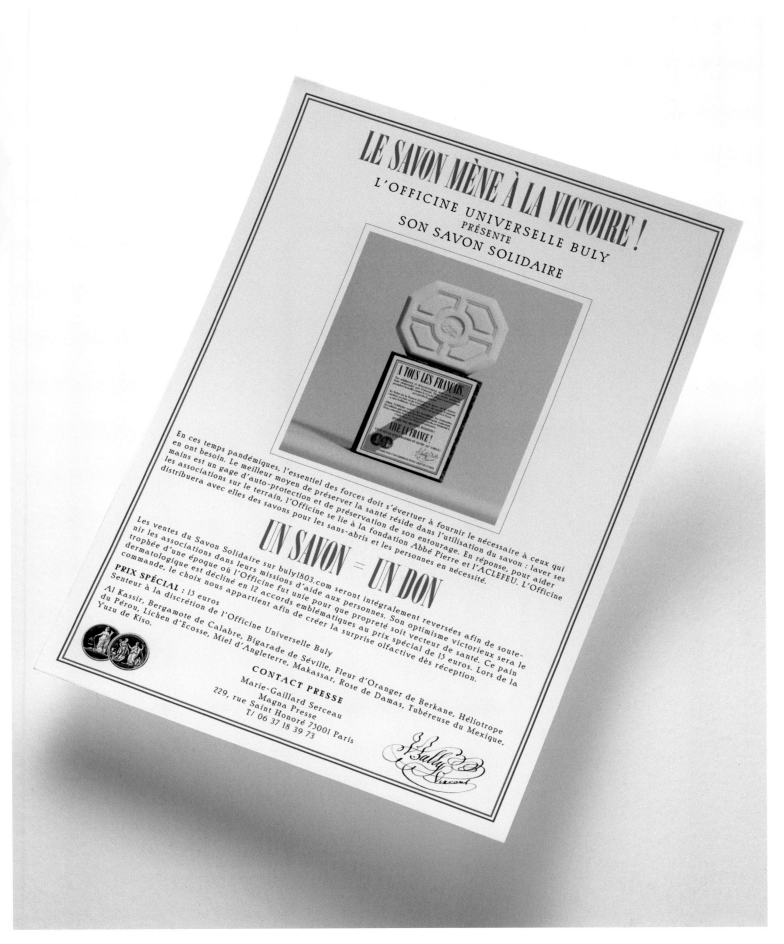

During the Covid-19 pandemic, the sequences shot to promote the use of masks and antibacterial gel mimicked French politics and the statements made by President Macron, who said we were "at war" with the virus; hence, soaps were temporarily adorned with military-style graphics, and typefaces and messages were made in a martial, commanding tone. The voiceover is serious, as if a general were speaking.

Trompe l'œil cake featuring the Seoul front store, made for the store opening.

Trompe l'œil cake in a scented candle shape displayed on the real marble candle counter during the rue de Saintonge opening in 2017.

A sequence about masks brings a certain caustic sense of humor, with just a faint whisper of derision, to fight against the morosity that has set in everywhere because of the pandemic. "We never take ourselves seriously. Buly is here to help people take care of themselves, not to save the world," notes Victoire de Taillac.

Tears of Chios: Ramdane Touhami wanted to pay homage to the blunt, caustic, slightly absurd sense of humor that Jean Yanne had popularized in his films in the 1970s.

"Buly has been serving the world since 1803." Against a backdrop of a performance by a philharmonic orchestra, our sales staff, the *officiers-préparatrices*, stroll through a Paris filmed in the style of Paolo Sorrentino. With their pleated skirts, Peter Pan collars, and high heels hitting the pavement, they slowly take over the city.

Illustration for the Opiat Dentaire, a toothpaste by Officine Universelle Buly, 2019.

Illustration for combs.

Illustration for Pommade Concrète, a hand and foot nourishing cream by Officine Universelle Buly, 2019.

Illustration for Pommade Virginale, a softening face cream.

RETAIL AS A GAME

Cross interview between Ramdane Touhami and Shinichi

One of the initial goals of Ramdane Touhami was to create special space and structures for Buly's employees, with singular rules following the Shinto philosophy of *honmono*, a virtuous circle linking the designer, the manufacturers, the salesmen, and the customers in a relation of pride, authenticity, and quality as seen previously. He sat with Shinichi Nakazawa, director of the Institute for Art Anthropology at Meiji University in Japan, who develops the theory of game as an ideal social system for everyone to take part and gain pride, to discuss how gamification can be applied to *honmono* philosophy in retail.

R.T   I read your discussion on gamification which illustrates how our daily act can be assimilated to gaming.

S.N   Human culture originated in various forms of game. Game which is not about fighting to win, but close to play in which everyone feels fulfillment. Fundamentally, our primitive form of economic transaction started with the fun game of exchanging goods, from agricultural produce to hand-crafted tools for everyday use. I say fun games, because Japanese artisanal workers particularly feel joy in showing their work, which one can see in various form of traditional crafts.

R.T   Do you think that is the reason for Japanese artisanal workers to be adamant about sticking to their own way of working and not flexible to the request of a client?

S.N   For artisanal workers, their work is about joy, fulfillment and self-expression. So to a certain extent, they will persist in what they do and are not in favour of negotiating. However, that is a story of the past. Unlike older generations, younger artisans are more receptive to contemporary society: they enjoy the game of living now.

R.T   For those artisans, their work is not about the exchange of time they spent on their work? From an economic perspective, we are trading the time of others. Our life is about the transaction of time: I pay for the amount of time someone spent on creating one product.

S.N   In the Edo period (1603–1868), there were small-scale manufactures of daily tools. As the population increased in Edo, there was a huge need for daily tools for a household: like electrical appliances now. People who made these tools were all artisans: before the concept of the factory worker was introduced in a later period. These artisans didn't consider what they are doing as labor. In the Edo period, these artisans were no different from the painter who paints, or author who writes: making tools and everyday objects were an act of fulfillment of their own expression hance an artisan become completely immersed in what he is doing forgetting the time. Just like painting or a book doesn't reflect the amount of hours a painter or an author put into creating their work, artisans can't put a price tag on things by the amount of time a craft person took to create.

R.T   Everyone in those days was like an artist.

S.N   Indeed.

R.T   If crafts people all take pride in their work and try incessantly to improve their craft, was there competition between crafts people?

S.N   They may compete with one another, which will improve each other's skill as well as create a rich culture. But winning is not the main objective.

R.T   It is intriguing to see how game structure in general is incorporated into the majority of companies' payroll systems: employees get more salary when they achieve a certain targeted goal. It is exactly like adding scores in playing a game. Gaming and our lives overlap.

S.N   What is particular to Japanese games is that they don't place emphasis on winning. Even when the games rules are based on accumulating points and scores, that is not the utmost goal. Many games have a plot during which players gain scores, but a player's main motivation to play is in enjoying the adventure of going through the plot: the process is important in Japanese games.

Nakazawa, under the supervision of Kanae Hasegawa.

R.T   You developed a theory that Japanese games as a system don't create a sole or an absolute winner.

S.N   The structure of many Japanese games is based on adventure through which each game player participates in the development of a game character rather than combatting or fighting with other characters. The Pokémon game, which consists of several hundred non-human creatures of Pokémon trained by game players, can be seen as microcosmos of Japanese society that tries to find joy without winning or losing: game creatures act as firefighters or great housekeepers, helping each other while the game plot develops. During the adventure, game players swap their Pokémon creature with other creatures. This can be related to trade, but more than the simple exchange of goods. There is no battle involved here: every player feels a sense of achievement. This can be said as the underlying philosophy of Japanese games.

R.T   I like the idea that everyone involved in the game feels pleasure and earns pride. Japanese games reflect my ideal philosophy of creating *honmono* (the essential). By *honmono* I mean a product or an object which brings joy and pride to all the stakeholders involved in creating it: the designer who comes up with the idea, crafts people who produce and realize the designer's idea, the sales assistant who sells those products in the store, and the customer who buy those products. No one should be exploited. When all the people involved in the life of a product feel enchanted with the product, that product is *honmono*: it becomes a loop. It is like the Japanese approach to game playing.

S.N   Interesting point to relate retail enterprise to the fulfillment of all the game players without the apparent notion of a winner and loser.

R.T   If I go to select stores in Japan: multi-brand stores, the service of the sales assistant, the way they treat customers, the way people wrap items, is so high that I feel these people must have such a pride in their work of shop keeping. They are playing their own game and the customers who are treated well in the store will feel enchanted and enjoy shopping. It is like a game.

S.N   The Japanese place value on losing the game. Analyzing why this person lost the game, finding out what was wrong, is considered to bring significant outcome to the loser: more significant than winning. The loser gains more from losing. Some Japanese Shogi players try to search for different ways of how to lose the game when he already knows he will lose. That is because by trying different ways of losing, the player will learn: it is a very fruitful experience. We call this approach the "aesthetic of losing".

R.T   So, it is more about finding ways to avoid mistakes for the future rather than considering one as a game loser.

S.N   More than finding mistakes: the player sees the act of analysing the lost game significant and enriching experience. This attitude towards games can be related to Japanese crafts people's approach to their work.

R.T   That explains the Japanese obsession with their crafting process.

S.N   One thing is different from the game world to crafts. There is an end to a game. Every game will finish at some point. However, there is no end to crafts people's art: they will not stop their endeavor for better craft.

"Some Japanese S ways of how to lose lose. That is because player will learn. this approach 'aesth

ogi players try to search for different
he game when he already knows he will
y trying different ways of losing, the
t is a very fruitful experience. We call
c of losing.'"

Shinichi Nakazawa

BECOMING G
REMAINING

sparkling water

OBAL WHILE OCAL

Respecting the city where you open a shop, an essay by Ramdane Touhami

The design of a Supermarket is the same wether its brand or its geographical localisation.
Above: Supermarket in the 1960s.

No matter in which city center I find myself these days, I generally come to the same conclusion: everything looks rather the same. One single style appears to have colonized any number of culturally diverse spaces. Cafes from New York to Seoul, from Beijing to Berlin all have the same minimalist decor, readily identifiable at first glance: terrazzo, brass, marble, decorative metal frames, imitation Scandinavian or industrial furniture, vintage Edison bulbs... All of these materials and furnishing styles, which no longer represent any specific, local identity, have now been exported the world over.

There is a global circulation of styles, each one specific to a certain place, that have mixed and invaded the major cities of the world to form a large, incoherent amalgam of trends that are reproduced ubiquitously, almost to the letter. In the long run, we risk living in an extremely insipid world, destroying the specific heritage of any given place in the process. Why should anyone travel if the world's cities all lose their aesthetic specificity? Why should we continue to shop in neighborhood stores if they all start to look alike?

We are overtaken with boredom when faced with this routine. Yet, I believe that each city has its own aesthetic specificity, its own identity, where the styles that characterize the various phases of its development manifest themselves like different visual strata to form the urban landscape. This identity is a veritable trademark, instantly recognizable among others, so much so that when you arrive in certain cities, you know immediately where in the world you are: in Paris for its Haussmann, Restoration, and Empire facades, in New York for its cast-iron buildings, and Art Deco and International Style skyscrapers, or in Berlin for its mixture of Bauhaus, Prussian palaces, and Soviet-era architecture. The visual appearance of objects, interior designs, and buildings shapes the local character of any given place at any given time. And this uniqueness contributes to the gradual, cultural development of societies. The aesthetic specificity of places and the populations who inhabit them is intangible and it is constantly in the process of unfolding. It is what often inspires us to travel: to go see styles of production that are unfamiliar. It concretizes our relationship to the other through a visual language that a community shapes and breathes life into, ultimately transmitting it to future generations.

For that matter, when we visit a city, our sole contact with other people is often with salespeople in stores or waiters in restaurants. As ambassadors of the city, they are the representatives of their culture and an important intermediary for foreign visitors. Before the globalization of our contemporary era, each place, whether understood as a city, a region, or even a country, had its own specific aesthetic trajectory. Its architectural style was always tied to the access to local materials and specific modes of production. Subsequent periods each adopted their own style, with their canons that everyone acknowledges. "That doesn't exist anymore. It's the major characteristic of our new modernity: there no longer is a shared doctrine." [1] In Europe, for example, a continent that boasts centuries-old traditions of craft, things are now mostly made "American-style," because the United States now dictates most fashion and visual trends. We must revitalize this local culture, this aesthetic specificity in time and space, even at the risk of evoking certain unwanted nativist specters. Because the French style of the past, for example, is a visual trace, a living memory of our heritage, a bulwark against the amnesia that the era of cultural uniformity brings with it.

I believe that the wealth of any society resides in the uniqueness of what it produces, what we might call its aesthetic specificity. So, how can we make sure that we do not lose this cultural diversity at an international scale? I believe it is essential that we uphold the idea of an aesthetic heritage as a guiding stylistic thread, one that we nevertheless continue to revisit and renew.

1. Christian de Portzamparc, "Toute architecture engage une vision de la ville", *Le Monde*, February 3, 2006.

Today, more than ever, we have to rely on our spatial and temporal context to design new projects to live alongside the things that form our past. This also applies to the creation of a new store; we should examine its coherence with the plan for the city where it will open, in accordance with this notion of aesthetic heritage. A boutique should be unique and yet appropriate for its surrounding architectural styles, unlike chain stores, which all reproduce a single construction model. When you visit a Louis Vuitton, Hermès, or Christian Dior boutique, whether you are in Taiwan or Toulouse, you will find the same products displayed in the same windows at the same time.

But people should instead be confronted with the local character of any given place. To do this, long before any development project is undertaken, people have to think long and hard about the locally available materials, the history of that city, and its local know-how to design a project that is intelligent and well adapted—the impetus of my work stems from this curiosity. We must ultimately value the local natural and human resources that any given place has to offer.

Every territory has its specific resources that also induce specific artisanal know-how.

Avoiding using the standard whatever, subcontracting from far off, not shifting and exporting productions to developing countries, surrounding oneself with a team: this creates a healthy economic environment where even money circulates on a more local basis.

It means ensuring that these experts remain connected to the project over the long term and not just as the works are carried out, consulting them when there is a problem, asking for their advice, establishing a bond of trust.

Designing a shop is a human adventure: meeting a Japanese glassmaker to set up a wall of glass flasks and test tubes for a Japanese shop, discovering the ancestral art of Alsatian earthenware to construct a counter in Luxembourg or being surrounded by ornamental painters for the ceiling of a Parisian boutique. At Officine Universelle Buly, I prefer choosing singularity and opting for a culture of detail. Our boutiques are aesthetic tributes to the cities that host them.

Let's go back to our know-how, and not to "what the entire world expects!"

Ramdane Touhami

Next page: Supermarket Viale Zara's official opening, Milan, Italy.

IF NO ONE CAN DO IT, DO IT YOURSELF!

From printing to typography, how to become your own supplier

Heidelberg Cylinder Machine, used for typography and printing at Société Helvétique d'Impression Typographique, Paris.

Inspired by the unrivaled excellence of 19th-centu

of perfectionism as far as possible. To create the subt

which cannot be made using standard processes toda

come a printer? In looking at and collecting prod

incredible the details were and how unique the expe

the time when typography revolutionized printing;

made for excellent letterpress. Aesthetics were alwa

inexpensive books. People did not spare any time o

precision, and at times, extraordinary creativity. Fo

printing was so fine and chiseled, silver on a black

large part of their time refining their technique in pu

peared, replaced by a simpler, faster, but less beauti

resemble these marvelous labels from my own archiv

touch. The contemporary era tends to make everythi

these new forms of digital or offset printing. So, I

tent is to work only with noble materials: glass, m

At a certain point, once people get over their surprise,

who still uses an old Nokia cell phone, but this init

sense of respect. I'm playing by other rules with the

come back to these fundamentals, and that time will

to preserve these disappearing techniques, crafts such as p

inting, Ramdane Touhami has pushed his sense
complex labels for Officine Universelle Buly,
e decided to buy old printing presses. "Why be-
and books from the 19th century, I realized how
in printing was during this era. This was also
xample, they began using lead for the type, which
nprivileged and exalted, even for labels, cards, and
ffort in producing with a sense of perfection and
xample, I found a book at the Louvre whose
ckground, absolutely delicate. Printers spent a
it of excellence. This heritage has all but disap-
mode of production. I wanted Buly's labels to
Our products deserve this rendering, this special
uniform, and it's becoming impossible to escape
lecided to ignore these inventions. My obsessive in-
l, paper with typography and old-style printing.
hey think you're being a bit original, like someone
l perception of an eccentricity finally gives way to a
firm conviction that at a certain point, we will
nrove us right. In the medium-term, we also want
nting or the manual fabrication of combs, for example."

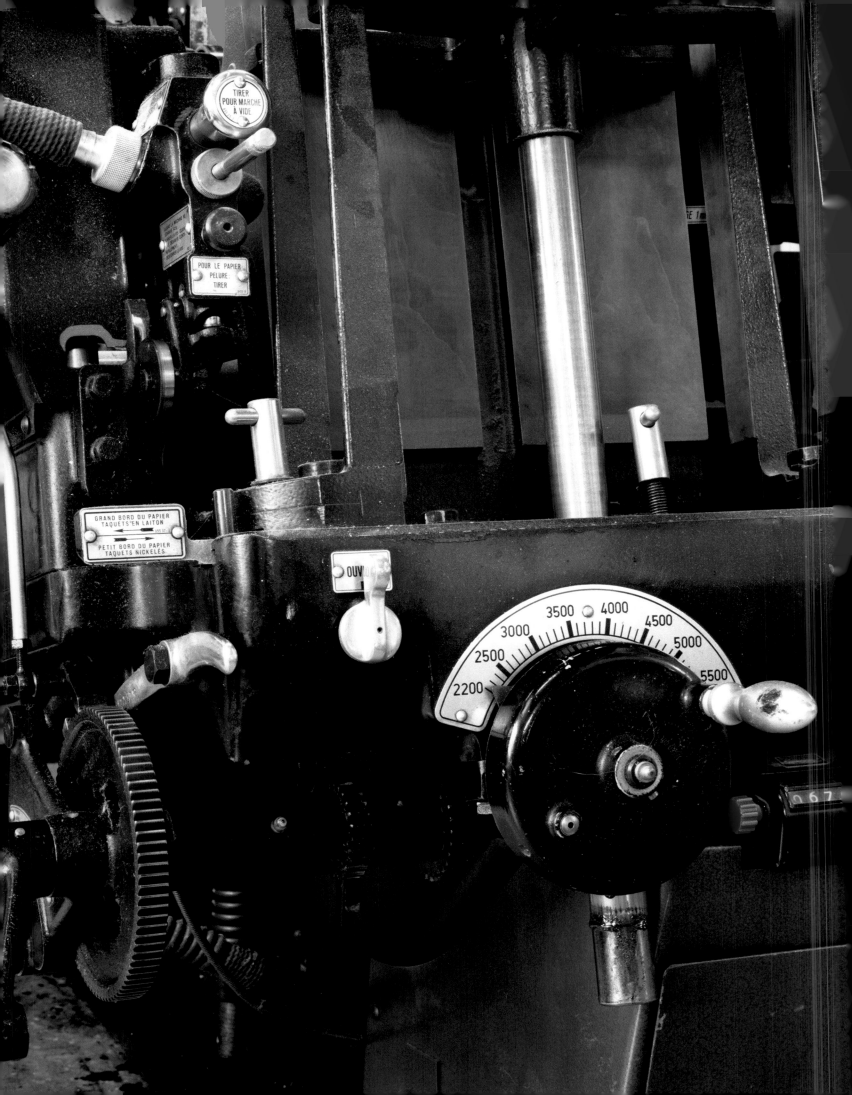

THE SOCIETE HELVETIQUE D'IMPRESSION TYPOGRAPHIQUE, AS KNOWN AS S.H.I.T.

No one was able to print labels that met Ramdane Touhami's expectations, so he circumvented the problem by buying his own printing press, but not just any press! With its age-old expertise, the press founded by Mr Heraldo in 1963 in the town of Puidoux, Switzerland was the ideal candidate, which Ramdane purchased in 2018, when its founder finally retired. Based in the Vaud canton and in a workshop in Paris, the Société Helvétique d'Impression Typographique (whose acronym in French is SHIT) is one of the last remaining institutions in Europe to work using typographic presses and a number of related procedures, including four-color, multilayer gilding, goffering, embossing, gilding, cutting, and monograms. Ramdane Touhami worked with Benoist Dallay, a printer well-versed in these old techniques and the use of very rare Heidelberg machines, including a compact, complex, but marvelous press from the 1960s, which is now used to print the labels for Eau Triple on an Italian paper. The Société Helvétique d'Impression Typographique's unique approach makes it an exception, both culturally and aesthetically. These outdated techniques that form the core of the printing system that Gutenberg first dreamt into being exalt colors, reflections, and depths, such that all the letters, which express their own particular nature once on paper, become a suite of incredibly refined artworks. Société Helvétique d'Impression Typographique has achieved a consistency, splendor, and a sense of physicality to its printing that is unrivaled. Graphic designers, editors, publishers, and writers can come here to find an antidote to the chromatic monotony and weak imprint of offset printing. Faced with the omnipresence of digital and its symptomatic dematerialization, the Société Helvétique d'Impression Typographique wants to restore the nobility of artisanal printing's letters. It protects a trade: the art of printing and its methods, which are sadly in the process of disappearing once and for all.

SOCIETE HELVETIQUE D'IMPRESSION TYPOGRAPHIQUE HAS ACHIEVED A CONSISTENCY, SPLENDOR, AND A SENSE OF PHYSICALITY TO ITS PRINTING THAT IS UNRIVALED.

Details of the Heidelberg Cylinder printing press. This tool is regarded as the Swiss Army knife of printing.
Next page: The Heidelberg Cylinder printing press on the left. Behind it, boxes for lead typography and at the right, the hot stamping machine.

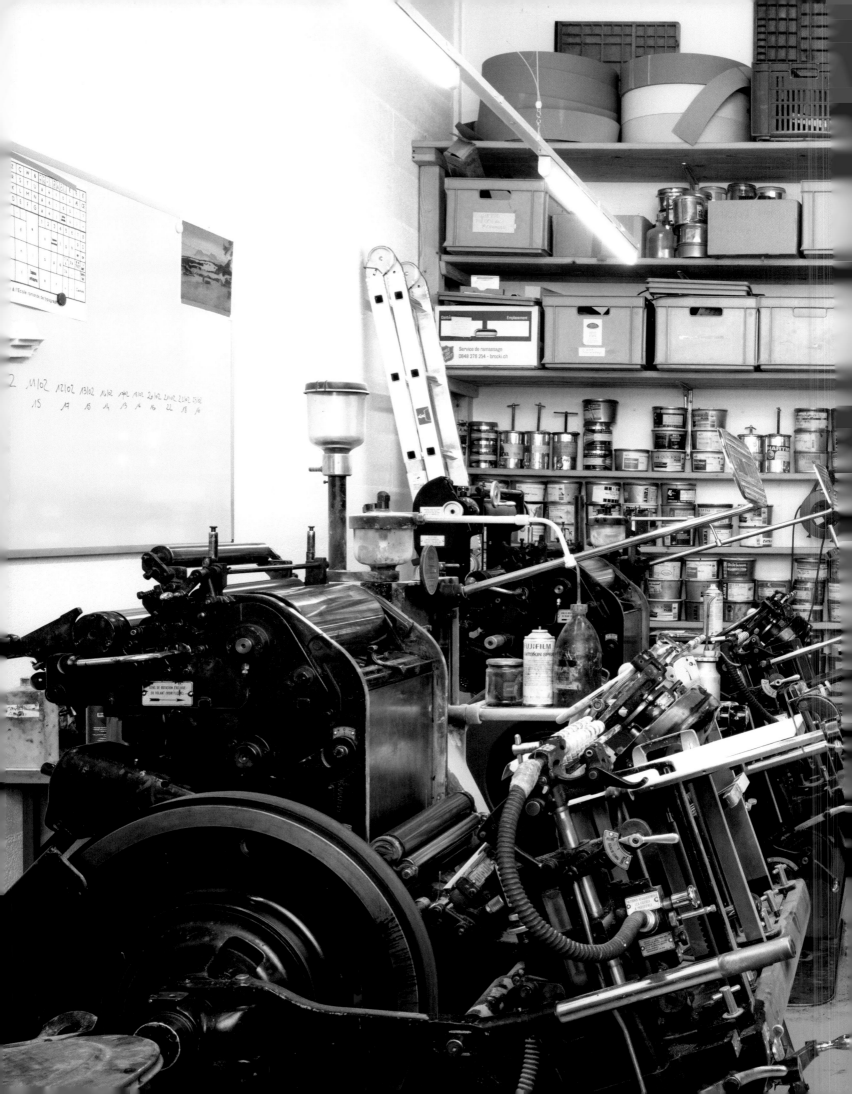

THE
TYPOGRAPHY

The typefaces used by Officine Universelle Buly and the Société Helvétique d'Impression Typographique are designed and produced in-house. A true paradox at a time when all the graphic identities in the world of luxury are becoming more and more alike. Ramdane Touhami advocates for complexity and diversity as a remedy for our boredom: "In the late 1960s, legendary graphic designers like Lou Dorfsman (creator of the CBS logo) and Herb Lubalin (responsible for the graphic design and typography of counterculture magazines such as *Eros*, *Fact*, and *Avant-Garde*) envisioned different typefaces for each individual client, sometimes for each item. It was very creative, unlike the lazy processes we now see becoming the norm." This obsession for a rich and inventive typography led him to form an outstanding team of graphic designers who are constantly working on dozens of projects inspired by anything and everything, ranging from a typeface found on an old tombstone to a title card from a silent film (see Chapter IV). The magazine *WAM*, edited and published by Ramdane Touhami in record time in 2020, is an ode to typography with its variety and multitude of extraordinary details that are often not noticeable to the uninitiated, and which don't even exist anymore in what we would call "niche" media. This obviously all comes at a certain price; the cost of producing a box for Officine Universelle Buly's Eau Triple is three to four times that of "normal" packaging. But these details are essential for Ramdane Touhami at a time when everything is dematerializing, even interpersonal relations. He fervently believes in paper, in objects as aesthetic standards, and in the power of an expertise that is as different as it is flamboyant. "If you present a client with a project that has been executed with all the precision, perfection, and creativity in the world, let's say a booklet, the impact is exceptionally powerful. The astonishment is always long-lasting."

RAMDANE TOUHAMI FERVENTLY BELIEVES IN PAPER, IN OBJECTS AS AESTHETIC STANDARDS, AND IN THE POWER OF AN EXPERTISE THAT IS AS DIFFERENT AS IT IS FLAMBOYANT.

The Ice Cream font is based on an industrial car logo and was used for several project presentations. Developed by Art Recherche Industrie in 2020.

ARMORIAL

70 PTS

LE LUXE EST UNE AFFAIRE D'ARGENT. L'ÉLÉGANCE EST UNE QUESTION D'ÉDUCATION.

The Armorial font was created in 2021 by Art Recherche Industrie. This font is based on a 19th-century logo.

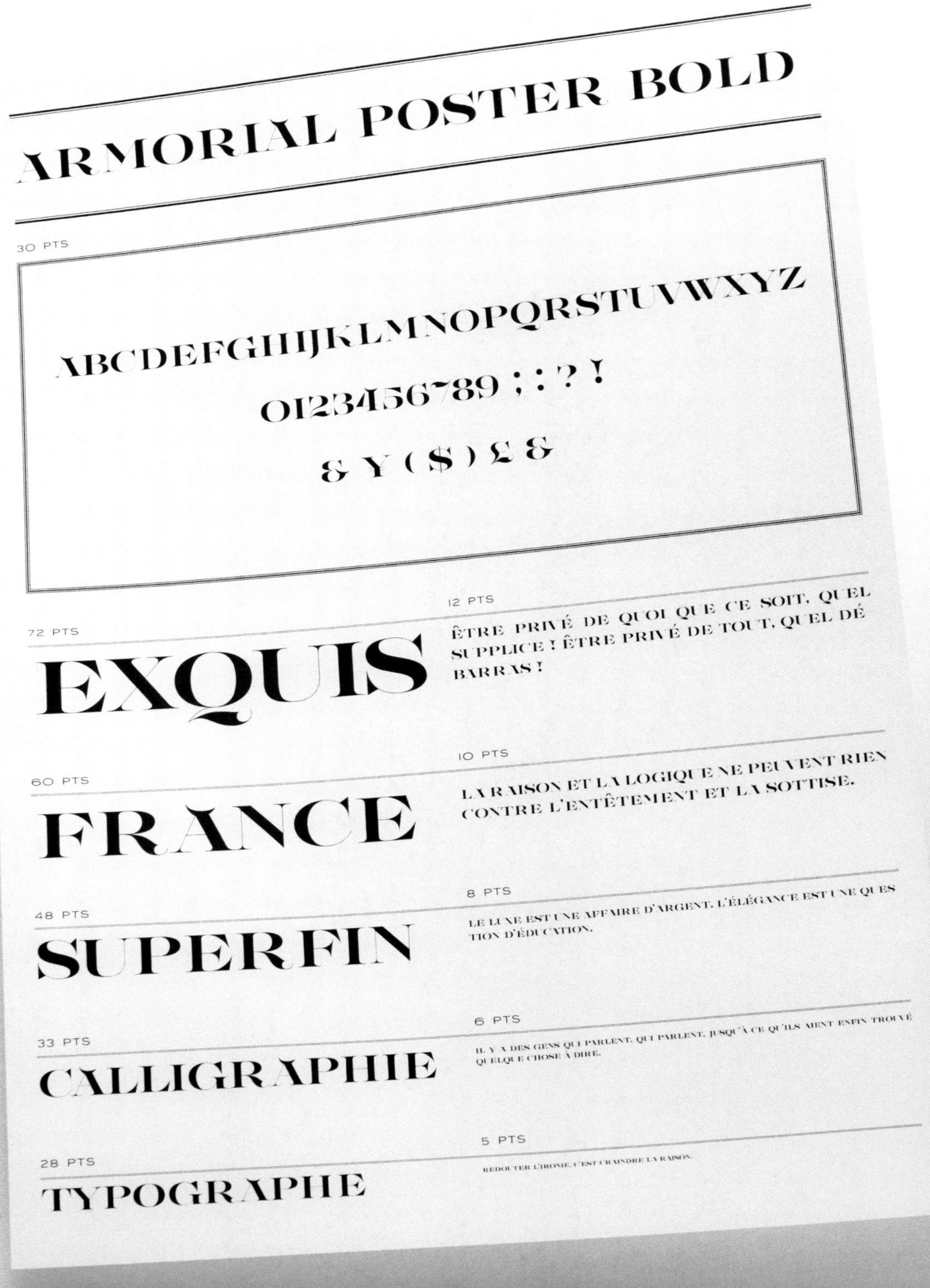

ARMORIAL POSTER BOLD

30 PTS

ABCDEFGHIJKLMNOPQRSTUVWXYZ

0123456789 ; : ? !

& Y ($) £ &

72 PTS

EXQUIS

12 PTS

ÊTRE PRIVÉ DE QUOI QUE CE SOIT, QUEL SUPPLICE ! ÊTRE PRIVÉ DE TOUT, QUEL DÉBARRAS !

60 PTS

FRANCE

10 PTS

LA RAISON ET LA LOGIQUE NE PEUVENT RIEN CONTRE L'ENTÊTEMENT ET LA SOTTISE.

48 PTS

SUPERFIN

8 PTS

LE LUXE EST UNE AFFAIRE D'ARGENT. L'ÉLÉGANCE EST UNE QUESTION D'ÉDUCATION.

33 PTS

CALLIGRAPHIE

6 PTS

IL Y A DES GENS QUI PARLENT, QUI PARLENT, JUSQU'À CE QU'ILS AIENT ENFIN TROUVÉ QUELQUE CHOSE À DIRE.

28 PTS

TYPOGRAPHE

5 PTS

REDOUTER L'IRONIE, C'EST CRAINDRE LA RAISON.

Lanserhoff

58 PTS

L'un des mensonges les plus fructueux, les plus intéressants qui soient, et l'un des plus faciles en outre, est celui qui consiste à faire croire à quelqu'un qui vous ment qu'on le croit.

The Lanserhoff font was inspired by a De Vinne typeface, a revival of a font found in a book of beauty recipes. Developed in 2019.

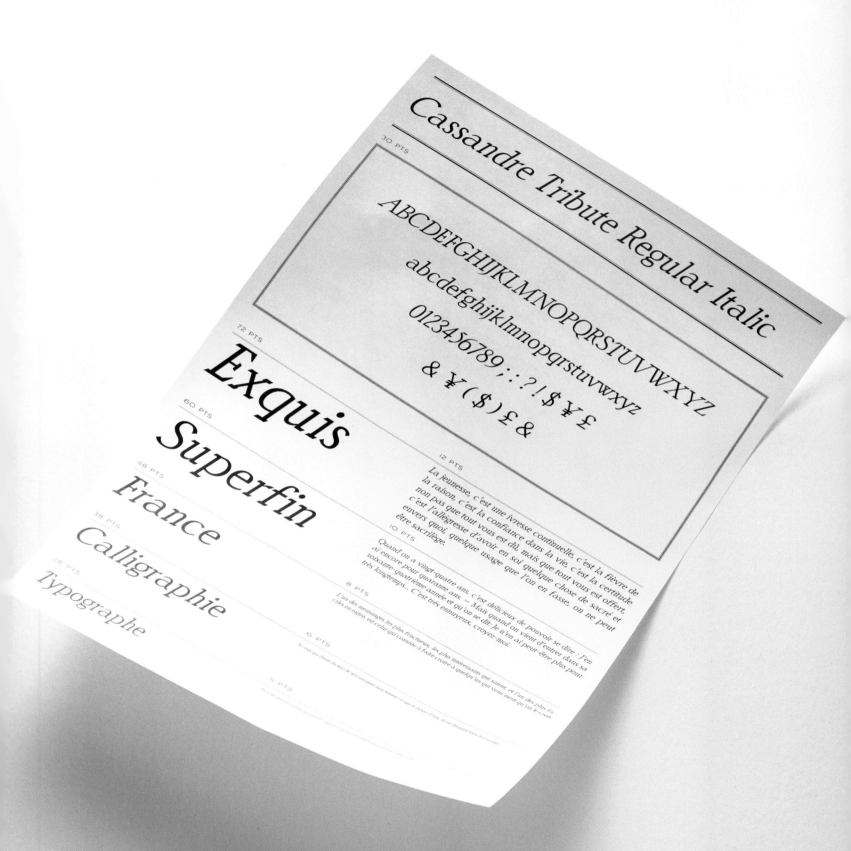

Cassandre Tribute Regular Italic

30 PTS

ABCDEFGHIJKLMNOPQRSTUVWXYZ
abcdefghijklmnopqrstuvwxyz
0123456789;:;?!§¥£
& ¥ ($) £ &

72 PTS

Exquis

60 PTS

Superfin

48 PTS

France

38 PTS

Calligraphie

28 PTS

Typographe

12 PTS

La jeunesse, c'est une ivresse continuelle, c'est la fièvre de la raison, c'est la confiance dans la vie, c'est la certitude non pas que tout vous est dû, mais que tout vous est offert, c'est l'allégresse d'avoir en soi quelque chose de sacré et envers quoi, quelque usage que l'on en fasse, on ne peut être sacrilège.

10 PTS

Quand on a vingt-quatre ans, c'est délicieux de pouvoir se dire : J'en ai encore pour quarante ans. — Mais quand on vient d'entrer dans sa soixante-quatrième année et qu'on se dit: Je n'en ai peut-être plus pour très longtemps... C'est très ennuyeux, croyez-moi.

8 PTS

L'un des mensonges les plus fructueux, les plus intéressants qui soient, et l'un des plus fa- ciles en outre, est celui qui consiste à faire croire à quelqu'un qui vous ment qu'on est ou le croit.

6 PTS

Si c'est qui donne du mal, de moi n'essayent méchamment, c'est que je pense c'était, eh ou illusion bien décourager.

5 PTS

The Cassandre Tribute font is based on a unfinished typeface designed by AM Cassandre for the Olivetti typewriter company. Developed in 2019.

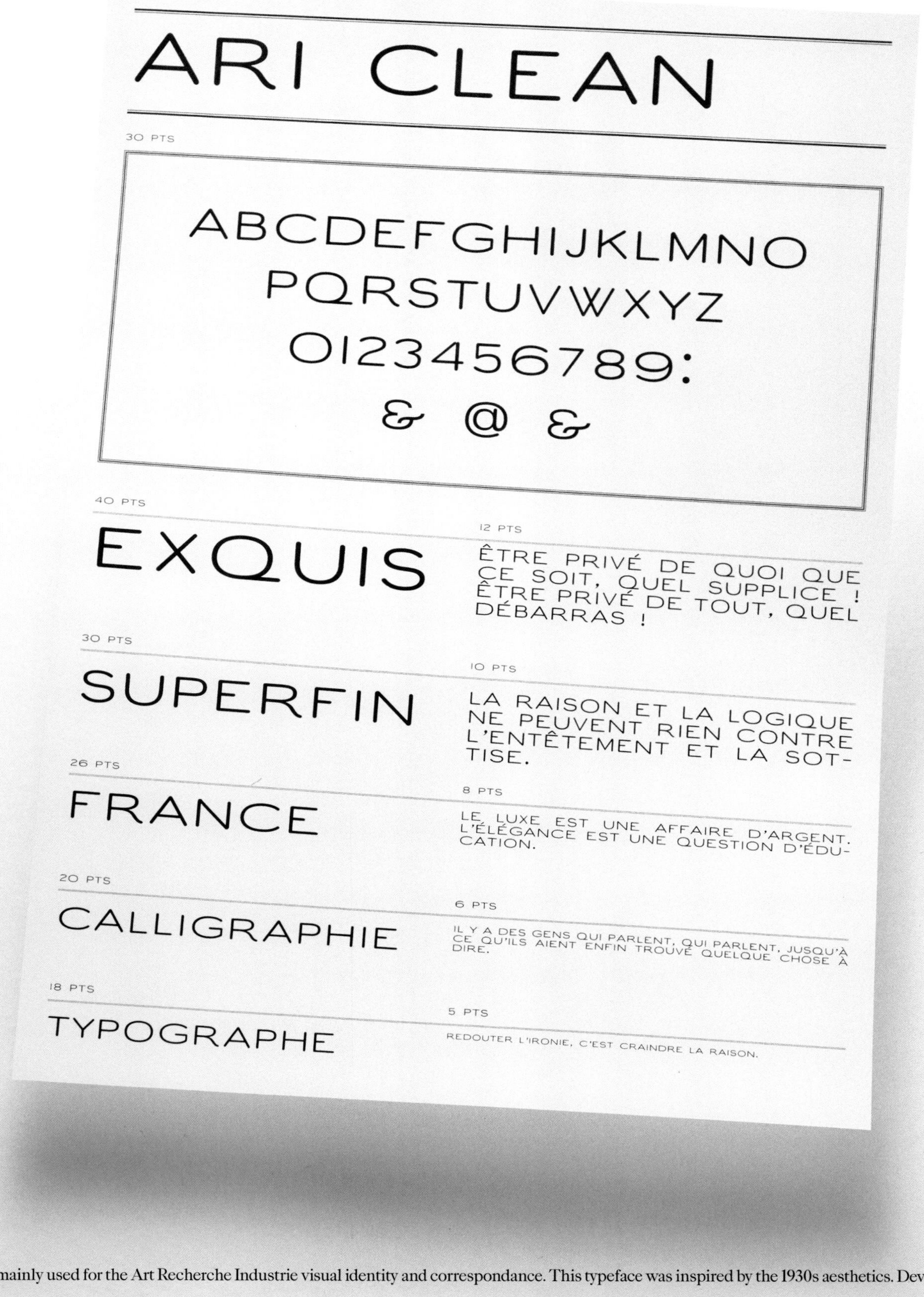

ARI CLEAN

30 PTS

ABCDEFGHIJKLMNO
PQRSTUVWXYZ
0123456789:
& @ &

40 PTS

EXQUIS

12 PTS

ÊTRE PRIVÉ DE QUOI QUE
CE SOIT, QUEL SUPPLICE !
ÊTRE PRIVÉ DE TOUT, QUEL
DÉBARRAS !

30 PTS

SUPERFIN

10 PTS

LA RAISON ET LA LOGIQUE
NE PEUVENT RIEN CONTRE
L'ENTÊTEMENT ET LA SOT-
TISE.

26 PTS

FRANCE

8 PTS

LE LUXE EST UNE AFFAIRE D'ARGENT.
L'ÉLÉGANCE EST UNE QUESTION D'ÉDU-
CATION.

20 PTS

CALLIGRAPHIE

6 PTS

IL Y A DES GENS QUI PARLENT, QUI PARLENT, JUSQU'À
CE QU'ILS AIENT ENFIN TROUVÉ QUELQUE CHOSE À
DIRE.

18 PTS

TYPOGRAPHE

5 PTS

REDOUTER L'IRONIE, C'EST CRAINDRE LA RAISON.

The ARI font is mainly used for the Art Recherche Industrie visual identity and correspondance. This typeface was inspired by the 1930s aesthetics. Developed in 2019.

ARI DIRTY MIX

30 PTS

ABCDEFGHIJKLMNO
PQRSTUVWXYZ
0123456789:
& @ &

40 PTS

EXQUIS

30 PTS

SUPERFIN

26 PTS

FRANCE

20 PTS

CALLIGRAPHIE

18 PTS

TYPOGRAPHE

12 PTS

ÊTRE PRIVÉ DE QUOI QUE
CE SOIT, QUEL SUPPLICE !
ÊTRE PRIVÉ DE TOUT, QUEL
DÉBARRAS !

10 PTS

LA RAISON ET LA LOGIQUE NE
PEUVENT RIEN CONTRE L'ENTÊ-
TEMENT ET LA SOTTISE.

8 PTS

LE LUXE EST UNE AFFAIRE D'ARGENT.
L'ÉLÉGANCE EST UNE QUESTION D'ÉDUCA-
TION.

6 PTS

IL Y A DES GENS QUI PARLENT, QUI PARLENT, JUSQU'À
CE QU'ILS AIENT ENFIN TROUVÉ QUELQUE CHOSE À
DIRE.

5 PTS

REDOUTER L'IRONIE, C'EST CRAINDRE LA RAISON.

The ARI Dirty Mix font is a destroyed version of the ARI font, for a handmade stamp print effect.

Avant-Guerre

70 PTS

Si ceux qui disent du mal de moi savaient exactement ce que je pense d'eux, ils en diraient bien d'avantage.

The Avant-Guerre font is a serif typeface based on a perfume or beauty product packaging from the 1920s-1930s. Developed in 2017.

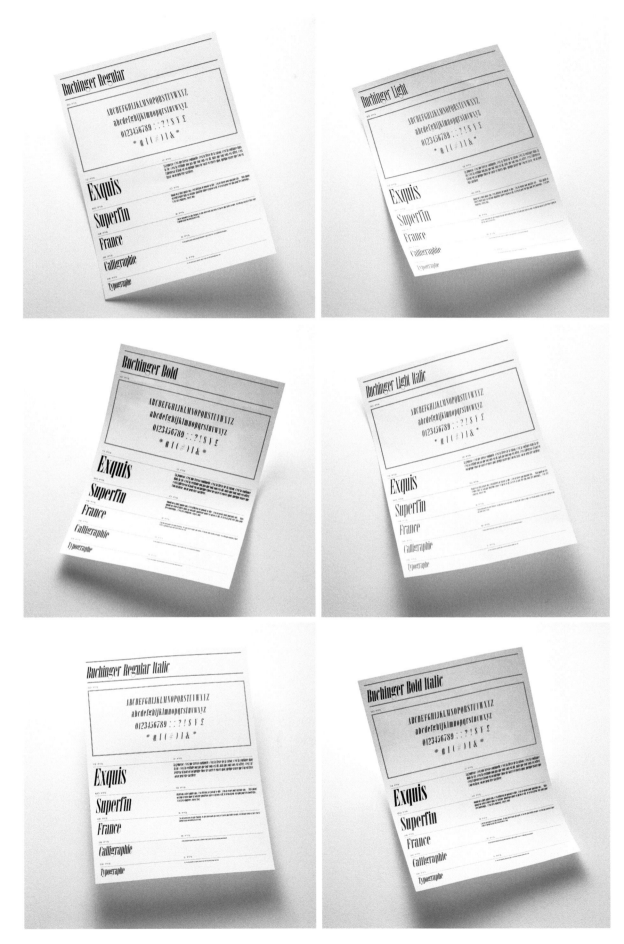

The Buchinger fonts, a revival of a typeface from the Swiss foundry Haas (who created Helvetica for example), has a Swiss administration in the 1890s look. This condensed serif typeface was obviously developed during a stay at Buchinger in Switzerland by the ARI team, in 2020.

E PUBLICATION
UALISÉE, ÉCRITE ET R

RECHERCHE INDUS
IS ET À LAUSANNE.
TÉ IMPRIMÉE PAR LA
E D'IMPRESSION TYPOGRAPH
N FÉVRIER 2020
OGRAF

ART
RECHERCHE
INDUSTRIE

*T*his core requirement for aesthetics and for a brand's identity and development is something that Ramdane Touhami places at the disposal of other brands through his unique creative firm, Art Recherche Industrie, based in Paris and in Switzerland, which he founded in 2018 together with Jan Abellan. It works in the main fields of art and aesthetics (architecture, typography, graphic design, photography, writing, product creation, the development of brand philosophies, and the redefining of identities) and distinguishes itself for its very individual approach of advocating for the homemade and for zero outsourcing. Ramdane Touhami strives for absolute artistic and aesthetic coherence in a project, from start to finish, with no dilution of the creative process, from the time when the idea arises to when the client receives the final product. The name Art Recherche Industrie, or Art Research Industry, pays homage to the 1950s and to the research laboratories of the time that were once so emblematic of French *savoir-faire*. One of the firm's impetuses is to create connections between the worlds of art (the search for materials, colors, aromatics, woodworking techniques, typographic printing, etc.) and industry. It has won a number of design prizes such as the WWD Award and first prize in the Frame Awards for Officine Universelle Buly's extraordinary boutiques, for retail (Best Retail Experience in HK Stores), and many of the 900 items in Buly's catalog have been awarded beauty and cosmetics prizes, such as the Allure Prize, Tatler Beauty, and in *GQ*, among others.

This game, conceived by Art Recherche Industrie, offers an ironic variation of famous "business" board games, but this time about the luxury and fashion world, limited edition of 100, 2019.

GO WHERE NO ONE EXPECTS YOU TO GO: THE VARENNE SERVICE STATION

In 2021, Ramdane Touhami once again went where no one expected him to, taking on a surprising project: a luxury service station that is at once ideal, funny, and surprising. These stations have been disappearing in France in the last four decades (there were more than 40,000 in 1980 and in 2018, only 11,000), especially in the center of Paris (where there is one service station for every 5,000 cars!). They have become as rare and precious as they are indispensable.

The Varenne service station project consists of re-establishing the quality and expertise of the service stations of yore, with the added codes of luxury. Located in Paris' seventh arrondissement, one of the city's wealthiest, the Varenne service station is already an institution, an essential stop for chauffeurs and valets, as well as locals who have their habits and requirements in terms of quality and services. The Varenne service station project integrates perfectly into the *art de vivre* of Paris' Left Bank. The station attendants provide customers with full service, borrowing codes from the world of luxury, and restoring the quality of services from yesteryear. One no longer needs to step out of one's car, because the attendants do everything. Filling up one's tank with gas and performing a spot check of the vehicle while ordering a cappuccino, an organic ice cream or a bento prepared by a Japanese chef is now possible, all at once.

Ramdane Touhami's Varenne service station is striving to become a landmark that offers both high-end gas station services as well as a boutique with a very personalized selection of varied objects, sometimes quirky but always beautiful, such as accessories for the car or the driver, sunglasses, umbrellas, magazines, stickers, or restyled maps of Paris, all designed to have visitors discover rarities from the world over. Connected to Officine Universelle Buly, the Varenne service station will also be the perfect place to showcase one of Officine Universelle Buly's new collections: the Car Fragrance range. A dedicated space will let visitors perfume their vehicle on the spot and buy various brand products. The service station's diversity emulates the general store of another time, a place where everyone stops in for a chat, the kind that used to fill our small towns. With the added extra of an impeccable, friendly service. Ramdane Touhami is reinterpreting the notion of French *art de vivre* with this project, luxurious in its form, but accessible to everyone.

AFTERWORD

by Victoire de Taillac
and Ramdane Touhami

Officine on the move

436

We set up Officine Universelle Buly with a clear vision for our Parisian boutique, which would house a selection of quality skincare, water-based perfumes, oils, and clays from across the world as well as timeless beauty accessories.

Today, our ambitious goal remains the same: to achieve, with each product, a perfect balance between efficiency, aesthetic harmony, and use.

We invent with inspiration from the 19th century, the golden age of French perfumery, and the know-how of the best French manufacturers. "Excellence of the past and the best of the present," as we declare in our catalog.

Officine uses its voice to speak differently about beauty, weighing its words, informing and embodying a vision of natural beauty that is pragmatic but also respectful. A word that we value and which is illustrated in the catalog, on our website, social media, and soon in a magazine.

Officine is designed as an urban oasis where time stands still for our customers, where we competently advise them on how to take care of themselves, where purchase is both conversation and performance.

As soon as it opened, our first store experienced extraordinary enthusiasm—and it hasn't slowed down since. We imagined the Officine in rue Bonaparte as a standalone boutique, but the enthusiasm of our customers has decided otherwise; the wave carried us and led us to open other Officines all over the world. We had to improvise in order to better reinvent ourselves and let Officine Universelle Buly grow in terms of references and sales counters.

Each Officine is an embassy of this French beauty that we hope will contribute to embellishing the city and its inhabitants. As soon as you push the door open, you are greeted with a delicious and indescribable scent. Dressed in their uniforms, our salespeople, the pillars of our approach and highly esteemed team members, listen to you and provide you with advice. Over the first years, we remained in our Officine every day to sell and achieve a better understanding of the wishes of our customers. Today, we still spend time in our stores during each trip to other countries or to experience the intense festive season in our Parisian boutiques. Knowing precisely what life is like in our boutiques is a fundamental element of our work.

Every day, Officine Universelle Buly follows its inspirations and builds its universe in complete freedom. The choice of uniqueness is one of our founding principles. Unlike any other brand, we are proud of being detached from this industry.

The future of Officine Universelle Buly will follow the same path.

Victoire de Taillac and Ramdane Touhami

THIS BOOK IS DEDICATED TO MY WIFE VICTOIRE DE TAILLAC AND MY CHILDREN SCHERAZADE, ADAM, AND NOOR TOUHAMI.

THANKS FOR THEIR INCREDIBLE SUPPORT TO VICTOIRE DE TAILLAC AND MY BROTHER, JAN ABELLAN.

SPECIAL THANKS TO THOSE WHO BELIEVED IN BULY FROM THE BEGINNING,
ARNAUD MONTEBOURG, PHILIPPE PARRENO, MUSTAPHA BOUHAYATI, ABDEL BOUNANE, MICHEL DYENS, YAMING FENG, MR OH, MR KOO, AND THE LATE MR OH.
AND TO OUR BANKS SOCIÉTÉ GÉNÉRALE, HSBC ET BPI.

THANKS FOR THEIR GREAT SUPPORT TO ALL THE SUPPLIERS WHO FOLLOWED US, TO THE LOUVRE MUSEUM TEAM, AND THE DEPARTMENT STORES AND MALLS TEAMS AROUND THE WORLD.

THANK YOU INFINITELY TO ALL THE FAMILY OF OFFICINE UNIVERSELLE BULY.
"NOTHING IS IMPOSSIBLE WITH A VALIANT HEART" AS YOU PROVE IT EVERY DAY.

HITOMI ANDO, KONATSU ANDO, SOUMAYA EL ALAMI, CHIE AKASHI, HITOMI AKANE, ERI AKIYAMA, KOJIRO AO, YUMI ARAKAWA, SAKURA ARIGA, SOFIA BARROUCHE, ELISABETH BASINI, FERYEL BEJI, SONIA BEN MADHKOUR, JULIE BERCOVY, KATIE BICKLEY, CLÉMENCE BOUVET, CHARLOTTE DE BROGLIE, ALICE BUREAU, NICOLAS CHAUVELOT, AYOUNG CHOI, GAELLE LE COZE, EARDA CUMANI, BENOIST DALLAY, ORNELLA DELATTRE, IVONE DESCLOZEAUX, JAWAD DOUIR, MAX DRACON, CAROLINE DUONG, SAYAKA ENDO, YAMING FENG, HARRISSON FAUMUINA, ANNE FLAMAND, TAKAKO FUKUSHIMA, RYO FUJIMURA, KEN FULK, MOMO FURUKAWA, MYRIAM GARCETTE, ROSIE GARCIA, DAPHNÉ GAUTIER, CAROLINE GEORGE, JACKY GEORGES, BRUNO GIGAREL, HALIMATA GRAILLE, SATOKO GOTO, HYO HAN, SEINA HAYAKAWA, MINORI HASHIZUME, GABRIELLA HEARST, MAYUMI HISAJIMA, ERIKO HOSONO, IROHA HIRAKAWA, STÉPHANIE HUSSONNOIS, BORA HWANG, LISA ISHII, SAYAKA ISHIGURO, MIZUKI ITO, MAKO IZUTSU, DELPHINE JACQUEMART, KATE JEON, SOFIA JERGNER, MAI KAGEYAMA, ENA KIM, SAYURI KIRIYAMA, EMI KOZAKURA, SACHIKO KUROBANE, RYOKO KUSAMA, FLORA LE SAINT, ISABELLE LINDQWISTER, JOAN MADERA, RYOSUKE MAEDA, KURUMI MATSUDA, SARAH DE MAVALEIX, STÉPHANIE MAZAN, GAËTAN MERCIER, SHOGO MISUMI, SHIERI MIYAKE, ERI MIYAHARA, KANAE MORI, MAKIKO MORISHIGE, MISUZU MORIMOTO, MURIEL MORISSET, RIDA MOUMEN, MAIKO MOURI, AGATHE MYARD, YOKO NAITO, AKI NAKATSU, HINA OGAWA, EMIKO OGURI, HARUKO OHARA, YUKA OKAMOTO, YUUKI ONO, CHRISTIAN PAULY, AMAELLE PINTUREAU, CHLOÉ PHAM VAN HOA, CAROLINE POUJOL, JULIO RAMEAUX, NARIMAN SABEUR, SATOE SAZAWA, NAMIKO SEKINE, JITSUKA SHIMAZAKI, WAKAKO SHIMOMURA, NAOKO SHIROTA, EMI SUGAHARA, HYUNSOO SON, SOPHIE SONANN SONG, WEN SONG, NOBU SUZUKI, TOMOMI TAKAOKA, MINA TAKAYAMA, HARUKA TAKAYANAGI, KAZUFUMI TAKIKAWA, TAKAKO TANAKA, KEIKO TAKENAKA, PAULA TEATIN, CHIKAKU TERAZAWA, VALÉRIE THERON, EMI TSUNEHISA, YUKA TSUTSUMI, YOHANNA TODD-MOREL, REI TOMINAGA, AZUSA UJIKE, YURI UNNO, AI USUI, FLORIAN VAZ, SYOGO YADA, YURI YAMADA, MAYUKI YAMAGUISHI, KURUMI YAMAMOTO, TAKAAKI YAMAMURO, HYEJIN YANG, KAYOKO YOKOTANI, AIRI YONEYAMA, MAI YOSHIKAWA, HARUNA WAKUISHI, MOEKO WATANABE, VIVAN WONG... OUR SINCERE APOLOGIES FOR THE NAMES THAT MAY HAVE ESCAPED OUR MEMORY.

WE SINCERELY THANK ALL THE TEAM OF ART RECHERCHE INDUSTRIE,
WITH THEIR CREATIVITY AND ENERGY IN ABUNDANCE,
JAN ABELLAN, ANNA BARTOLOMEI, PIERRE BOURRÉ,
HÉLÈNE DEVRED, YANN GARIN, GUILLAUME JEAN-MAIRET,
SALASSA MITSUI, FLORENT REVELLIN, DELPHINE VALLOIRE, AND PIOTR WIDELKA.

A VERY SPECIAL THANKS TO THE CONTRIBUTORS OF THIS BOOK,
JINA KHAYER, KANAE HASEGAWA, DELPHINE VALLOIRE AND FLORIAN VAZ.

ENGLISH TRANSLATION PROVIDED BY CLAUDIO CAMBON, LAURE CHANDÈZE-FITZPATRICK AND KEVIN ST JOHN.

PHOTOGRAPHIC WORK FOR OFFICINE UNIVERSELLE BULY BY
JAN ABELLAN, YANN GARIN, MARTIN HOLTKAMP, HIROSHI IGARASHI, MINEUN KIM, ARTUS DE LAVILLÉON, PIERRE MAHIEU, CHRIS MATTA, CALIXTE MOISAN, FABIAN PARKS, DAISUKE SHIMA, AND KOZO TAKAYAMA.

MERCI.

THE BEAUTY OF TIME TRAVEL
THE WORK OF RAMDANE TOUHAMI
AND THE AGENCY ART RECHERCHE INDUSTRIE
FOR OFFICINE UNIVERSELLE BULY

THIS BOOK WAS CONCEIVED BY AGENCY ART RECHERCHE INDUSTRIE.
EDITED BY AGENCY ART RECHERCHE INDUSTRIE AND GESTALTEN

INTRODUCTION AND CHAPTER XV (PP. 408–413) BY RAMDANE TOUHAMI
FOREWORD BY VICTOIRE DE TAILLAC AND RAMDANE TOUHAMI
(PP. 436–437)
FEATURE TEXTS BY JINA KHAYER
(PP. 52–57, 70–73, 110–119, 272–289),
KANAE HASEGAWA
(PP. 8–15, 404–407),
DELPHINE VALLOIRE
(PP. 58–69, 120–133, 414–435),
AND FLORIAN VAZ
(PP. 16–51, 74–109, 134–271, 290–403)

TRANSLATION FROM FRENCH TO ENGLISH
CLAUDIO CAMBON
(PP. 4–7, 58–69, 120–133, 312–341, 368–403, 408–435),
LAURE CHANDÈZE-FITZPATRICK
(PP. 134–271),
AND KEVIN ST. JOHN
(PP. 16–51, 74–109, 290–311, 342–367)

ART DIRECTION BY RAMDANE TOUHAMI

EDITORIAL MANAGEMENT
HÉLÈNE DEVRED AND DELPHINE VALLOIRE FOR AGENCY ART RECHERCHE INDUSTRIE
ANDREA SERVERT AND LARS PIETZSCHMANN FOR GESTALTEN

DESIGN AND LAYOUT BY RAMDANE TOUHAMI AND JAN ABELLAN
FOR AGENCY ART RECHERCHE INDUSTRIE

ALL TYPEFACES BY RAMDANE TOUHAMI, JAN ABELLAN, AND GUILLAUME JEAN-MAIRET
FOR AGENCY ART RECHERCHE INDUSTRIE

COVER PHOTOGRAPHY
2017 OFFICINE UNIVERSELLE BULY

PRINTED BY OFFSETDRUCKEREI KARL GRAMMLICH GMBH, PLIEZHAUSEN
MADE IN GERMANY

PUBLISHED BY GESTALTEN, 2021
ISBN 978-3-96704-019-7

FOR MORE INFORMATION, AND TO ORDER BOOKS, PLEASE VISIT WWW.GESTALTEN.COM
BIBLIOGRAPHIC INFORMATION PUBLISHED BY THE DEUTSCHE NATIONALBIBLIOTHEK. THE DEUTSCHE NATIONALBIBLIOTHEK LISTS THIS
PUBLICATION IN THE DEUTSCHE NATIONALBIBLIOGRAFIE, DETAILED BIBLIOGRAPHIC DATA IS AVAILABLE ONLINE AT WWW.DNB.DE

THIS BOOK WAS PRINTED ON PAPER CERTIFIED ACCORDING TO THE STANDARDS OF THE FSC®.

MIX
Paper from
responsible sources
FSC
www.fsc.org   FSC® C011712